A Handbook of Digital Library Economics

CHANDOS
INFORMATION PROFESSIONAL SERIES

Series Editor: Ruth Rikowski
(Email: Rikowskigr@aol.com)

Chandos' new series of books is aimed at the busy information professional. They have been specially commissioned to provide the reader with an authoritative view of current thinking. They are designed to provide easy-to-read and (most importantly) practical coverage of topics that are of interest to librarians and other information professionals. If you would like a full listing of current and forthcoming titles, please visit our website, www.chandospublishing.com, email wp@woodheadpublishing.com or telephone +44 (0) 1223 499140.

New authors: we are always pleased to receive ideas for new titles; if you would like to write a book for Chandos, please contact Dr Glyn Jones on gjones@chandospublishing.com or telephone +44 (0) 1993 848726.

Bulk orders: some organisations buy a number of copies of our books. If you are interested in doing this, we would be pleased to discuss a discount. Please email wp@woodheadpublishing.com or telephone +44 (0) 1223 499140.

A Handbook of Digital Library Economics

Operations, collections and services

WRITTEN AND EDITED BY

DAVID BAKER AND WENDY EVANS

CHANDOS
PUBLISHING

Oxford Cambridge New Delhi

Chandos Publishing
Hexagon House
Avenue 4
Station Lane
Witney
Oxford OX28 4BN
UK
Tel: +44 (0) 1993 848726
Email: info@chandospublishing.com
www.chandospublishing.com
www.chandospublishingonline.com

Chandos Publishing is an imprint of Woodhead Publishing Limited

Woodhead Publishing Limited
80 High Street
Sawston
Cambridge CB22 3HJ
UK
Tel: +44 (0) 1223 499140
Fax: +44 (0) 1223 832819
www.woodheadpublishing.com

First published in 2013

ISBN: 978-1-84334-620-3 (print)
ISBN: 978-1-78063-318-3 (online)

© The editors and contributors, 2013

British Library Cataloguing-in-Publication Data.
A catalogue record for this book is available from the British Library.

Typeset by Domex e-Data Pvt. Ltd., India.
Printed in the UK and USA.

Printed and bound in Great Britain by 4edge Ltd, Hockley, Essex.

Contents

Foreword

Professor Sir Timothy O'Shea

Libraries are changing. We now have digital libraries of increasing scale and value. Nearly all conventional libraries also have a digital library component. At the same time there are new open access digital resources of tremendous value, the key example being, of course, Wikipedia. The challenge for library professionals and also for library users is to understand the nature of these new digital libraries and how best to operate and use them. David Baker and Wendy Evans have performed a very valuable service in producing the useful *Handbook of Digital Library Economics*. I would recommend this book to anyone who works in a library and to anyone who is interested in taking advantage of the new opportunities that digital libraries present.

The first chapter of the book provides a very accessible overview and the remaining chapters contain 14 contemporary case studies which cover the full gamut of digital library developments. This book is also, of course, important to people with jobs like mine who have to prioritise the allocation of resources in colleges and universities. David and Wendy have many years of successful professional work related to the development of digital libraries and their experience is reflected in the high quality of this handbook.

Preface

Despite the extensive developments over the last ten years, there is remarkably little published on the economic and financial management of digital libraries, their operations, collections and services. This book aims to address this gap by attempting to provide a 'manual' for all those involved – or expecting to be involved – in the development and management of digital libraries. While it is based on theory and research, it takes a practical approach to the subject, focusing on the key challenges associated with the economic and financial aspects of digital developments.

The handbook therefore concentrates on the 'how to' of managing digital collections and services of all types with regard to their financing and financial management. The emphasis is on case studies and practical examples drawn from a wide variety of contexts. We hope that the book – designed as a companion to our 2009 title *Digital Library Economics: An Academic Perspective*, from which we have drawn extensively – will be of particular value to the practitioner or the student of practice of the various topics, though we expect that it will also be of interest to all involved in digital library developments and digital collections and services, whether or not library based.

All web links were correct at the time of checking (April 2013).

David Baker and Wendy Evans
May, 2013

Acknowledgements

The authors are especially grateful to all who made this book possible: to Professor Sir Timothy O'Shea for writing the foreword; to the authors of the case studies for their rich input, based as it is on substantial experience, knowledge and expertise over many years; to Nina Hughes, research assistant for the project, and to Sharon Holley for her help and support during the final stages; to the University of St Mark & St John for their support; to Peter Williams, copy editor; and to Chandos Publishing for their help in preparing the book.

David Baker and Wendy Evans

List of abbreviations

1B1U	One Book, One User
1B3U	One Book, Three Users
1BUU	One Book, Unlimited Users
AAF	Annual Access Fee
ACF	Archive Capital Fee
ALA	American Library Association
API	Application Programming Interface
ARK	Archival Resource Key
APC	Article Processing Charge
ARL	Association of Research Libraries
BMCC	Borough of Manhattan Community College
CD	Compact Disc
CDL	California Digital Library
CICF	Central Indiana Community Foundation
CILIP	Chartered Institute of Library and Information Professionals
COUNTER	Counting Online Usage of Networked Electronic Resources
CRL	Centre for Research Libraries
CUNY	City University of New York
CVM	Contingent Valuation Method
DANS	Data Archiving and Networked Services Institute
DEFF	Denmark's Electronic Research Library
DFG	Deutsche Forschungsgemeinschaft

DiCoMo	Digitization Costs Model
DIY	Do It Yourself
DL(s)	Digital Library (Libraries)
DOI	Digital Object Identifier
DRM	Digital Rights Management
EBL	Electronic Book Library
EDS	EBSCO Discovery Service
ECM	EBSCO*host* Collection Management Tool
ESPIDA	An Effective Strategic Model for the Preservation and Disposal of Institutional Digital Assets
FTE	Full Time Equivalent
FRPAA	Federal Research Public Access Act
HEI	Higher Education Institution
HERON	Higher Education Resources ON-demand
HESA	Higher Education Statistical Agency
HoDs	Heads of Departments
ICT	Information and Communications Technology
IDF	International DOI Federation
IFLA	International Federation of Library Associations
IMLS	Institute of Museum and Library Services
iRODS	The integrated Rule-Oriented Data System
ISO	International Organization for Standardization
IT	Information Technology
IUPUI	Indiana University-Purdue University Indianapolis
JHUP	Johns Hopkins University Press
JISC	Joint Information Systems Committee
JSTOR	Journal Storage
KNAW	Royal Netherlands Academy of Arts and Sciences
KRDS	Keeping Research Data Safe
LIFE	Lifecycle Information for E-Literature
LOCKSS	Lots of Copies Keep Stuff Safe

LSRNs	LifeScience Resource Names
LSTA	Library Services Technology Act
MARC	Machine Readable Cataloging
MIT	Massachusetts Institute of Technology
MOU	Memorandum of Understanding
MVP	Minimum Viable Product
NARCIS	National Academic Research and Collaborations Information System
NCAR	National Center for Atmospheric Research
NDIIPP	National Digital Information Infrastructure and Preservation Program
NIH	National Institutes of Health
NLP	National Licensing Programme
NWO	Netherlands Organisation of Scientific Research
OA	Open Access
OAI-PMH	Open Archives Initiative – Protocol for Metadata Harvesting
OAIS	Open Archival Information System
OAPEN	Open Access Publishing in European Networks
OCR	Optical Character Recognition
OpenDOAR	Directory of Open Access Repositories
OSTI	Office of Strategic and Technical Information
OTPS	Other Than Personnel Spending
PDA	Patron Driven Acquisition
PDF	Portable Document Format
PDL	Patron Driven Lease
PEAK	Pricing Electronic Access to Knowledge
R&D	Research and Development
RCI	Research Cyberinfrastructure
RFP	Request for Proposal
ROI	Return on Investment
SCONUL	Society of College, National and University Libraries

SDSC	San Diego Supercomputer Center
SHEDL	Scottish Higher Education Digital Library
SIO	Scripps Institution of Oceanography
SLA	Service Level Agreement
SPARC	Scholarly Publishing and Academic Resources Coalition
STM	Science, Technology, Medicine
TB	Terabyte(s)
TEACH	Technology, Education and Copyright Harmonization
TOC	Table of Contents
UC	University of California
UCL	University College London
UI	User Interface
UMIACS	University of Maryland Institute for Advanced Computer Studies
UPCC	University Press Content Consortia
UPeC	Association of American University Presses
XML	Extensible Markup Language

List of figures and tables

Figures

Tables

About the authors

David Baker was Principal of University College Plymouth St Mark & St John (now the University of St Mark & St John) 2003–9. He is Emeritus Professor of Strategic Information Management there. He has published widely in the field of Library and Information Studies, with 15 monographs and some 100 articles to his credit. He has spoken at numerous conferences, led workshops and seminars and has undertaken consultancy work in most countries in the European Union, along with work in Ethiopia, Kuwait, Nigeria and the Sudan. He was Deputy Chair of the Joint Information Systems Committee (JISC) until December 2012, also having led a number of large technology-based projects, both in relation to digital and hybrid library development and content creation for teaching and learning. He has published the following books with Chandos: *Strategic Information Management, Strategic Change Management in Public Sector Organisations* and (with Bernadette Casey) *Eve on Top: Women's Experience of Success in the Public Sector* and co-produced (with Wendy Evans) *Digital Library Economics: An Academic Perspective, Libraries and Society: Role, Responsibility and Future in an Age of Change* and *Trends, Discovery and People in the Digital Age.*

Laura Brown is the executive vice president for Ithaka and the JSTOR managing director. Laura previously served as the managing director of Ithaka S+R where she oversaw work on a number of research programmes and consulting projects, including the sustainability of academic initiatives, new models for library collaboration, changing faculty attitudes and publishing behaviours, open courseware and university-sponsored online courses, and new e-book publishing models for university presses. Brown is the author of the Ithaka report *University Publishing in a Digital Age.* Prior to joining Ithaka, Brown was the president of Oxford University Press, USA, where she spent most of her professional career. She has led a variety of publishing divisions, including scholarly, professional, reference, trade and textbook operations, and helped Oxford to make the transition to digital publishing. Brown currently serves on the Yale University Press Board of Governors and the Meserve-Kunhardt Foundation Board of Trustees. She holds a Bachelor of Arts from Goucher College, a Master of Arts from Johns Hopkins University, and a Master of Fine Arts in painting from Indiana University.

Mark Dahl is the Director of the Aubrey R. Watzek Library at Lewis & Clark College, a private liberal arts college in Portland, Oregon in the United States. His professional career in libraries began in systems and technical services, an area in which he has published and presented extensively. In recent years his interests have focused on library digital initiatives and the evolving role of the academic library in the US liberal arts college sector. He blogs at *liberalartslibrary.blogspot.com*.

Sidney Eng is currently Chief Librarian at the Borough of Manhattan Community College (City University of New York) and has been in that position for 17 years. He is also an adjunct associate professor at Hofstra University Library, Long Island, New York. In addition to college and university libraries, he has worked in a public library, a high-school library and an opinion magazine. He holds a BA (Sociology) from Bishop's University, Quebec, Canada, an MA (Sociology) from New York University and an MLS from St John's University, New York. He began a sabbatical leave in September 2012 to conduct further research on managing library technologies.

Wendy Evans is Head of Library at the University of St Mark & St John. She has a keen interest in the Internet and electronic resources and in particular access to journals and databases. She also has an expertise in data protection and freedom of information. Evans has published, lectured and researched in the field of electronic journal and database usage and also access versus ownership of journals. She has co-authored and edited *Digital Library Economics: An Academic Perspective*, *Libraries and Society: Role, Responsibility and Future in an Age of Change* and *Trends, Discovery and People in the Digital Age*. Wendy is an Associate member of the Higher Education Academy and has recently been awarded an Associate Teaching Fellowship of UCP Marjon.

Michael Gorrell, the Executive Vice President of Technology and Chief Information Officer of EBSCO Publishing, is responsible for managing all technology operations for EBSCO Publishing as well as providing key leadership in strategic product direction for the EBSCO*host* platform. Michael joined EBSCO Publishing in August 1994 to help usher in EBSCO*host*, responsible for building a high-performance system that meets the highest industry standards for performance and availability. Michael has been instrumental in making usability testing central to the product design of the EBSCO*host* platform, overseeing an industry-leading end-user testing programme that has yielded tremendous feedback and enhancements to EBSCO's interfaces. Under his direction, EBSCO Publishing has become the industry leader in website accessibility for users with various physical and visual disabilities. Michael has led EBSCO Publishing's involvement in Internet2's Shibboleth project since 2002. He has been a driving force behind EBSCO Discovery Service technical developments and directed the beta programme through to its successful conclusion in December 2009. Following EBSCO's acquisition of NetLibrary, the technology teams were charged with the mission of integrating e-books into the EBSCO*host* platform and Michael's direct involvement helped accomplish this within one year, including new functionality that had never before been available for e-books.

José-Marie Griffiths is Vice President for Academic Affairs at Bryant University in Smithfield, Rhode Island. She has previously served as Dean of the School of Information and Library Science at the University of North Carolina at Chapel Hill, Chief Information Officer at the University of Michigan, Vice Chancellor at the University of Tennessee-Knoxville and Vice President for King Research, Inc. She has a BA with honours in Physics, a PhD in Information Science and a Post-Doctorate in Computer Science and Statistics, all from University College, London.

Dr Griffiths has spent over 30 years in research, teaching, public service, corporate leadership and higher education administration. She has been awarded presidential appointments from two United States Presidents that have included the National Science Board, the US President's Information Technology Advisory Committee, and the US National Commission on Libraries and Information. She has had appointments to multiple projects as lead or key personnel for over 28 United States federal agencies, departments and offices. Dr Griffiths has carried out projects and/or advisory roles with over 20 major corporations on projects in science and technology, as well as seven major international organisations, including NATO and the United Nations. She is the recipient of over 20 significant awards in science, technology, teaching and the advancement of women in these fields.

Arjan Hogenaar has studied biology and was a researcher in the embryology of the pea before getting involved in the world of libraries and documentary information (in 1982). In the first years of his career he was active as a biomedical collection developer and information broker for the Royal Netherlands Academy of Arts and Sciences (KNAW). Later on, his scope broadened into the social sciences and into content management for information portals. Since 2011 Arjan has worked for DANS, an institute of both KNAW and the Netherlands Organisation for Scientific Research. In this environment his focus has changed somewhat in the direction of policy development in the field of sustainable access to information.

John W. Houghton is currently Professorial Fellow at Victoria University's Centre for Strategic Economic Studies (CSES) and Director of the Centre's Information Technologies and Information Economy Program. He has many years experience in information technology policy, science and technology policy and more general industry policy-related economic research. He has published and spoken widely, and is a regular consultant to the Organization for Economic Cooperation and Development (OECD) in Paris. In 1998, John was awarded a National Australia Day Council, Australia Day Medal for his contribution to IT industry policy development. John's research is at the interface of theory and practice with a strong focus on the policy application of economic and social theory and of leading-edge research in various relevant fields. Consequently, his contribution tends to be in bringing knowledge and research methods to bear on policy issues in an effort to raise the level of policy debate and improve policy outcomes. Major foci for John's recent research have been a series of studies exploring the economic implications of alternative scholarly publishing models, studies of the costs and benefits of open access to public sector information, and studies of the curation and sharing of research data.

Jennifer A. Johnson is the Digital Initiatives Project Coordinator at IUPUI University Library. She has worked professionally in the area of digital libraries for 11 years focusing on community outreach. Johnson works with community organisations to guide them through the processes of funding, and digital library best practices to make historical documents and artifacts available online. Recent partners include the Indianapolis Recorder, the Indianapolis Museum of Art and the Indianapolis Motor Speedway. Johnson also participates in the library's

Campus Outreach Group and enjoys interacting with the IUPUI faculty and students to better understand their research needs.

Donald W. King is Honorary University Professor, Bryant University and Adjunct Professor, University of Tennessee. He received an MS (1960) in statistics from the University of Wyoming. In 1961, he was co-founder of Westat, Inc. which received government contracts to evaluate retrieval systems and information services. This led to a National Science Foundation contract to prepare a book (*Evaluation of Information Services and Products*, 1971, with E.C. Bryant). In 1976 he founded King Research, Inc. which focused on science communication (*Scientific Journals in the U.S.*, 1981, with N.K. Roderer and D.D. McDonald; *Towards Electronic Journals: Realities for Scientists, Librarians and Publishers*, 2000; *Communication Patterns of Engineers*, 2004, with C. Tenopir), information professionals (*The Information Professional*, 1981, with A. Debons, U. Mansfield and D.L. Shirey; *New Directions in Library and Information Science*, 1986, with J.M. Griffiths) and assessment of libraries (*Keys to Success: Performance Indicators for Public Libraries*, 1989; *Evaluation of Information Centers and Services*, 1991; *Special Libraries: Increasing the Information Edge*, 1991; *A Strong Future for Public Library Use and Employment*, 2011, with J.M. Griffiths). In addition, he has over 300 other publications. He has received many awards and honours in recognition of his work including Pioneer of Science Information, Chemical Heritage Foundation, Research Award and Award of Merit, American Society for Information Science and Technology, Fellow, and American Statistical Association.

Amy Kirchhoff has been the Archive Service Product Manager for Portico since 2006. She is responsible for the creation and execution of archival policy and oversees the operation and development of the Portico website. Prior to her work at Portico, Kirchhoff was director of technology for JSTOR and also served as a member of the shared software development group at Ithaka. She has published articles on Portico's preservation methodology and policies in several publications including most recently *Learned Publishing* and *The Serials Librarian*.

Ardys Kozbial is Director of the Research Data Curation Program in the University of California, San Diego Library where her current work is focused on building services that support the research data lifecycle of this new library programme. Through the Research Data Curation Program, the UC San Diego Library is a partner in the UC San Diego cross-campus, collaborative effort, called Research Cyberinfrastructure (RCI) which has been charged and funded by the UC San Diego Chancellor to provide data services to campus researchers, ranging from centralised storage to data curation to research computing. She works on collaborations with faculty and organised research units (ORUs) at UC San Diego as well as grant-funded projects, with responsibilities ranging from grant writing to project management, depending on the needs of a particular project. Before coming to UC San Diego, Ardys spent 12 years working in architecture collections at Harvard University, UC Berkeley, the University of Texas at Austin, and Payette Associates (a Boston-based architecture firm) as a librarian and archivist. She received a BA from the University of Michigan and an MS in Library and Information Science from Simmons College.

Derek Law is Emeritus Professor of Informatics at the University of Strathclyde. He was chair of the JISC Advance Board, has worked in several British universities and has published and spoken at conferences extensively. He is a regular project evaluator for the EU and has undertaken almost fifty institutional reviews. Most of his work has been to do with the development of networked resources in higher education and with the creation of national information policy, and he has been PI on some twenty research projects. Recently he has worked on the future of academic information services. This has been combined with an active professional life in professional organisations related to librarianship and computing. A committed internationalist he has been involved in projects and research in over forty countries. He was awarded the Barnard Prize for contributions to Medical Informatics in 1993, Fellowship of the Royal Society of Edinburgh in 1999, an honorary degree by the Sorbonne in 2000, the IFLA medal in 2003 and Honorary Fellowship of CILIP in 2004, and was an OCLC Distinguished Scholar in 2006.

David Minor works at the University of California, San Diego (UCSD), where he is the Director of Digital Preservation Initiatives at the UCSD Library. In this role he helps define current and future work needed for the preservation of vital resources. He is also the programme manager of Chronopolis, a national-scale digital preservation network that originated with funds from the Library of Congress's NDIIPP Program. He also has a joint working relationship between the UCSD Libraries and the San Diego Supercomputer Center. In this role he works as co-lead on the

Curation Services Program in the Research Cyberinfrastructure Initiative on the UCSD campus.

Professor Sir Timothy O'Shea became Principal of the University of Edinburgh in 2002. A computer scientist, he is a graduate of the Universities of Sussex and Leeds. In his early career he was a Research Fellow at the University of Edinburgh and has worked in the United States and for the Open University where he was appointed Pro-Vice-Chancellor in 1993. He was elected Master of Birkbeck in 1997 and subsequently appointed Provost of Gresham College and Pro-Vice-Chancellor of the University of London, holding the three posts concurrently until returning to Edinburgh as Principal.

Professor O'Shea is Chair of the Joint Information Systems Committee (JISC) and Chair of the Board of Directors of the Edinburgh Festival Fringe. His fellowships are from Birkbeck, the University of the Highlands and Islands Millennium Institute, the European Co-ordinating Committee on Artificial Intelligence and the Royal Society of Edinburgh. He holds an honorary degree from Heriot-Watt University, the University of Strathclyde and McGill University.

Professor O'Shea was awarded a knighthood in the Queen's 2008 New Year Honours in recognition of his services to higher education.

Kristi L. Palmer earned a BA in History from Ball State University in 1999 and a Masters in Library Science from Indiana University in 2001. She has worked professionally in the arena of digital collection organisation and metadata creation for 12 years supporting the creation of faculty, student and community-driven digital scholarship and cultural heritage collections. Palmer's research interests include open access, scholarly communication and Indianapolis history, with her publications and presentations on the topics earning her recognition as one of Library Journal's Movers & Shakers in 2009. In addition to leading IUPUI University Library Digital Scholarship Team, Palmer also provides collection development and research instruction for the Department of History, and Programs of Women's Studies and American Studies.

Dean Smith, Director of Project MUSE, brings a wealth of experience in leading digital publishing initiatives, global sales and marketing expertise, and strategic planning skills. He spearheaded the launch of the University Press Content Consortium in 2012 – a multi-publisher e-book initiative including 66 publishers and 15,000 titles. As Director of Content for the American Society for Training and Development, he created a digital publishing strategy for the society's periodical, book and research publications.

During a decade-plus tenure with the American Chemical Society, Smith oversaw dynamic growth in worldwide electronic access to the Society's publications, designing innovative pricing models, emphasising library customer relations and implementing effective internal management systems. He previously led electronic publishing efforts for a variety of medical publication products at Chapman & Hall, and led traditional STM journal publishing programmes at C&H and Springer-Verlag. An accomplished writer and published poet, he holds a BA from the University of Virginia and an MFA in Creative Writing from Columbia University.

Joan A. Smith has been an enthusiastic technophile since programming her first computer in 1982 (an Atari). She quickly became a keen supporter of digital preservation, having witnessed the rapid rate of technology change over the past several decades. Her work in industry and the academy has focused on the impact of file format migration, component obsolescence and long-term accessibility together with the substantial costs involved in developing and maintaining systems for public and private use. By turns an academic (at Emory University and Old Dominion University) and an industry practitioner (INRI, Northrup Grumman, Linear B Systems and others), Dr Smith has sought to bring practical and affordable solutions to real-world problems. Her background includes a degree in Philosophy from KU Leuven (Belgium) and a PhD in Computer Science from Old Dominion University (USA). For more information, visit her website at: *http://www.joanasmith.com*.

Joan Starr manages the EZID service for the California Digital Library (CDL), a service that makes it easy to create and manage unique, long-term identifiers. Joan is Chair of the Metadata Working Group at DataCite, an international organisation working for easier access to and increased acceptance of research data in scholarly communications. She engages with a wide range of data management stakeholders, including researchers, libraries, data centres, archives and repositories. She is also Strategic and Project Planning Manager for the CDL.

Kate Wittenberg is the Managing Director of Portico, the digital preservation service provided by Ithaka. Before joining Portico, Kate served as Project Director, Client and Partnership Development for

Ithaka S+R, where she worked with libraries and publishers to develop innovative and sustainable resources, products and services.

Kate spent much of her career at Columbia University, where she was the Editor-in-Chief of Columbia University Press until 1999, and then went on to found and direct EPIC (Electronic Publishing Initiative at Columbia), a pioneering initiative in digital publishing, and a model partnership for libraries, presses and academic IT departments. Kate speaks and writes frequently on issues at the intersection of digital technologies, academic libraries and scholarly communication.

Martin Woodhead started his first company, Woodhead-Faulkner (Publishers) Limited, in Cambridge in 1972 which grew successfully until its acquisition by Simon & Schuster in 1987. In 1989 he started Woodhead Publishing Limited to specialise in books on the latest science and technology in the fields of materials science, engineering, textiles, food, biomedicine, energy and the environment, currently publishing over 100 titles per year. In 2009 the company acquired Chandos Publishing, based in Witney, a leading publisher of books on library and information science and Asian Studies, now publishing 50 titles per year. The company also has a joint venture business in India, Woodhead Publishing India (Private) Limited, producing around 20 titles per year. Overall, Woodhead Publishing employs 40 people and exports account for 80 per cent of sales, the largest markets being the United States, China, Germany and India. In 2010 the company launched its online platform Woodhead Publishing Online followed in 2012 by Chandos Publishing Online. Martin Woodhead is on the board of the Independent Publishers Guild and takes a keen interest in copyright, licensing and piracy issues. In 2012 the company won the London Book Fair International Achievement of the Year Award at the Independent Publishing Awards dinner.

Digital economics:
introduction and overview

Abstract. Chapter 1 provides an overview of digital library economics, describing the main areas to be discussed in more detail in subsequent chapters and case studies. It provides definitions of the term 'digital library' and a literature review of recent history and relevant works. It concludes with the key themes relating to all aspects of digital libraries: sustainability, economic models, business plans and resource allocation, and cost-effective decision-making.

Keywords: business plans, cost-effective decision-making, digital library, economic models, history of digital libraries, resource allocation, sustainability

Introduction

This opening chapter aims to provide an overview of digital library economics, describing the main areas to be discussed in more detail in subsequent chapters. It is complemented by Chapter 4, a résumé and critique by Derek Law of the case studies that form an integral part of the later chapters of this publication. For a fuller contextual and environmental analysis of the subject, see *Digital Library Economics: An Academic Perspective* (Baker and Evans, 2009), especially the first two chapters.

Defining the digital library

In 'an era of unprecedented technological innovation and evolving user expectations and information-seeking behaviour, we are arguably now an online society, with digital services increasingly common and increasingly preferred' (Buchanan, 2010; see also Castelli, 2006). Moreover, there continues to be an exponential growth in digital content and an ever greater divergence in its provenance. There is clearly a significant role for digital libraries which, ideally, should 'enable any citizen to access all human knowledge anytime and anywhere, in a friendly, multi-modal, efficient, and effective way, by overcoming barriers of distance, language, and culture and by using multiple Internet-connected devices'.[1]

> The 'Library' is being de- and re-constructed, with a digital future being seen as the norm in many environments. Digital libraries will not necessarily be linked to a physical space or a single organization, though many have grown – and will continue to grow – out of a single entity, which may have a physical base, collections and services as well as digital ones. In most cases, the digital library will bring together content and services from a range of suppliers, both commercial and non-commercial. In the digital library, physical location is immaterial and formats are diverse. (Baker, 2006)

What will the library be for, what will it be doing, in 20 years time? What are the things done now that should be distilled and preserved for the future, the unique roles and tasks that should continue, however technology might develop, and which are so demonstrably vital that funders and policy-makers will want to pay for them? A number of definitions of a digital library have been put forward in recent years. The most popular were analysed in *Digital Library Economics* (Baker and Evans, 2009). The working definition of the Digital Library Federation is regularly cited and appears to have a wide currency:

> Digital libraries are organizations that provide the resources, including the specialized staff, to select, structure, offer intellectual access to, interpret, distribute, preserve the integrity of, and ensure the persistence over time of collections of digital works so that they are readily and economically available for use by a defined community or set of communities. (Digital Library Federation, 1998)

The definition from the Joint Information Systems Committee (JISC) stresses the distributed nature of electronic library provision:

> A 'digital library' provides access to digital collections (as opposed to print, microform, or other media) using one or more interlinked information retrieval systems. The digital content may be stored locally within the institution, in a repository or stored remotely for example in a JISC data centre or a national repository and accessed via the Janet network.[2]

More recently, Candela et al. (2011) have provided another variant on the basic definition, as follows:

> A potentially virtual organisation, that comprehensively collects, manages and preserves for the long depth of time rich digital content, and offers to its targeted user communities specialised functionality on that content, of defined quality and according to comprehensive codified policies.

Our definition of a 'digital library' remains much the same as it was in *Digital Library Economics: An Academic Perspective* (Baker and Evans, 2009):

> ... an organizational entity that brings together a wide range of ... assets, including metadata, catalogues, primary source materials, learning objects, datasets and digital repositories – in a structured and managed way. It will be a place to search for these assets, to discover their existence, to locate them and then, if required, receive them. It will also recognize and support the core authoring functions of creation, iteration, finalization and publication. (Baker, 2006, cited in Baker and Evans, 2009)

In addition, digital libraries must maintain, store and preserve in ways not envisaged in a traditional library set-up. Elements of a digital library may include the conversion of existing services into digital mode or the creation of new services, for example 'online delivery, portals, personalised services, online teaching modules, online reference, digitised collections, or electronic publishing' (Poll, 2005). The emphasis will vary depending upon context, need and priority, though the basic elements identified here are typically always present (see, for example, Digital Library Federation, 1998; Seadle and Greifeneder, 2007).

The need for economics

Libraries – of all types – face an uncertain future (Feather, 2004; Grant, 2010). So do publishers and others involved in the creation, publication and dissemination of information and knowledge (see, for example, Paulson, 2011; Johnson, 2012). Continuing global economic difficulties and increased competition from other services and alternative means of provision mean that libraries will have to fight for resources, including through the development of strategic approaches and partnerships (Rasmussen and Jochumsen, 2003). In *Digital Library Economics* (Baker and Evans, 2009) we stressed the importance of the financial and related aspects of digital library management and development:

> Economics is a complex subject, and there are close links with other elements of the sophisticated and subtle value chain that is library provision and usage. It is more than just being about finances. Information has an economic value, not least in terms of added value, and in particular what it enables people to do once they possess information. (Baker and Evans, 2009)

However, it is only since the late 1990s that the need for a better understanding of all economic aspects of digital libraries – and notably cost, funding, long-term financial implications and the need to ensure sustainability – has been fully recognised. The drive to ensure sustainability has become ever more important and prevalent:

> And more and more new projects are being created with the premise that they should develop into sustainable services. Regardless of the initial intention, if the projects cannot achieve financial sustainability, they will either limp along or fail altogether. (Guthrie et al., 2008)

In *Digital Library Economics* (Baker and Evans, 2009), we discussed in some detail the key themes surrounding the development of the digital library in the first decade of the twenty-first century, as do the other authors in that volume. Those themes were further developed and broadened in *Libraries and Society: Role, Responsibility and Future in an Age of Change* (Baker and Evans, 2011) and even more so in *Trends, Discovery and People in the Digital Age* (Baker and Evans, 2013). The future of libraries – of all kinds – will be as dependent on economic and financial sustainability as on technological developments, though having said that it is clear that the two key themes of sustainability and innovation are inextricably linked. As both Eakin and Pomerantz (2009) and Koehn and Hawamdeh (2010) point out, libraries are in yet another phase of belt tightening and this situation is likely to continue for some considerable time.

All library systems are required to be efficient, effective and relevant, and economic pressures (see, for example, Martinez et al., 1998; Hutchings 2009; Koehn and Hawamdeh, 2010) are leading to the questioning of received wisdom and accepted models, the development and implementation of radical solutions and a resulting trend towards discontinuous change simply because existing ways of doing things can no longer be afforded (Hyams, 2010). Digital library developments are no longer an adjunct to traditional provision and access; they replace it – for good (Curtis et al., 2012) – though 'the justifications for delivering cultural resources digitally can rarely be made on purely financial grounds as the fiscal returns on investment are relatively small, but the returns for culture, education and prestige are high' (Tanner, 2004).

It is clear that change is already well under way (Keiser, 2010), with a wide range of pathfinder and exemplar projects exploring new futures for libraries. Indeed, librarians have often been some of the earliest adopters of new technologies (Walter, 2010), paving the way for more widespread adoption by other public and private sector organisations, though a number of commentators have observed that progress is neither consistent nor coherent. Nevertheless, librarians have evolved 'from mere content providers to sophisticated service suppliers' (Markscheffel, in CILIP, 2007) and in consequence, Buchanan (2010; see also Chowdhury, 2010) argues that, as a trusted information provider, libraries are in an advantageous position to respond to this much-changed environment, but this requires 'integrated strategic and enterprise architecture planning' across a complex matrix of variables, of which economic factors are a fundamental aspect. 'While challenging, such integrated planning should be regarded as an opportunity for the library to evolve as an enterprise in the digital age, or at minimum, to simply keep pace with societal change and alternative service providers' (Buchanan, 2010). It needs to be stressed, though, that once libraries enter the online world, they 'are moving from a relatively sheltered environment, operating at the pace of the academic enterprise, into one that operates at the speed of web commerce' (JISC, 2008) and away from the 'dependency culture' which Derek Law describes in Chapter 4. In any case, 'the pervasive nature of economics [means that it is something that is] influencing every decision, technology, implementation and evaluation' (Tanner, 2004), hence the need for a full and clear understanding of the economic management of the digital library. As Cathro puts it:

> A digital library, like any library, is more than a mere aggregation of information resources: it is a service which is based on principles of selection, acquisition, access, management and preservation, related to a specific client community . . . Thus any analysis of the economic aspects of digital libraries will need to take account of the costs of all of the above activities, while also examining issues of value and benefit . . . (Cathro, 2009)

However, as Tanner (2004; see also Lee, 1997; Deegan and Tanner, 2002; O'Connor, 2005; Jubb, 2007; Law, 2009; Creaser, 2011) goes on to say, the economic aspects of managing digital content and establishing digital libraries are proportionately underrepresented in the relevant literature, to the point where it is not necessarily clear or certain that digital solutions are always the most cost-effective or that they are economically sustainable (Marcum, 2001; Baker, 2006; Boukacem-Zeghmouri and Kamga, 2008; Lavoie, 2008). Indeed, the final evaluation of the UK's major eLib programme[3,4] makes almost no reference to the economic benefits of the initiative, though the subsequent assessment of the Joint Information Systems Committee's impact since its setting up in the wake of eLib suggested significant savings as a result of JISC's spend on electronic resources (Dolphin and Walk, 2008).

What is the value of libraries? Without robust answers to this question, it will be difficult to justify continued investment. Yet much progress still needs to be achieved if convincing cases are to be made. There are nevertheless some notable contributions to the subject area (see, for example, Lesk, 1997, 1999, 2005; Butler and Kingma,1999; Beagrie et al., 2008) and a number of earlier case studies show that a range of digital library developments have considered the financial implications, their evaluation and their management (see, for example, Martinez et al., 1998; Brewer, 2002; Choy, 2005; Hickox et al., 2006; Franklin and Plum, 2008; Poll, 2010; Steinberger, 2010; Walmiki, 2010). Tanner

(2009) stresses, however, that information and communications technology (ICT) in digital libraries is not always showing the immediate return on investment (ROI) delivered in the 1980s and 1990s, such that future developments will not necessarily instantly save staff time or reduce costs, certainly not if there is no overarching framework within which cost-effective decisions can be taken. Without coherent economic strategies and realistic business, funding, costing and pricing models, then rapid and effective digital library development could well be stifled (Carr, 2009). Financial considerations become ever more crucial in such circumstances.

Recent history and relevant work

Carr (2009) provides a useful history of digital library economics, noting that the financial sustainability of early digital library projects – as, for example JSTOR, discussed in Case Study 1 – was 'by no means certain' in their early years. Indeed, Carr stresses that there were many who did not believe that such initiatives would survive. Philanthropic funding made a big difference to such projects. Not all of them, though, put the question of long-term sustainability to one side in their early days. The California Digital Library (CDL) recognised as early as 1996 that the traditional provision of 'comprehensive research collections' across a distributed campus system was financially unsustainable. Both 'operational efficiencies' and 'additional cost savings' were required, at least in the longer term (Ober, 1999). This seems to have been achieved, at least partly, by the development of a number of equitable co-investment funding models that have been 'the basis for sharing the financial responsibility for providing access to . . . digital resources . . . on all ten campuses' (French, 2004). Business models were developed by publishers in order to calculate the total cost to the university of the digital resources, including a unit cost model based on full-time equivalent student numbers, the cost of print plus an electronic access fee and a flat fee plus a fee for ongoing access. CDL's involvement in digital library projects is discussed further in Case Studies 7 and 11. Carr (2009) notes other early successes, such as the 'Making of America' project:[5] 'Although few details have been published about the economics of this large digital collection – now containing almost four million digitised pages – the fact that it is still freely available and publicly searchable suggests that the costs of sustaining it have proved manageable.'

Kollöffel and Kaandorp (2003) describe the development of a model for academic libraries that can be used to give detailed insight into the library's current financial structure and to quantify the impact of the transition to a digital environment. Moving forward, certain library services, activities and costs will decrease whereas others will increase. How will this affect the library budget? The project gave all participants detailed insight into library costs before and after such a transition, and showed that the added value of library services increases. The model is a cooperation of the libraries of the universities of Utrecht in the Netherlands, Luleå in Sweden and Bremen in Germany. Elsevier commissioned the project; Atos KPMG Consulting delivered the methodology (Rapid Activity Based Costing) and financial expertise. Franklin and Plum (2008; see also Choy, 2005) surveyed early attempts by libraries to assess the value and impact of digital content on users. Among these were projects to standardise the measurement of digital content use, user satisfaction with digital content, cost–benefit analyses, and determination of the demographics and purpose of use of digital content.

Pomerantz et al. (2008) traced the history of digital libraries (DLs) in the United States through the funding sources that have supported DL research and development over the past decade and a half. A set of related questions are addressed: How have the mission and goals of funding agencies affected the types of projects that have been funded? What have been the deliverables from funded projects and how have the goals of the funding agencies shaped those deliverables? Funding agencies have exerted strong influence over research and development in DLs, and different funding agencies have funded different types of projects, with varying sets of concerns for driving the various fields that feed into DLs.

One great assistance to the development of DLs has been the ability to measure usage relatively easily. The development of the COUNTER (Counting Online Usage of Networked Electronic Resources) Code of Practice has helped. It has been possible to undertake many research projects aimed at analysing cost and usage and assessing relative value for money (King et al., 2003; Cooper, 2006).

Without exception, the advantage always lies with electronic publications, for several reasons: 'Big Deals' and consortium purchasing provide more titles for little more expenditure and the previously unsubscribed material always finds use; users make more use of texts now that they can access them from their own offices or homes and do not have to visit the library; more than one user can use the same material at the same time. (Woodward and Rowland, 2009)

Case Study 9 summarises and develops this kind of work.

In 2004, Pung et al. assessed the British Library's contribution to the UK national economy using the contingent valuation method (CVM) discussed in more detail in Chapter 3 and Case Study 9. Their study was the first of its kind and provided not only a comprehensive evaluation of the collections and services, but also a demonstration of how the technique could best be used, not least in a digital library context. Missingham (2005) followed this up by examining CVM not only at the British Library but also by public library services in the United States, and reviewed value studies of national bibliographic services in Canada and New Zealand.

Yet in 2007 the work of the Research Information Network on digital provision led to the conclusion that 'we lack the key components in the evidence base on which we might build an effective strategy for the future (Jubb, 2007). The Ithaka report *Sustainability and Revenue Models for Online Academic Resources* (Guthrie et al., 2008) thus examined the key mindsets needed to run a digital project and the success drivers and challenges of several revenue models, giving an overview of many of the issues which are pertinent to digitisation initiatives, including creating the culture and structure for success, leveraging value and some of the pros and cons of revenue-generating options. At much the same time, Joint (2008) examined the impact on library funding of 'budget holders' idiosyncratic understanding of three important principles of technological innovation: the more you use a technology, the less staff you need, the better the service becomes and the lower the cost of the service'. He found that there were 'common misunderstandings' about not only 'service-enhancing impacts' but also the real costs of supposedly free digital library provision – a major challenge still.

With the support of the Joint Information Systems Committee (JISC), the US National Endowment for the Humanities and the US National Science Foundation, Ithaka selected a range of projects to illustrate the various business models being employed (Maron et al., 2009). This new work focused on how project leaders were implementing these models, including advertising income, author fees, content licensing, corporate sponsorship, endowment, memberships, subscriptions, premium services and more. How did project leaders define their organisational mission and their sustainability goals? What steps did they take to build business models that generated revenue and controlled costs while also serving users? What contributed to the success of different models and what challenges were encountered?

The Blue Ribbon Task Force (2008) was set up to look at sustainable digital preservation and access, looking at economic sustainability, the cost of preserving valuable data and the identification of who will pay for it. The final report of the Task Force (2010) provides general principles and actions to support long-term economic sustainability; context-specific recommendations tailored to specific scenarios analysed in the report; and an agenda for priority actions and next steps, organised according to the type of decision-maker best suited to carry that action forward.

Digital preservation is concerned with the long-term safekeeping of electronic resources. How can we be confident of their permanence if we do not know the cost of preservation? One of the first attempts to look at lifecycle costing was the LIFE (Lifecycle Information for E-Literature[6]) Project (Watson, 2005; Davies et al., 2007; Wheatley and Hole, 2009), based at University College London. It has made a major step forward in understanding the long-term costs because it aimed at a comprehensive analysis of activities related to the management of content from selection, through licensing and acquisition to ingest, metadata creation, adding links, access, user support, storage costs and preservation. The project developed at least the basis for a robust methodology to model the digital lifecycle and to calculate the costs of preserving digital information for the next five, ten or 100 years. Libraries can now apply this process and plan effectively for the preservation of their digital collections.

Research into long-term preservation costs has also been explored in *Keeping Research Data Safe – A Cost Model and Guidance for UK Universities* (Beagrie et al., 2008). The study made a major contribution to the understanding of the long-term preservation costs for research data by developing a cost model and indentifying cost variables for preserving research data in UK universities. The conclusion was that it may be difficult to identify clearly digitisation costs without a full contextual understanding, not least because an initiative may be part of a set of activities, therefore making it difficult to isolate the cost model. The Keeping Research Data Safe 2 (KRDS2) project (Beagrie et al., 2010) built on this work and delivered the following:

1. A survey of cost information for digital preservation was carried out, collating and making available 13 survey responses for different cost datasets.

2. The KRDS activity model was reviewed and its presentation and usability enhanced.

3. Cost information for four organisations (the Archaeology Data Service, the National Digital Archive of Datasets, the UK Data Archive and the University of Oxford) was analysed in depth and presented in case studies.

4. A benefits framework was produced and illustrated with two benefit case studies from the National Crystallography Service at Southampton University and the UK Data Archive at the University of Essex.

Walters and Skinner (2010) describe one economically sustainable digital preservation model in practice, the MetaArchive Cooperative, a distributed digital preservation network that has been in operation since 2004. The MetaArchive has built its financial sustainability model and has experienced successes with it for several years, with an emphasis on cooperative models. Where possible, the approach taken by JISC is to sustain project outputs and the synthesis of knowledge, learning and lessons across a number of projects through existing JISC services or other agencies. An example of this approach can be seen in the toolkits created by JISC infoNet.[7]

The JISC-funded ESPIDA (An Effective Strategic model for the Preservation and Disposal of Institutional Digital Assets) project was completed in January 2007.[8] The initial aim was 'the creation of a model that could help the digital preservation community achieve sustained funding'. The plan was to develop a model of the relationships, roles and responsibilities, costs, benefits and risks inherent in institutional digital preservation and implement this model by selling it to all the stakeholder groups, including senior management, administrative and clerical staff and academic teachers and researchers. 'In particular, the project sought to identify the cost and benefits to the institution of developing a coherent, managed and sustainable approach to the preservation of its digital assets in a way that is transparent to all stakeholders.' The model that ESPIDA has developed can help make business cases for proposals that may not necessarily offer immediate financial benefit to an organisation, but rather bring benefit in more intangible spheres. While it was designed initially to be used within the area of digital resource management, it has potential for far wider application (decision-making, performance measurement, change management).

Ithaka are currently working on two projects directly focusing on sustainability. *Digital Content and Host Institution Support Strategies (UK)* is supported by JISC. The emphasis is on financial sustainability post launch of a project beyond the initial up-front costs. There are two phases to the project:

1. *Landscape research desk* – research and interviews with those involved in supporting digital resources with the aim of providing the research team with an understanding of the practices and expectations of project leaders, university administration and funders.

2. *In-depth assessment of three host institutions* – UCL, Imperial War Museums and the National Library of Wales – to provide a detailed view of how digitised projects are initiated, funded and supported in both academic and cultural heritage settings.

The final report *Sustaining Our Digital Future: Institutional Strategies for Digital Content* was published early 2013.

Sustaining the Digital Humanities: Host Institution Support Beyond the Start-up Phase is also an Ithaka project and builds upon the JISC-funded work. It is supported by the National Endowment for the Humanities. It commenced in October 2012; the final paper will be published March 2014. The project also has two stages:

1. *Sector-wide research* – interviews and research with stakeholders at a variety of HE institutions (in the US).

2. *Deep-dive research* – extensive analysis of two institutions that have created and managed several of their own digital projects allowing Ithaka S+R to develop a map of the full scope of activities, costs and value they offer and dynamics that drive decision-making.

Reference must also be made to the significant work of Houghton and others (Houghton et al., 2009) on the economic implications of alternative scholarly publishing models, with special reference to costs and benefits. Houghton discusses this work further in Case Study 7. Hall provides a useful critique of the research and the subsequent discussion of the main findings.[9]

Key themes

As we noted in *Digital Library Economics* (Baker and Evans, 2009):

The key themes are generally the same regardless of the resources in question . . . because there is always the need to juggle diverse needs with limited resources in a constant quest for sustainability. Libraries of all kinds . . . must be efficient and productive along with the rest of the economy. As a result, they have to increase efficiency and decrease costs in order to survive in any economic climate, and to ensure that information is available as cheaply as possible . . .

In that book, we identified what we regarded as the key themes relating to all aspects of digital libraries. Those relating particularly to their economic aspects form the basic framework of this book. They are briefly reviewed here before being discussed in more detail in later chapters and through the case studies.

Sustainability

The 'secret' to success in attaining long-term viability of a resource is in the development and successful implementation of a coherent sustainability plan: the steps a project commits to taking in order to deliver value to its users and, as a result, generate the resources it will need to survive and continue to grow. (Maron and Loy, 2011)

Arguably the most fundamental aspect of digital library development and management, then, is the question of sustainability (see, for example, Bond, 2006; Dawson, 2006; Blue Ribbon Task Force, 2008 and 2010; Maron et al., 2009; Walmiki, 2010; Walters and Skinner, 2010). As also evinced by the case studies in this handbook, the drive towards sustainability is of paramount importance. If a digital library cannot be sustained for the longer term, then the work of setting up the collections, services and/or other elements of the entity will have been in vain and there will be no transfer of any permanent benefit to the relevant user community/ies (see, for example, Ball, 2009). The whole question of sustainability is discussed in more detail in Chapter 2, while every one of the case studies looks at the challenge of sustaining a project, collection, service or other activity. But sustainability is only achievable through the development and implementation of robust models (see, for example, Dempster and Grout, 2009). 'Sustainable economics . . . is not just about finding more funds. It is about building an economic activity firmly rooted in a compelling value proposition, clear incentives to act, and well-defined ... roles and responsibilities' (Blue Ribbon Task Force, 2010), though 'there is no formulaic answer or single approach to achieving sustainability' (Guthrie et al., 2008). The future existence of libraries will depend to a high degree on their continued positive impact (Alwis and Fühles-Ubach, 2010) and the extent to which they create social, cultural and economic capital (Aabo and Audunson, 2002; Chung, 2008; Goulding, 2004, 2008; Varheim et al., 2008; Halpern, 2009), especially in the digital age (Aabo, 2005).

Models

> Economic models have changed hugely over the last decade and the search by both librarians and publishers for 'perfect' economic and business models will continue apace. (Woodward and Rowland, 2009)

> The requirements of ongoing sustainability demand at their base a source of reliable funding, necessary to ensure that the constant, albeit potentially low level, support ... can be maintained for as long as it is required. (Cathro, 2009)

Economic, business, financial, funding and pricing models are all considered in Chapter 3 and Case Studies 6–8, though most of the other studies also make at least some reference to some aspect of financial modelling. Shrinking budgets and the greater availability of material and information means that there must be a consistent and continuous search for increasing value for money, including as a means of creating funds to develop and exploit new resources and new technologies. A number of writers suggest the creation of frameworks as the best way of ensuring that the best use is made of resources, as for example Lavoie (2004) with his framework of 'responsibilities, incentives and organization', though one size most definitely does not – and will not – fit all.

Business plans and resource allocation

The development of effective and robust business plans supported by well thought-out and appropriately targeted resource allocation is deemed by many to be the key to sustainability in digital library provision and management (Poll, 2005; Brindley, 2009; Blue Ribbon Task Force,

2010). The realisation of financial objectives through the development of business plans and resource allocation – including the assignment of cost and value – is considered in Chapter 3 and Case Studies 3, 8, 9, 10 and 14.

Cost-effective decision-making

Effective decision-making should be based on basic questions such as: what is being used, by whom, in what way, when, with what outcome? All this is in addition to the many 'how' questions that need to be pursued, not least in terms of funding and resourcing. The decision-maker should be making choices based on priorities and criteria underpinned by strategic priorities which, most importantly, bring an appropriate return on investment (Baker and Evans, 2009). Determining what to fund and what not to fund needs to be based on cost-benefit analysis and the extent to which value – and not simply economic value – is added longer term through the investment being made (see, for example, Rauch and Rauber, 2005; Shearer et al., 2009). In this context, the ability to cover ongoing costs (the fundamental question of sustainability) must be tested. Costs therefore need to be understood in order to be as efficient and economical as possible, to attract and manage income and to respond to risk in the most robust way possible. Chapters 2–4 and the various case studies consider these issues further.

Conclusion

These, then, are the main areas covered in this handbook. The 'wordles' at the start of each case study – and perhaps especially that associated with Derek Law's summary in Chapter 4 – show both the complexity of the subject on the one hand and the commonality of the key areas on the other. There can be no one right answer and no perfect solution to the many problems posed in any digital library project. However, the last ten years have seen many positive developments that need to be used as the basis of robust collection and service development for the longer term. As we said in the companion volume to this handbook:

> Digital library approaches offer significant potential for altering existing ways of doing things, reducing costs and making real use of the digital revolution that is already well under way . . . But it

must be more than simply repackaging traditional processes and materials. Innovative thinking is required in terms of a whole range of developments focusing on the provision of value added services. (Baker and Evans, 2009)

As Derek Law comments in Chapter 4, the digital library world is populated by naturally collaborative innovators, as evinced by the case studies, so there is much cause for optimism in terms of meeting the challenges identified in this chapter and throughout the rest of the publication. The emphasis is on practical applications based on as wide a range of experience and know-how as we have been able to assemble, using key contributions from experts in the field, whether on the basis of the available literature or the specific contributions to this handbook.

Notes

1. *http://www.delos.info/index.php?option=com_content&task=view&id =299 &Itemid=26*
2. *http://www.jisc.ac.uk/whatwedo/topics/digitallibraries.aspx*
3. *http://www.jisc.ac.uk/media/documents/publications/elibimpactstudyreport. pdf*
4. See also *http://lcweb2.loc.gov/ammem/dli2/html/cbedl.html*
5. *http://quod.lib.umich.edu/m/moagrp/*
6. *http://www.life.ac.uk/*
7. *http://www.jiscinfonet.ac.uk/infokits*
8. *http://www.jisc.ac.uk/media/documents/programmes/preservation/espida projectjiscfinalreport.pdf*
9. *http://dx.doi.org/10.1080/08109021003676375*

References

Aabo, S. (2005) 'The role and value of public libraries in the age of digital technologies', *Journal of Librarianship and Information Science*, 37 (4): 205–11.

Aabo, S. and Audunson, R. (2002) 'Rational choice and valuation of public libraries: can economic models for evaluating non-market goods be applied to public libraries?' *Journal of Librarianship and Information Science*, 34 (1): 5–16.

Alwis, R.S. and Fühles-Ubach, S. (2010) 'Success factors for the future of information centres, commercial and public libraries: a study from Germany', *Interlending and Document Supply*, 38 (3): 183–8.

Baker, D. (2006) 'Digital library futures: a UK HE and FE perspective', *Interlending and Document Supply*, 34 (1): 4–8.

Baker, D. and Evans, W. (eds) (2009) *Digital Library Economics: An Academic Perspective*. Oxford: Chandos Publishing.

Baker, D. and Evans, W. (eds) (2011) *Libraries and Society: Role, Responsibility and Future in an Age of Change*. Oxford: Chandos Publishing.

Baker, D. and Evans, W. (eds) (2013) *Trends, Discovery and People in the Digital Age*. Oxford: Chandos Publishing.

Ball, R. (2009) 'Digital library economics: international perspectives: the German perspective', in D. Baker and W. Evans (eds), *Digital Library Economics: An Academic Perspective*. Oxford: Chandos Publishing.

Beagrie, N., Chruszcz, J. and Lavoie, B. (2008) *Keeping Research Data Safe: A Cost Model and Guidance for UK Universities*. Bristol: JISC. Online at: *http://www.jisc.ac.uk/publications/publications/keepingresearchdatasafe.aspx*.

Beagrie, N., Lavoie, B. and Woollard, M. (2010) *Keeping Research Data Safe 2*. Bristol: JISC. Online at: *http://www.jisc.ac.uk/media/documents/publications/reports/2010/keepingresearchdatasafe2.pdf*.

Blue Ribbon Task Force (2008) *Sustaining the Digital Investment: Issues and Challenges of Economically Sustainable Digital Preservation*, Interim Report of the Blue Ribbon Task Force on Sustainable Digital Preservation and Access. Online at: *http://brtf.sdsc.edu/biblio/BRTF_Interim_Report.pdf*.

Blue Ribbon Task Force (2010) *Sustainable Economics for a Digital Planet: Ensuring Long-Term Access to Digital Information*, Final report of the Blue Ribbon Task Force on Sustainable Digital Preservation and Access. Online at: *http://brtf.sdsc.edu/biblio/BRTF_Final_Report.pdf*.

Bond, T.J. (2006) 'Sustaining a digital collection after the grants: the Early Washington Maps Project', *OCLC Systems and Services*, 22 (1): 56–66.

Boukacem-Zeghmouri, C. and Kamga, R. (2008) 'La consultation de périodiques numériques en bibliothèque universitaire: état des lieux', *Bulletin des Bibliothèques de France*, 3: 48–60.

Brewer, G. (2002) 'Case study: the University of Derby Electronic Library, a case study of some economic and academic aspects of a local digitised collection', *Electronic Library and Information Systems*, 36 (1): 30–7.

Brindley, L. (2009) 'Foreword: digital library economics: an introduction', in D. Baker and W. Evans (eds), *Digital Library Economics: An Academic Perspective*. Oxford: Chandos Publishing.

Buchanan, S. (2010) 'Planning strategically, designing architecturally: a framework for digital library services', *Advances in Librarianship*, 32: 159–80.

Butler, M.A. and Kingma, B.R (1999) *The Economics of Information in the Networked Environment*. New York: Haworth Press.

Candela, L., Athanasopoulos, G., Castelli, D., El Raheb, K., Innocenti, P., Ioannidis, Y., Katifori, A., Nika, A., Vullo, G. and Ross, S. (2011) *The Digital Library Reference Model*. Online at: *http://bscw.research-infrastructures.eu/pub/bscw.cgi/d222816/D3.2b%20Digital%20Library%20Reference%20Model.pdf*.

Carr, R.P. (2009) 'A history of digital library economics', in D. Baker and W. Evans (eds), *Digital Library Economics: An Academic Perspective.* Oxford: Chandos Publishing.

Castelli, D. (2006) 'Digital libraries of the future – and the role of libraries', *Library Hi Tech*, 24 (4): 496–503.

Cathro, W. (2009) 'Digital library economics: international perspectives: the Australian perspective', in D. Baker and W. Evans (eds), *Digital Library Economics: An Academic Perspective.* Oxford: Chandos Publishing.

Chowdhury, G. (2010) 'From digital libraries to digital preservation research: the importance of users and context', *Journal of Documentation*, 66 (2): 207–23.

Choy, F.C. (2005) 'Preparing for the future: academic libraries in the beginning of the 21st century', *ICOL*. Online at: *http://dr.ntu.edu.sg/bitstream/ handle/10220/6134/ICOL-2005-CFC.pdf;jsessionid=6DAD448FBD986B6 DE5AF856A68B4E8C5?sequence=1.*

Chung, H.-K. (2008) 'The contingent valuation method in public libraries', *Journal of Librarianship and Information Science*, 40 (2): 71–80.

CILIP (2007) 'Online information 2007', *Library and Information Update*, 6 (11): 21.

Cooper, M.D. (2006) 'The cost of providing electronic journal access and printed copies of journals to university users', *Library Quarterly*, 76 (3): 323–51.

Creaser, C. (2011) 'Open access to research outputs – institutional policies and researchers' views: results from two complementary surveys', *New Review of Academic Librarianship*, 16 (1): 4–25.

Curtis, G. et al. (2012) *Academic Libraries of the Future: Scenarios Beyond 2020.* British Library, JISC and others. Online at: *http://www.futurelibraries. info/content/system/files/Scenarios_beyond_2020_ReportWV.pdf.*

Davies, R., Ayris, P., Mcleod, R., Shenton, H. and Wheatle, P. (2007) 'How much does it cost? The LIFE Project – costing models for digital curation and preservation', *Liber Quarterly*, 17 (3/4). Online at: *http://eprints.ucl.ac. uk/18872/1/18872.pdf.*

Dawson, A. (2006) 'Issues, principles and policies for creating high-quality digital resources with low-cost methods', *New Review of Information Networking*, 12 (1/2): 87–91.

Deegan, M. and Tanner, S. (2002) *Digital Futures: Strategies for the Information Age.* London: Library Association Publishing.

Dempster, S. and Grout, C. (2009) 'Digitisation – trends in the economics of retro-conversion', in D. Baker and W. Evans (eds), *Digital Library Economics: An Academic Perspective.* Oxford: Chandos Publishing.

Digital Library Federation (1998) *A Working Definition of Digital Library.* Online at: *http://www.diglib.org/about/dldefinition.htm.*

Dolphin, I. and Walk, P. (2008) 'Towards a Strategic Approach to the Integrated Information Environment'. Unpublished JISC discussion document.

Eakin, L. and Pomerantz, J. (2009) 'Virtual reference, real money: modelling costs in virtual reference services', *Portal: Libraries and the Academy*, 9 (1): 133–64.

Feather, J. (2004) *The Information Society: A Study of Continuity and Change*, 4th edn. London: Facet.

Franklin, B. and Plum, T. (2008) 'Assessing the value and impact of digital content', *Journal of Library Administration*, 48 (1): 41–57. Online at: *http://dspace.nitle.org/bitstream/handle/10090/7643/FranklinPlumAssessing ValueDigitalContent.pdf?sequence=1*.

French, B. (2004) 'The economics and management of digital resources in a multi-campus, multi-library university: the shared digital collection', *Collection Management*, 28 (1/2): 45–54.

Goulding, A. (2004) 'Libraries and social capital', *Journal of Librarianship and Information Science*, 36 (1): 3–6.

Goulding, A. (2008) 'Libraries and cultural capital', *Journal of Librarianship and Information Science*, 40 (4): 235–7.

Grant, C. (2010) 'How librarians can shape the future', *Public Library Quarterly*, 29 (2): 95–103.

Guthrie, K., Griffiths, R. and Maron, N. (2008) *Sustainability and Revenue Models for Online Academic Resources*. Ithaka. Online at: *http://sca.jiscinvolve.org/files/2008/06/sca_ithaka_sustainability_report-final.pdf*.

Halpern, D. (2009) 'Capital gains', *RSA Journal*, Autumn, pp. 10–14.

Hickox, C., Jackson, R., Markham, G. and Cox, C. (2006) 'Going broke, going digital: a preliminary cost analysis of building a digital library', *Internet Reference Services Quarterly*, 11 (1): 51–66.

Houghton, J. et al. (2009) *Economic Implications of Alternative Scholarly Publishing Models: Exploring the Costs and Benefits*. Bristol: JISC.

Hutchings, C. (2009) *Impact of the Economic Downturn on University Library and IT Services*, Final Report. JISC, SCONUL and UCISA. Online at: *http://www.jisc.ac.uk/media/documents/publications/libsitimpacts.pdf*.

Hyams, E. (2010) 'Where next for the serials crisis?', *Library and Information Gazette*, June, p. 4.

JISC (2008) 'Libraries unleashed', *Guardian Supplement*, 22 April.

Johnson, L. (2012) 'Permission for growth', *Management Today*, September, p. 23.

Joint, N. (2008) 'It is not all free on the web: advocacy for library funding in the digital age', *Library Review*, 57 (4): 270–5.

Jubb, M. (2007) 'Supporting the research base: the research information network and scholarly communications in the UK', *New Review of Academic Librarianship*, 13 (1/2): 35–50.

Keiser, B.E. (2010) 'Library of the future – today!', *Searcher*, 18 (8): 18–54.

King, D., Boyce, P., Montgomery, C., Tenopir, C., Liu, L. and Allen, B. (2003) 'Library economic metrics: examples of the comparison of electronic and print journal collections and collection services', *Library Trends*, 51 (3): 376–400.

Koehn, S. and Hawamdeh, S. (2010) 'The acquisition and management of electronic resources: can use justify cost?', *Library Quarterly*, 80 (2): 161–74.

Kollöffel, J. and Kaandorp, A. (2003) 'Developing a cost/benefit financial model for hybrid libraries', *Serials*, 16 (1): 41–9.

Lavoie, B. (2004) 'Of mice and memory: economically sustainable preservation for the twenty-first century', *Access in the Future Tense*, CLIR Reports Publication 126. Online at: *http://www.clir.org/pubs/reports/pub126/lavoie.html*.

Lavoie, B. (2008) 'The fifth blackbird: some thoughts on economically sustainable digital preservation', *D-Lib Magazine*, 14 (3/4). Online at: *http://www.dlib.org/dlib/march08/lavoie/03lavoie.html*.

Law, D. (2009) 'Digital library economics: aspects and prospects', in D. Baker and W. Evans (eds), *Digital Library Economics: An Academic Perspective*. Oxford: Chandos Publishing.

Lee, S. (ed.) (1997) *Economics of Digital Information: Collection, Storage and Delivery*. New York: Haworth Press.

Lesk, M. (1997) *Practical Digital Libraries: Books, Bytes and Bucks*. San Francisco: Morgan Kaufman.

Lesk, M. (1999) 'The organisation of digital libraries', *Science and Technology Libraries*, 17 (3–4): 9–25.

Lesk, M. (2005) *Understanding Digital Libraries*, 2nd edn. San Francisco: Morgan Kaufman.

Marcum, D. (2001) *Development of Digital Libraries – An American Perspective*. Westport, CT: Greenwood Press.

Maron, N. and Loy, M. (2011) *Revenue, Recession, Reliance: Revisiting the SCA/Ithaka S+R Case Studies in Sustainability*. Bristol: JISC.

Maron, N., Smith, K. and Loy, M. (2009) *Sustaining Digital Resources: An On-the-Ground View of Projects Today*, Ithaka Case Studies in Sustainability. Bristol: JISC. Online at: *http://www.jisc.ac.uk/media/documents/publications/general/2009/scaithakaprojectstoday.pdf*.

Maron, N., Yun, J. and Pickle, S. (2013) *Sustaining Our Digital Future: Institutional Strategies for Digital Content*. London: Strategic Content Alliance.

Martinez, J., Newsome, K. and Sheble, M. (1998) 'Planning and budgeting the transition to a digital tomorrow', *Serials Librarian*, 34 (3): 353–60.

Missingham, R. (2005) *Libraries and Economic Value: A Review of Recent Studies*. Online at: *http://www.nla.gov.au/openpublish/index.php/nlasp/article/view/1213/1498*.

O'Connor, S. (2005) 'The economics of repository libraries in the context of the future conventional libraries', *Library Management*, 26 (1/2): 18–25.

Ober, J. (1999) 'The California Digital Library', *D-Lib Magazine*, 5 (3). Online at: *http://www.dlib.org/dlib/march99/03ober.html*.

Paulson, K. (2011) 'E-books procurement: a disruptive business', *CILIP Update*, April, pp. 20–2.

Poll, R. (2005) 'Measuring the impact of new library services', *World Library and Information Congress: 71st IFLA General Conference and Council*, Oslo, 14–18 August.

Poll, R. (2010) 'Digitisation in European libraries: results of the NUMERIC Project', *Liber Quarterly*, 19 (3/4): 248–58. Online at: *http://liber.library.uu.nl/index.php/lq/article/view/7964*.

Pomerantz, J., Choemprayong, S. and Eakin, L. (2008) 'The development and impact of digital library funding in the United States', in A. Woodsworth (ed.), *Influence of Funding on Advances in Librarianship, Advances in Librarianship, Vol. 31*. UK: Emerald Group, pp. 37–92.

Pung, C., Clarke, A. and Pattern, L. (2004) 'Measuring the economic impact of the British Library', *New Review of Academic Librarianship*, 10 (1): 79–102.

Rasmussen, C.H. and Jochumsen, H. (2003) 'Strategies for public libraries in the 21st century', *International Journal of Cultural Policy*, 9 (1): 83–93.

Rauch, C. and Rauber, A. (2005) 'Anwendung der Nutzwertanalyze zur Bewertung von Strategien zur langfristigen Erhaltung digitaler Objekte', *Zeitschrift für Bibliothekswesen und Bibliographie*, 52 (3/4): 172–83. Online at: *http://www.ifs.tuwien.ac.at/~andi/publications/pdf/rau_zfbb05.pdf*.

Seadle, M. and Greifeneder, E. (2007) 'Defining a digital library', *Library Hi Tech*, 25 (2): 169–73.

Shearer, B., Klatt, C. and Nagy, S. (2009) 'Development of a new academic digital library: a study of usage data of a core medical electronic journal collection', *Journal of the Medical Library Association*, 97 (2): 93–101. Online at: *http://www.ncbi.nlm.nih.gov/pmc/articles/PMC2670205/*.

Steinberger, N. (2010) 'Building a virtual library – a case study at the library of the Jewish Theological Seminary', in K. Bor Ng and J. Kuscma (eds), *Digitization Projects in the Real World*. New York: Metropolitan New York Library Council. Full chapter postprint available online at: *http://eprints.ecs.soton.ac.uk/21471/1/Chapter_8_Swan_postprint.doc*.

Tanner, S. (2004) 'Economic factors of managing digital content and establishing digital libraries', *Journal of Digital Information*, 4 (2). Online at: *http://journals.tdl.org/jodi/article/viewArticle/98/97*.

Tanner, S. (2009) 'The economic future for digital libraries: a 2020 vision', in D. Baker and W. Evans (eds), *Digital Library Economics: An Academic Perspective*. Oxford: Chandos Publishing.

Varheim, A., Steinmo, S. and Ide, E. (2008) 'Do libraries matter? Public libraries and the creation of social capital', *Journal of Documentation*, 64 (6): 877–92.

Walmiki, R. (2010) 'Libraries' response to changing information environment: a study of Karnataka State University Libraries', *SRELS Journal of Information Management*, 47 (4): 449–63.

Walter, V. (2010) *Twenty First Century Kids, Twenty First Century Librarians*. Chicago: American Library Association.

Walters, T. and Skinner, K. (2010) 'Economics, sustainability, and the cooperative model in digital preservation', *Library Hi Tech*, 28 (2): 259–72.

Watson, J. (2005) *The LIFE Project Research Review: Mapping the Landscape, Riding a Life Cycle*. Online at: *http://eprints.ucl.ac.uk/archive/00001856/01/review.pdf*.

Wheatley, P. and Hole, B. (2009) 'LIFE3: predicting long-term digital preservation costs', *iPRES 2009: The Sixth International Conference on Preservation of Digital Objects*. California Digital Library, UC Office of the President, 5–6 October. Online at *http://escholarship.org/uc/item/23b3225n*.

Woodward, H. and Rowland, F. (2009) 'E-journals and e-books', in D. Baker and W. Evans (eds), *Digital Library Economics: An Academic Perspective*. Oxford: Chandos Publishing.

2

Sustainability

Abstract. Chapter 2 considers the fundamental issue in digital library management and development: that of sustainability. It provides a definition of the term and looks at the basics of a sustainable approach, drawing on the authors' own research, key relevant literature and the case studies.

Keywords: digital library development, digital library management, sustainability

Introduction

This chapter and the ensuing case studies look at how best to make digital libraries, collections and services economically viable and financially sustainable, drawing on research and experience to date. John Robinson describes some of the challenges of ensuring sustainability:

> Librarians have always been engaged with the problem of sustaining their infrastructures ... The generic challenges are the same: capital-intensive infrastructure which must be replaced every five or ten years; teams of people with the high-level systems administration and programming skills required to operate the infrastructure; new approaches to revenue budgeting which take into account the new operating costs and the requirement by the institution to defend these costs ... (Robinson, 2009)

As we wrote in *Digital Library Economics* (Baker and Evans, 2009), there are a good many different activities (all of which cost) that need to be taken into account in order to ensure sustainability:

> Paying for access to the information is only the first step, whether or not the costs are passed on to the user. It is then necessary to make it

accessible, as for example by: marketing the existence of the resources to users; by developing good search and classification functions; by training staff in accessing the information and instructing others in how to access, evaluate and reference information. These overheads or 'extras' also cost money and may not be affordable on top of purchasing costs.

Defining sustainability

Abby Smith (2003) sums up the main challenge as being 'how to pay for it all', especially after the initial grants have finished (Bond, 2006). As Derek Law points out in Chapter 4, even projects that are set up for the public good have to be sustainable, for without sustainability there is no long term, and any benefits envisaged can either not be realised or realised only fleetingly. But, important though finding the money is, there is more to it than that. It is about thinking and planning for the long term, not least in order to ensure that up-front investment results in long-term benefit for the key stakeholders – funders, users, subscribers and so on. 'Ensuring sustainability requires taking long hard looks at the environment and the service or collection required, including in relation to costs . . . sustainability is also about preservation and the risks associated with losing data if financial sustainability is not achieved' (Baker and Evans, 2009). Sustainability is not the same as independent continuation, however:

> Start-ups in the private sector aim for independent profitability but they also consider it a success to sell their companies to a larger enterprise with the means to take those assets forward. They may also seek to merge with complementary businesses. Not-for-profit projects should think similarly about their options and pursue different forms of sustainability based on their particular strengths, their competition, and their spheres of activity. It is enormously difficult to survive in a competitive environment with a single product aimed at a single market. (Guthrie et al. 2008)

Basics of a sustainable approach

The way in which sustainability should be addressed will depend on the context, the type of project, service or resource, and the desired outputs and outcomes. Table 2.1 lists what are widely seen as the basic requirements for a sustainable service or resource.

Table 2.1 Basic requirements for sustainability

Valuable products	'The key to sustainability . . . is to reach a position where the digital library is no longer regarded as an add-on but as part of this integral core.' (Bennett, 2001) 'The starting point of your campaign towards sustainability has to be a product that is valuable, and not just to you and your colleagues . . . Beware the attractions of the technology-driven project: just because something can be done, does not mean it should be.' (Hamilton, 2004) 'Products must add value in order to create competitive advantage, attracting and retaining audience, for example by building up a strong presence in the marketplace or by providing tools and/or content that becomes integrated into the user's workflows.' (Baker and Evans, 2009)
Robust business models/cases	Sustainability has to be 'supported by a robust business model – whether this be through 100 per cent funding by the taxpayer or through the monetarisation of the content.' (Dempster and Grout, 2009) 'Economic viability for the production and distribution of information goods and services requires appropriate mechanisms for the recovery of costs and pricing mechanisms that are acceptable to users.' (Brindley, 2009)
Strong set of processes and organisational structures	'Sustainability is most likely to be achieved if there is a strong set of processes and organisational structures in place that takes initiatives beyond the project and start-up stages.' (Baker and Evans, 2009)
Understanding of the users (secondary as well as primary) and their interests/needs	'Looking at the "fringe benefits" – the benefits to users outside the immediate community – as well will help, for example the general public or school children as well as academics. This will be one way of increasing value at little extra cost.' (Baker and Evans, 2009) Project MUSE (Case Study 2) suggests continuous engagement with key communities and users.

Table 2.1 Basic requirements for sustainability (*cont'd*)

Market research	'Providing access to the digital world is expensive . . . and limited financial resources means informed targeting of resources, and a continual review of market penetration.' (Macdonald and Kebbell, 2004) 'Identification procedures to highlight services, resources and materials that are the most useful and are therefore likely to be funded [or income generating are needed]. This will be not just an understanding of the technology and the environment in which one is working but an understanding of demand as well as supply gained through market research.' (Baker and Evans, 2009)
Technology assessment	'Just because technology has made developments possible does not mean that they become feasible economically. The technology needs to be thought about before proceeding. It is necessary to make sure that the technology will add value. It is inappropriate just to use the same processes in a new environment. Rather, it is important to make sure that the process is appropriate for the digital environment.' (Baker and Evans, 2009)
Evidence of positive effects/ impact measures	'Libraries need to justify the investment in change and to prove the efficiency and positive impact of the new resources and services . . . funding institutions want evidence of positive effects . . . [in order to] gain a basis for resource allocation.' (Poll, 2005) 'New services always cost money. This may be needed for specific new resources or equipment, staff training, changes to workflows or work practices, new or different physical space, and so on. It will always be important to measure the impact of such services to see if they are worth it. For example, on the positive side, do they reduce the time taken, enlarge the scope or lower the costs associated with, say, the learning and teaching or the research process? On the negative side, do they result in information overload, technical problems, or the over-reliance on one type of resource, for instance? The impact will depend on the goals of the library and the reasons the users patronise it: what the library wants to achieve – and therefore the link between its aims and the actual end result.' (Baker and Evans, 2009)
Cost-efficiency and affordability	'The economic challenge [is one] of making our information systems both cost-efficient and affordable.' (Bennett, 2001)

Capital programme (rolling, as necessary)	'Digital library managers must accept that capital spend will not be a one-off: there will be a requirement for rolling programmes of updates to software, hardware and other core infrastructural elements, together with basic running costs including commodities such as electricity and related bills. Otherwise, digital library provision will become increasingly unreliable, ending up as a greater financial risk to the providing institution.' (Baker and Evans, 2009)
Collaboration	'The digital world not only makes collaboration possible, it may make it economically imperative.' (Lee, 1997) For institutions, the attractions will be: cost savings, or at least cost avoidance in the future; cost/time efficiency, providing more information for the same level of effort; and less investment risk. Suppliers may gain a bigger market share, a ready market or one bill or licence through collaboration. (See also Anglada and Comellas, 2002; Anderson, 2008.) 'The shared approach and the shared ownership of the repository resource makes real economic sense.' (O'Connor, 2005) 'Collaboration on many levels (local, regional, national, international and with non-academic and commercial partners) and coherence between groups and areas will make the . . . sector sustainable in the longer term.' (Baker, 2006) Partnership provision – as noted in Table 3.1 – can often provide the necessary financial sustainability through the development of shared-risk business models (Cox, 2007), though agreements need to be in place to ensure equity. 'We all benefit from (and generate) economies of scale, pooled expertise, larger funding, and more robust infrastructure when we collaborate.' (Zorich, 2007). 'On-line content is now an essential resource where significant economies of scale can be found by national procurement and delivery' (JISC, 2007). Managed licensing agreements and central negotiation have led to better deals and good terms and conditions that allow the utilisation of materials for the benefit of research, learning and teaching development and also relationship management with other key stakeholders such as publishers.

Table 2.1   Basic requirements for sustainability (*cont'd*)

'Responding to the challenges must include assessing and realising the potential for mergers or the aggregation of the offer through partnerships, public and private, with others . . . [also] collective licensing is increasingly valued and valuable as a way of ensuring both cost-effective provision and long-term sustainability.' (Baker and Evans, 2009; see also Middleton, 2005)

'Collaboration will also help with preservation. Much of the cost is fixed so the more people who collaborate, the more spread out the fixed costs are, and the more materials that utilise the fixed cost, the lower the cost per usage. No one institution can know whether it will be able to fund preservation indefinitely, so collaboration lowers the risk that money will be spent on digitising and archiving materials that might suddenly become unreachable if the institution stops funding the preservation programme.' (Baker and Evans, 2009)

'Collaborative activities can influence the economics of digital libraries in several ways. Development of shared infrastructure and shareable software can assist in reducing the costs of developing and maintaining digital library services. Collaborative activities can also increase the value of digital libraries from the user perspective.' (Cathro, 2009)

'There is also an increasing emphasis on shared services, at regional, national and international level, though the ability to have localised – and indeed personalised – flexibility seems to be crucial to the success of such collaborative projects. The benefits are considerable, both in terms of cost efficiency and enhanced services to users.' (Baker and Evans, 2009; see also Collier, 2004, 2005)

'Linking in more closely with commercial providers and players is a way of dealing with declining budgets and rising costs as well as the opportunities provided by digital approaches. It is also a way of ensuring that library mechanisms remain up to date and attractive to users, both by utilising the existing interface styles such as Google and by getting hold of market research to ensure the targeting of key groups – for example students – successfully. There may be new costs here as well, for example staff time management of collaborative

	partnerships or the loss of the ability to develop internal economies of scale. Arguably, prospective collaborators should be judged on a cost-benefit analysis: do they add enough value to be worthwhile? Collaboration will thus help everyone to access these resources and to utilise them fully as well as spreading the costs for their development and maintenance. Many authors suggest that the way forward may be to merge and to share resources, accessing them via aggregated tools, for example with metadata harvesting aggregators or with regional repositories. Collective licensing (as for example with the SHEDL initiative) is increasingly valued and valuable as a way of ensuring both cost-effective provision and long-term sustainability.' (Baker and Evans, 2009) Walters and Skinner (2010) 'consider in detail the cooperative model and the path it provides toward sustainability as well as how it fosters participation by cultural memory organizations and their administrators, who are concerned about what digital preservation will ultimately cost and who will pay.'
Flexibility	A product or service will need to be adaptable in respect of the environment that is emerging around it, and adept enough to respond to those changes that are perceived as being important for the future. 'In a fast-changing environment [with constantly developing technology], it is crucial to ensure flexibility, continually finding ways of monetising the value of the product going forward, understanding the fact that costs are ongoing.' (Baker and Evans, 2009)
Good risk management	There will always be a risk with any new (technology) development. The five categories of suggested response to risks are:* Prevention Terminate the risk – by doing things differently and thus removing the risk, where it is feasible to do so. Countermeasures are put in place that either stop the threat or problem from occurring or prevent it having any impact on the project or business.

Table 2.1 Basic requirements for sustainability (*cont'd*)

Reduction	Treat the risk – take action to control it in some way where the actions either reduce the likelihood of the risk developing or limit the impact on the project to acceptable levels.
Transference	This is a specialist form of risk reduction where the management of the risk is passed to a third party via, for instance, an insurance policy or penalty clause, such that the impact of the risk is no longer an issue for the health of the project. Not all risks can be transferred in this way.
Acceptance	Tolerate the risk – perhaps because nothing can be done at a reasonable cost to mitigate it or the likelihood and impact of the risk occurring are at an acceptable level.
Contingency	These are actions planned and organised to come into force as and when the risk occurs.

* Office of Government Commerce (2005) 'Managing Successful Projects with PRINCE2', Management of Risk.

Sustainability criteria

Fulfilling the basic requirements listed in Table 2.1 will not necessarily guarantee sustainability. A number of more specific criteria typically need to be met in order to ensure – as far as it is possible to do so – that a project or service will be sustainable in the longer term. Table 2.2 aims to list and describe the key criteria. It is not expected that all of these questions can necessarily be answered or be relevant for every project or service.

Table 2.2   Key sustainability criteria

Area	Key questions
Strategic fit	How closely does the product or service align with relevant strategies (funders, organisational and individual stakeholders)?
Demonstrable impact	What (positive) impact is likely to be demonstrated over a reasonable time period, as expected by the key stakeholders?
Differentiation	Where there is competition for resources, it will be important to ensure that the project, product or service can be differentiated from that of rival ones, whether by added value, competitive pricing or other attractant(s) or benefit(s) as listed in this table.
Value for money	Will the product or service provide good value for money, as perceived by all the key stakeholders?
Return on investment	Will the return on the initial or ongoing investment be deemed to be sufficient by those doing the investing?
Product or service performance	Is the product or service performing as well as it needs to do to fulfil other key criteria? Will it continue to perform well in the longer term?
User need	Is there evidence of user need? What do users value? What are their perceptions? Is there a developing market to deliver similar services freely or under different business models? Is there sufficient evidence of continuing user demand?
Level of innovation/ obsolescence	How leading edge are the products or services? (This includes enabling innovative research or teaching to take place through lowering the barriers to take up of new types of resource, for example.) Are new products or technologies emerging that may render the product or service redundant or inefficient? Are more innovative approaches or technologies developing that could be adopted to improve the value or impact of the service? Can the product or service be re-engineered or refreshed if/when the technology being used starts to become obsolescent?
Competition	Is there evidence of emerging competition in the area, commercially or from other public sector organisations? Does acceptable alternative provision, either commercial or non-commercial, exist?
Consolidation	Are there opportunities for consolidation across operations, products or services, or between participating organisations?

Case studies

All the case studies in this book refer to long-term sustainability and the challenge of achieving it. However, we have selected four studies in particular to complement this chapter on sustainability in general.

Case Study 1

The JSTOR service has become ever more vital as pressure on traditional libraries increases – not only in terms of budgets and physical space but also increased user demand and exponential growth in publications. The case study exemplifies some of the critical success factors in ensuring long-term sustainability: having a robust and attractive value proposition with 'unique benefits'; ensuring that the products meet the needs both of the market and of the content suppliers; being flexible and open to change; emphasising collaboration. But it is the tiered pricing model that makes the JSTOR offer especially attractive for its users (including pricing stability) on the one hand and the organisation financially sustainable (not least in terms of JSTOR's ability to generate capital for renewal and regeneration purposes) on the other.

Case Study 2

As with the JSTOR project, part of the initial rationale for Project MUSE was to respond to the growing budgetary crisis in humanities academic publishing. Again, the critical success factor has been the organisation's vision, strategy and ability to evolve 'in dynamic ways', supported by collaborative approaches and tiered pricing structures. MUSE leaders were – and are – also willing to take risks. The end result has been an attractive product that people want to buy into because – as, for example, in the case of libraries and the need to make savings – it gives them what they want and need. In other words, it adds value at a price or a cost they can afford.

Case Study 3

One of the critical success factors most evident in this project is cooperation and collaboration on a community-wide scale. While grants and internal resource allocations provided the necessary start-up funds, partnership working enabled the project leaders to lever additional funds from other sources. Here, success has bred success, with other partners wanting to participate as a result of initial achievement. Care needs to be taken, however, when there is multiple bidding for funds as a partner institution and clarity of role is required in applications.

Case Study 4

The study focuses on the decision-making points through the various stages of a project undertaken by Emory University Library, all the time emphasising the importance and necessity of long-term sustainability. Joan Smith comments: 'Sustainability is a recognised issue for academic research projects, particularly those in the humanities. Our intent was to creatively address the sustainability challenges of our own production system, thereby advancing digital library project sustainability more broadly.'

Other case studies

Attention is also drawn to:

- *Chronopolis* (Case Study 6) which only focused on funding for finite amounts of time as opposed to long-term sustainability. To address this, Chronopolis sought the support of an institution which is committed to a long-term existence. The authors also stress the need to build in work on sustainability from the start of any project rather than when it is well up and running.
- *Portico* (Case Study 8) where the free-rider problem – a challenge to sustainability in many cases – and how to respond to it is discussed. The project is also a good example of cooperation at work, with the emphasis being on a good balance between the key stakeholders and flexibility in the choice and use of business models.
- *NARCIS* (Case Study 14) where there is no arrangement yet for the sustainability of the research information (the information on researchers, research institutes, projects and programmes).

Conclusion

This chapter has considered the fundamental issue in digital library management and development: that of sustainability. It has provided a definition of the term and looked at the basics of a sustainable approach, drawing on our own research, key relevant literature and the case studies. Chapter 3 considers specific elements in a sustainability strategy for digital libraries.

References

Anderson, M. (2008) 'Evolving a network of networks: the experience of partnerships in the National Digital Information Infrastructure and Preservation Program', *International Journal of Digital Curation*, 3 (1): 4–14.

Anglada, L. and Comellas, N. (2002) 'What's fair? Pricing models in the electronic era', *Library Management*, 23 (4/5): 227–33.

Baker, D. (2006) 'Digital library futures: a UK HE and FE perspective', *Interlending and Document Supply*, 34 (1): 4–8.

Baker, D. and Evans, W. (eds) (2009) *Digital Library Economics: An Academic Perspective*. Oxford: Chandos Publishing.

Bennett, S. (2001) 'The golden age of libraries', *Journal of Academic Librarianship*, 27 (4): 256–9.

Bond, T. (2006) 'Sustaining a digital collection after the grants: the Early Washington Maps Project', *OCLC Systems and Services*, 22 (1): 56–66.

Brindley, L. (2009) 'Foreword: Digital library economics: an introduction' in D. Baker and W. Evans (eds), *Digital Library Economics: An Academic Perspective*. Oxford: Chandos Publishing.

Cathro, W. (2009) 'Digital library economics: international perspectives: the Australian perspective', in D. Baker and W. Evans (eds), *Digital Library Economics: An Academic Perspective*. Oxford: Chandos Publishing.

Collier, M. (2004) 'Development of a business plan for an International Co-operative Digital Library – The European Library (TEL)', *Program*, 38: 225–31.

Collier, M. (2005) 'The business aims of eight national libraries in digital library co-operation: a study carried out for the business plan of The European Library (TEL) project', *Journal of Documentation*, 61 (5): 602–22.

Cox, J. (2007) *Investigative Study Towards Establishing a Scottish Higher Education Digital Library for Scottish Universities*. Northants: John Cox Associates Limited. Online at: *http://its-ewds1.ds.strath.ac.uk/Portals/14/WG/SHEDL/documents/SCURLSHEDLREPORTfinal280907JE.pdf*.

Dempster, S. and Grout, C. (2009) 'Digitisation – trends in the economics of retro-conversion', in D. Baker and W. Evans (eds), *Digital Library Economics: An Academic Perspective*. Oxford: Chandos Publishing.

Guthrie, K., Griffiths, R. and Maron, N. (2008) *Sustainability and Revenue Models for Online Academic Resources*. Ithaka. Online at: *http://sca.jiscinvolve.org/files/2008/06/sca_ithaka_sustainability_report-final.pdf*.

Hamilton, V. (2004) 'Sustainability for digital libraries', *Library Review*, 53 (8): 393–5.

JISC (2007) *Corporate Plan*. Bristol: JISC.

Lee, S. (ed.) (1997) *Economics of Digital Information: Collection, Storage and Delivery*. New York: Haworth Press.

Macdonald, J. and Kebbell, A. (2004) 'Access in an increasingly digital world', *Electronic Library*, 22 (6): 498–508.

Maron, N., Yun, J. and Pickle, S. (2013) *Sustaining Our Digital Future: Institutional Strategies for Digital Content*. London: Strategic Content Alliance.

Middleton, K. (2005) 'Collaborative digitization programs: a multifaceted approach to sustainability', *Library Hi Tech*, 23 (2): 145–50.

O'Connor, S. (2005) 'The economics of repository libraries in the context of the future conventional libraries', *Library Management*, 26 (1/2): 18–25.

Poll, R. (2005) 'Measuring the impact of new library services', *World Library and Information Congress: 71st IFLA General Conference and Council*. Oslo, 14–18 August.

Robinson, J. (2009) 'Spinning the disks – lessons from the circus', in D. Baker and W. Evans (eds), *Digital Library Economics: An Academic Perspective*. Oxford: Chandos Publishing.

Smith, A. (2003) 'Issues in sustainability: creating value for online users', *First Monday*, 8 (5).

Walters, T. and Skinner, K. (2010) 'Economics, sustainability, and the cooperative model in digital preservation', *Library Hi Tech*, 28 (2): 259–72.

Zorich, D. (2007) *Webwise: Stewardship in the Digital Age: Managing Museum and Library Collections for Preservation and Use*. Conference proceedings, WebWise Conference on Libraries and Museums in the Digital World, 1–2 March, Washington, DC.

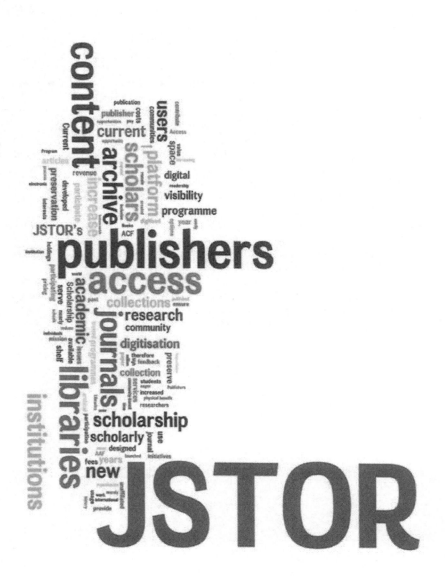

Case Study 1

The JSTOR platform
Laura Brown

Abstract. The JSTOR service has become ever more vital as pressure has increased on traditional libraries – not only in terms of budgets and physical space but also increased user demand and exponential growth in publications. The case study exemplifies some of the critical success factors in ensuring long-term sustainability: having a robust and attractive value proposition with 'unique benefits'; ensuring that the products meet the needs both of the market and of the content suppliers; being flexible and open to change; emphasising collaboration. But it is the tiered pricing model that makes the JSTOR offer especially attractive for its users (including pricing stability) on the one hand and the organisation financially sustainable (not least in terms of JSTOR's ability to generate capital for renewal and regeneration purposes) on the other.

Keywords: content, digitisation, future, JSTOR, preservation, publishers, sustainability, users

Introduction

Over the past few years, librarians, publishers and scholars in the academic community expressed with increasing frequency a need that had yet to be properly addressed: the availability of current academic scholarship on an integrated, powerful, convenient, affordable digital platform. Libraries wanted consolidated holdings that could be easily administered, publishers wanted to distribute current scholarship and increase visibility, and scholars wanted to access the full runs of academic journals. JSTOR is a community-based organisation, one that is responsive to new ideas and dedicated to helping the academic community discover, use and build upon a wide range of content on a trusted digital platform of academic content. JSTOR therefore solicited feedback from the three communities, considered ways to satisfy all interested parties, and, in 2010, launched its solution: the Current Scholarship Program. Through the Current Scholarship Program, publishers may now distribute current scholarship and increase visibility, libraries may now consolidate holdings and scholars may now access the full runs – archival and current issues – of academic journals.

The Current Scholarship Program is new to JSTOR, but JSTOR's method for generating such initiatives is not. In fact, JSTOR was founded in 1995 to serve the needs of libraries, publishers and scholars, and has for the past 15 years striven to serve these needs. As the needs change, so too does JSTOR. The formula is as simple as it is effective. More than 7,000 institutions worldwide participate in JSTOR. The JSTOR archive comprises more than 1,500 academic journals. In one year alone, JSTOR attracted nearly 600 million total accesses. By letting the needs of libraries, publishers and scholars shape our decisions, we maintain business models that are relevant and sustainable.

History and mission

William G. Bowen, then president of the Andrew W. Mellon Foundation, conceived JSTOR to help university and college libraries ingest an ever-growing amount of published scholarship into a finite amount of physical shelf space. Libraries could afford neither to limit academic scholarship nor to construct costly expansion after costly expansion. Bowen realised that by digitising the back files of printed scholarly journals, libraries could grow collections while obviating unnecessary expenses. These digitised journals could then be stored in a centralised digital archive and shared and accessed by libraries and their users on the Web. Participating libraries and their institutions could free local brick and mortar space, reduce capital and other costs associated with collection storage, and vastly improve access to scholarly papers and other content. JSTOR ensured that material would never be lost or checked out, small institutions could have access to large collections and, ultimately, the promotion of digital preservation could help to engender acceptance of, and faith in, electronic publication.

JSTOR might have remained a library digitisation and preservation service had Bowen's project not illuminated the dynamic web of interests that connected libraries, publishers and scholars and would later drive JSTOR's mission. The more that JSTOR explored ways for libraries to save shelf space, preserve content, increase holdings and reduce costs, the more we encountered corollary needs. Publishers who owned the rights to the digitised journals on JSTOR wanted to increase visibility, broaden usage and widen readership for their journals and authors. Researchers (faculty, students, independent scholars) who patronised the libraries wanted increased access to academic scholarship on a powerful, easy-to-use, trusted platform. Suddenly JSTOR was invested in three communities and three sets of interests, both conflicting and complementary. Faced with this new set of priorities, JSTOR articulated its mission and devised a list of guiding principles that encompassed all communities, principles that continue to inform our business decisions.

JSTOR is a not-for-profit service that enables discovery, access to and preservation of scholarly content. We collaborate with the academic community to achieve the following goals:

- To help libraries connect patrons to vital scholarship while increasing shelf space savings, lowering costs and guaranteeing preservation solutions for digital content.
- To help publishers reach new audiences and preserve their scholarly content for future generations.
- To help scholars, researchers and students discover, use and build upon a wide range of scholarly content on a dynamic platform that increases productivity and facilitates new forms of scholarship.

The element of collaboration is of particular importance for JSTOR. We refer to libraries, publishers and scholars as participants because these communities do not merely consume our product; they contribute to its formation. JSTOR has grown and evolved since its founding. We have added new programmes and modified existing ones. In the past two years alone, we have gone through some of the largest changes in our organisation's history. But all initiatives, no matter the size or scope, have been direct extensions of the needs of the communities we serve.

Libraries

JSTOR was originally conceived in order to help libraries save shelf space, increase holdings, preserve content and reduce costs. At the heart of our value proposition for libraries lies digitisation, for it is digitisation that enables libraries to remove physical copies of journals, receive electronic copies of journals and trust that all content is preserved in perpetuity. To achieve these aims, JSTOR invested in a robust digitisation process. Complementing JSTOR's digitisation process are our paper repositories. These repositories reinforce preservation efforts and ensure that the JSTOR archive is comprehensive. JSTOR's goal is to preserve at least one copy of a complete back run of each journal in the JSTOR archive in multiple and geographically separate paper repositories so that they remain available for re-digitisation and other unanticipated needs. JSTOR currently deposits one donated or purchased copy of a digitised volume into a paper repository at Harvard University. We also collaborate with the University of California on a second paper repository. Our stringent digitisation and preservation standards provide to libraries not just a replacement of standard stacks, but an archive that is more flexible, more interlinked, more searchable, more reliable and more complete than their predecessors. That the archive takes up no local physical space is a huge benefit to participating institutions.

Of equal importance to JSTOR's commitment to digitisation and preservation is the content we choose to digitise and preserve. When considering titles for inclusion, we maintain a selective collection development approach and take into consideration criteria that include a journal's historical significance, publishing life, number of institutional subscribers, citation frequency, reputation in the field and recommendations from scholars and librarians. Limiting the JSTOR archive to the most respected, most relevant journals allows libraries and scholars to participate with confidence in the quality of the content. But what good is an archive that is prohibitively expensive? High-quality digitisation is costly, and high fees restrict access. Fuelling our business while broadening access required a new pricing model, something never before seen in the field of archives: tiered pricing.

Participating JSTOR institutions pay two fees for each JSTOR collection: the Archive Capital Fee (ACF) and the Annual Access Fee (AAF). The ACF is a one-time fee per collection designed to ensure that JSTOR has the necessary resources to meet its archival obligation to migrate data and software systems as technology evolves. In practice, the ACF ensures the preservation and availability of content for the long term. The AAF is intended to cover the ongoing costs of maintenance, user services and administration required to support access to collections in JSTOR. The AAF is invoiced on a calendar basis.

Because institutions vary in size, research intensity and funding, JSTOR tiers the ACF and AAF according to the type and size of the institution. Full-time enrolment and Carnegie Classification contribute to five JSTOR size categories: Very Large, Large, Medium, Small, Very Small, while institution type such as higher education, public library, museum and not-for-profit research institution is also factored into every institution's fees. Secondary schools, for example, pay a considerably reduced fee for access to all JSTOR collections. Fees are also reduced according to international countries' gross national income, and all institutions in Africa pay nothing. Finally, JSTOR gives institutions the option of paying the ACF at the onset of participation or in smaller instalment payments over a number of years. This lowers the barrier to entry considerably for many types of institutions.

Throughout its history, JSTOR has kept prices stable, which demonstrates the extent to which we are committed to expanding participation and access. In fact, the fees for new collections keep dropping. Every year JSTOR releases new content into existing archive collections, which increases those collections' depth and value. And every year the fees remain constant. The culmination of these categories and payment options is a system that creates enough revenue for JSTOR to operate and enough opportunities for institutions at varying levels of financial strength to participate in JSTOR. Nearly 3,000 US institutions participate in JSTOR, as do more than 4,000 international institutions. Participation will continue to increase as we continue to incorporate feedback into our business model and hone our services, our digitisation processes, our collections and our pricing options to meet the needs of our constituency.

Publishers

JSTOR developed partnerships with publishers through our work with libraries: digitising a journal requires publisher consent. But we took what could have been little more than a simple transaction and created a network of mutually beneficial relationships and initiatives. Through publishers, JSTOR could increase the value of its archive, gather invaluable feedback about discipline-specific scholarship from the people who know it best and generate ideas for serving the needs of the entire publisher community. Through JSTOR, publishers could significantly increase the visibility and scholarly impact of their content, expand access and readership, and, in some cases, use JSTOR as their publishing platform. Publishers eager to increase visibility were, of course, delighted to be included in JSTOR. Our digital archive offered the unique opportunity to deliver to the world high-quality, searchable, nearly perfect electronic replications of their journals. And JSTOR digitised the journals at no cost to the publishers. All journals, no matter the circulation or publication history, benefited from that kind of exposure. That we strove to select only the most respected journals ensured that inclusion in JSTOR increased the journals' visibility as much as it increased our own.

Much of what draws publishers to JSTOR, however, is enumerated in the publication licence agreement, which was created with publisher interests in mind. JSTOR understands that publishers alone know what is best for their content. Journals in JSTOR Archive Collections, therefore, have 'moving walls' that define the time lag between the most current issue published and the most current issue available in JSTOR. The moving wall is designed to help protect the economic sustainability of our content providers. By not making the most current content available on JSTOR, publishers have been able to preserve revenue opportunities from current issues subscriptions while ensuring that archival content is preserved and made continually accessible to scholars.

Over the past 15 years, JSTOR has amended the publication licence agreement with programmes and services to increase further the value of publisher participation. When we first launched JSTOR in 1995, publishers wanted to understand how their content was being used. With that in mind, we created our first of many programmes and services for publishers: usage statistics. More than merely informative, usage statistics allowed publishers to learn about a myriad of audiences, what articles and issues were most popular and how best to connect with readers. Four years later JSTOR launched its Individual Access programme, which gave publishers the freedom to provide full-text online access of their content to individuals as a benefit of society or organisational membership, or as a complement to personal print subscriptions. Individual Access served the dual purpose of opening up access to users unaffiliated with participating institutions and giving to publishers more control of their own content. In 2001 we saw the inauguration of JSTOR's revenue-sharing programme. We owe the integrity of our archive to the journals that compose it and therefore offer to our publishers a monetary benefit for participation. Payment by title is based on several criteria, including page counts and the number of libraries with access to the title.

Finally, the aforementioned Current Scholarship Program was developed to provide a platform for publishers. Because of JSTOR's moving wall, the archive contained precisely that: a vast and deep well of archival content. But over the years, libraries had been urging JSTOR to complement the archive collections with current issues of those journals so that their patrons would be able to access full runs of titles, and a variety of publishers were eager to explore this opportunity. To this end, JSTOR developed a series of changes that would allow publishers not merely to contribute current scholarship to JSTOR, but also use JSTOR as the main distribution platform for their current scholarship. The JSTOR Current Scholarship Programme enables publishers to set their own pricing, offer flexible subscription options and fuel discovery through JSTOR's extensive network of participating institutions. In the first year alone, usage of many Current Scholarship titles has doubled through the exposure to researchers around the world that the JSTOR platform provides. More than 800 publishers contribute more than 1,400 journals and other scholarly content to JSTOR. We attribute much of this growth to our community-based initiatives. JSTOR's publisher programmes and services attract to JSTOR new publishers eager to make use of our unique benefits.

Users

The final community that JSTOR serves is in many ways the most central. We work tirelessly to serve the needs of libraries and publishers, and libraries and publishers work tirelessly to serve the needs of users. In that sense, every JSTOR initiative affects users, their research, their scholarship and their access. The JSTOR platform features a host of tools designed to aid users' research – from advanced searching to surfacing related content. And users may save citations and searches with a free MyJSTOR account. Every aspect of the research experience is tailored to the needs of scholars, and we continually solicit feedback to ensure that JSTOR remains the most useful, trusted resource for every stage of the research process. JSTOR is keenly aware that many independent scholars, other unaffiliated individuals and students and scholars at libraries that participate in only a subset of our collections do not have access to all of the content in our archive. Over time we have developed a number of programmes to expand access to these materials, working steadily to balance the interests of publishers and libraries towards this goal.

As part of our efforts to increase access to the scholarly journals in JSTOR, we developed the Publisher Sales Service. Through this optional programme, publishers may give to individuals who are not affiliated with JSTOR participating institutions the ability to purchase single articles. Our goals for this programme are to facilitate access to important scholarly material by unaffiliated researchers and to help publishers reach new readers and markets. The programme may also represent a new, if modest, revenue stream for publishers.

In 2009 JSTOR expanded access through its Alumni Access Pilot, which gives universities and colleges the opportunity to grant to their alumni JSTOR access. Nineteen schools currently participate in the pilot, opening access to thousands of graduates. In keeping with our mission to aid research, we also made journal content in JSTOR published prior to 1923 in the United States and prior to 1870 elsewhere freely available to anyone, anywhere in the world. This Early Journal Content, as we call it, includes discourse and scholarship in the arts and humanities, economics, politics, mathematics and other sciences, and comprises nearly 500,000 articles from more than 200 journals.

Users accessed JSTOR nearly 600 million times in 2010. But of equal importance to this number are the groups of researchers that compose our user base: scholars and students at domestic and international universities, four-year colleges and community colleges, high schools, scholarly societies, non-governmental organisations and cultural institutions. Expanding access has been and will continue to be one of JSTOR's top priorities and we are proud to have made considerable progress.

The future

In 2011 JSTOR announced plans to supplement its extensive collection of journals, pamphlets, book reviews, auction catalogues and primary source materials with books. Like the programmes before it, Books at JSTOR is community-based and designed to meet the needs of libraries, publishers and users. The inclusion of books saves additional shelf space, disseminates scholarship and aids research. Books will be cross-searchable with the millions of journal articles and primary sources on JSTOR, contextualised by more than two million book reviews on the platform, and provide an online research experience marked by personalised, user-driven functionality. Books at JSTOR will also engender new subscription, pricing and collection options aligned with our dedication to offer publishers more flexibility, control and opportunities for increasing both visibility and revenue.

Google and other search engines have increased the number of users who want access to JSTOR articles but are not associated with institutions that have licensed the collection. Our other impending initiative, therefore, is aligned with our dedication to expand access: Register & Read[BETA]. As the name suggest, users who register with JSTOR may read, but not print or download, content in the JSTOR archive. This programme is of particular interest to users unaffiliated with participating institutions. All registered users will have a digital 'reading shelf' that accommodates a set number of items at any given time. After a minimum number of days (14 days in the BETA), users may remove old items and select new items. This programme is also designed to help publishers increase visibility and readership, and learn more about the academic community. At the launch of the programme, only archive journal articles will be available through Register & Read.

Through this triangulated approach of valuing librarian, publisher and user perspectives, JSTOR tracks, balances and anticipates the issues affecting academic research today and employs smart technologies and business models to ensure the sustainability of the platform for the long term. JSTOR remains successful because we honour these relationships and have grown with evolving needs – from a trusted digital archive to an integrated research platform. This evolution underscores that the better we serve the needs of libraries, publishers and users, the more valuable – and by extension more sustainable – the JSTOR platform becomes.

Case Study 2

Project MUSE

Dean Smith

Abstract. As with the JSTOR project, part of the initial rationale for Project MUSE was to respond to the growing budgetary crisis in humanities academic publishing. Again, the critical success factors have been the organisation's vision, strategy and ability to evolve 'in dynamic ways', supported by collaborative approaches and tiered pricing structures. MUSE leaders were – and are – also willing to take risks. The end result has been an attractive product that people want to buy into because – as for example in the case of libraries and the need to make savings – it gives them what they want and need. In other words, it adds value at a price or a cost they can afford.

Keywords: community, content, digital transition, journals, Project MUSE, platform, pricing, sustainability

Introduction

> Project MUSE just keeps getting better. Inclusion in the database is essential to the success of any journal.[1]

Project MUSE is a thriving online content community of 500 scholarly journals, 133 not-for-profit publishers, 2,500 library subscribers and millions of users around the world in the humanities and social sciences. During 2013, the platform will expand to include more than 23,000 e-books from 83 publishers.

Project MUSE began in 1993 as a conversation between Jack Goellner, the Director of the Johns Hopkins University Press (JHUP), and

Scott Bennett, Director of the Milton S. Eisenhower Library at Hopkins, about how they could work together to find a solution to the growing crisis in scholarly publishing. Library budgets were shrinking and price increases for scientific, technical and medical (STM) journals were outstripping inflation. Books were losing money at the press and library monograph budgets were beginning to dry up. How could smaller journals in the humanities and social sciences afford to have a digital presence?

Johns Hopkins explored options for producing electronic versions of the 40 journals then in JHUP's programme. Grant funding to pursue prototypes was secured from the Carnegie-Mellon Foundation and National Endowment for the Humanities in 1995, and a MUSE pilot project ensued with eight journals published online in full text. Several libraries, including members of the Oberlin Group of Liberal Arts College Libraries and the Virtual Library of Virginia consortia, served as beta testers for the electronic journals, providing feedback on presentation and searching capabilities.[2] By the end of 1996, all of the JHUP journals had been produced online and a pilot offer of subscriptions to the MUSE collection was offered to libraries commencing in January 1997. In 2000, 11 additional university presses joined Project MUSE. These presses included Indiana University, the Massachusetts Institute of Technology (MIT) and the Universities of Toronto, Nebraska and North Carolina. Since 1995, its electronic journal collections have supported a wide array of research needs at academic, public, special and school libraries worldwide. In early 2011, Project MUSE began cooperating on its e-book initiative with the University Press Content Consortium (UPCC), an assembly of major university presses and related scholarly publishers that grew out of extensive research into a viable model for a collaborative university press electronic book offering.

What started as a conversation 15 years ago between a publisher and librarian continues to evolve and expand in dynamic ways. MUSE celebrated its 15th anniversary in 2010 and has been working to strengthen its leadership position and plan for the next 15 years of the Project. Amid sweeping change in academic publishing, Project MUSE has emerged as the archetype for the dissemination of premium journal content. MUSE has enabled academic publishers to generate valuable revenue and has paved the way for more than 100 presses profitably to reach global audiences with journal content. For librarians, Project MUSE's affordable, tiered pricing structure enables libraries to choose a customised offering that meets their budget, usage and research needs. We thought this was not only a way that the press and the library could collaborate but it was something that held great promise for the future of scholarly communication.[3]

The MUSE mission: a balancing act

Project MUSE has played a major role in transforming the scholarly journal landscape by staying close to its mission of balancing the interests of publishers, libraries and end-user communities to provide a sustainable model for ensuring delivery and widespread access to content in the humanities and social sciences. Since 2000, Project MUSE has distributed more than $84 million in royalties to publishers and generated $100 million in savings to libraries. Many publishers rely on these monies to sustain their publishing operations.

In an environment of information overload, where users increasingly value credentialled knowledge, every page of the MUSE site reinforces the quality of the content in the collection. Charles Wilkinson, Director of Purdue University Press, commented: 'And, unlike many nameless aggregations, MUSE pays a living wage.'[4]

Academic libraries have used these savings to withstand annual budget cuts and provide a diverse range of content to their patrons. Project MUSE is again poised for growth and expansion to meet the needs of a changing competitive market and stands apart as a resource designed by the academic community for the academic community. We are focused on achieving goals that will leverage our strengths and enhance the market position of Project MUSE. These strategic actions include:

- expanding the acquisition of high-quality content;
- driving usage and discoverability;
- broadening access worldwide; and
- engaging the MUSE community through continued innovation and results-driven collaboration.

Our staff has amassed over 100 years of experience working on the platform. We are librarians, engineers, architects, marketers, publishers and researchers. A debt of gratitude is owed to Wendy Queen (Publishing Technologies), Melanie Schaffner (Sales and Marketing), and Elizabeth Brown (Content Development) for their outstanding contributions on a daily basis to this enterprise.

The MUSE experience: managing the digital transition

Since its inception, MUSE has adapted and evolved with the needs of publishers, libraries and end users. Listening to our community since 1995, we have altered our approach to pricing for libraries and to the paying out of royalties to publishers, expanded our content offering to include current and now back issues of journals, developed technologies to improve the publisher experience and demonstrated a commitment to increased functionality for the end-user. By 2004, the MUSE product had been well received by the library market but the number of titles was growing beyond the budgetary limits of libraries. Pricing was based on the subscription list prices of the journals provided by the publishers. Librarians were sceptical of the sustainability of the model. The majority of the business (90 per cent) was driven by consortia who were receiving a 50 per cent volume discount. Using print prices as the basis for the subscription, the model called for every institution – large or small – to pay a similar price. During the period of rapid growth from 2000 to 2004, publishers received new revenues from inclusion in MUSE. Now they were seeing massive print cancellations by libraries because of increasing economic pressures and the electronic revenues were not covering the losses.

MUSE hired October Ivins and Judy Luther to develop a new approach. Usage was beginning to emerge as a proxy for value as a result of the COUNTER initiative and Carnegie Classifications were being used to determine the size of a particular institution. Engaging in intensive market research, Ivins and Luther developed a usage-based model that was decoupled from print and based on size of institution – from the largest Association of Research Libraries (ARL) library to the smallest community college – to enable participation from institutions of all types. Usage bands were created within the tiers to recognise high and low users of the content.

This new pricing approach provided substantial value for institutions. New collection options were introduced to make available smaller subsets of titles. The average 2013 subscription list price for titles on the platform was $120. For the largest ARL library, the MUSE average subscription per title is $85 which reinforces the value proposition to libraries. By providing more options for institutions to participate, Project MUSE has grown annual revenues by 70 per cent over the last five years from $12.8 to $22 million. Publishers receive 80 per cent of those revenues.

Table CS2.1 Top five users of Project MUSE 2011

Institution	Downloads	% of total hits
University of Toronto	198,762	1%
Ashford University	145,098	1%
University of Ottawa	88,475	1%
University of British Columbia	87,034	1%
Columbia University	68,839	1%

During this timeframe, Project MUSE also worked on a new royalty payout structure for publishers by developing a performance-based model for paying publisher royalties based on three factors: (1) usage, (2) bytes and (3) score. Usage accounts for 50 per cent of the publisher

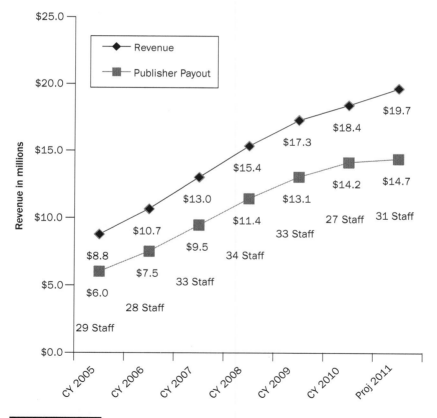

Figure CS2.1 Revenue/payout/staff from 2005 to 2011

payout; bytes or the amount of content on the platform 30 per cent, and a ten-point score that looks at a journal's market acceptance based on its inclusion in databases (20 per cent). This new model has been extremely effective in delivering meaningful revenues to publishers. In addition, MUSE will pay for three years' worth of cancellations as journals transition from print to web. Annual costs are split with publishers. Based on this new structure, Project MUSE has paid out 75 per cent of its revenues to publishers since 2008. For 2012, publishers received $16.9 million.

Project MUSE played an integral role in the acceleration from print subscriptions to electronic access for many publishers in the humanities and social sciences. Global markets for journals have opened in Western Europe, Asia, Japan, China and Latin America. There are 500 subscriptions in developing countries through the International Network for the Availability of Scientific Publications – Programme for the Enhancement of Research Information relationship including Honduras, Mauritius, Kenya, Nepal, Pakistan, Rwanda, Bangladesh and Ethiopia.

The MUSE experience: reinventing the platform at the article level

The Project MUSE technology staff have built the platform organically and without outside assistance since 1995. In 2007, Web 2.0 and social networking tools drove the reinvention of the MUSE platform. The focus of the redesign was to give the end-user more tools at the article level with the goal of increasing the amount of time a user spends on the site. In addition to a more flexible layout, social bookmarking links, journal alerts and linked subject headings were added for launch.

Usage statistics provided the metrics to learn further what tools are widely used and how users are engaging with the content. This helped create a commitment to continuous improvement and a streamlining of processes. In an effort to improve the granularity of content, speed of publication times and efficiency by over 50 per cent, MUSE also adopted an XML-workflow in 2007.

Project MUSE adds value at the article level through an indexing process by providing a controlled vocabulary and name authority recognition. As a result MUSE provides clickable subject headings on every article, as well as a table of contents and search results, which bring together topics and subjects in a more precise fashion. These are also used in the 'More Like This' algorithm and in the search relevance ranking. Overall article level enhancements have been a success. The creation of additional functionality has increased the amount of time a user spends on the site. The average session length has increased from 1.25 articles per session in 2008 to 2 articles in the first half of 2012.

MUSE has expanded the platform with the addition of e-book content in 2012 and will continue to deliver tools to create even greater connections between content and formats because driving usage is a critical activity that will increase revenues for publishers and lower cost per download for libraries. The cost per download for MUSE library customers was $1.75 in 2012. Publishers received $1.69 for every download of their content. Royalty per title in 2010 was approximately $30,000.

The MUSE experience: adopting a content neutral approach

At the 2010 MUSE Publisher meeting in Baltimore, we shared with our community a desire to develop an e-books platform with interested publishers. They had asked for this before and the topic was of great interest to the participants in the room. We viewed this as an opportunity once again to take a leadership position, just as we had done for journals fifteen years ago, and help save the scholarly monograph from extinction as the costs of print book publishing continue to increase in the face of diminishing sales. We had developed a request for proposal and had sent it to e-book vendors such as eBrary, NetLibrary and Electronic Book Library (EBL). A librarian raised her hand and stood up. 'This won't have any meaning unless these e-books are integrated on the Project MUSE platform,' said Deborah Slingluff, Associate Director of the Sheridan Libraries at Hopkins. 'Do for e-books what MUSE does for journals.'

Once again, a colleague from the Johns Hopkins University stepped forward to collaborate with us. More than fifteen years since the first conversations about a platform with notes written on napkins in a faculty board meeting we were back at the beginning of something special again. We had been exploring the Hopkins library search interface and had noticed that book and journal content appeared side-by-side in the search results but that it was difficult to tell whether it was a journal or book or even who had published it. Content was the critical driving factor of the result – not format or publisher brand, but information. This became our rallying cry and confirmed an idea that we had been kicking around – to create a research platform of e-book chapters and journal articles discoverable in the same search environment. We announced our programme shortly thereafter, Project MUSE Editions, to serve both MUSE Publishers and the Hopkins Fulfillment Service publishers.

We met with 20 prospective publishers at the 2010 Association of American University Presses Meeting in Salt Lake and explained our business model. The publishers would set prices based on the list price of the title and Project MUSE would assemble the collections in subject areas and in complete collections. We also met with the University Press e-book Consortium (UPeC) in Salt Lake. They were in the process of collecting 60 letters of intent from university press publishers and other not-for-profit entities. UPeC had received a Mellon Grant to move forward with research and modelling. They canvassed more than 1,000 librarians on multiple occasions over a two-year period to find out what the library community wanted as far as accessing e-books in a research setting. From their data, they developed a collection-based model to sell e-books to libraries in complete as well as subject-based collections. They had determined a market existed for it. Librarians wanted the same unlimited downloading privileges that existed for journals. They wanted limited to no digital rights management (DRM). They wanted ownership.

Alex Holzman (Temple University Press), Steve Maikowski (NYU Press), Marlie Wasserman (Rutgers University Press), Eric Halpern (Penn University Press) and Donna Shear (University of Nebraska Press) worked with consultants Raym Crow, October Ivins, and Judy Luther to bridge the gap between the academic library market and university press publishers. They were the true pioneers of university press e-book offerings because they journeyed where only vendors had gone before. Our models differed slightly when it came to pricing. UPeC derived their collection price using value-based metrics and an average price per title. This would be a requirement to win the Request for Proposal (RFP) they were developing in an effort to select an e-book vendor. It was believed that JSTOR, Cambridge University Press and HighWire were in the running for this business.

By fall of 2010, Project MUSE Editions had 28 agreements in place with publishers. We were moving forward and hoped to have a chance to bid on the RFP. We were honoured when the mail arrived in November and the extensive UPeC RFP was included. The programme we had developed had caught their attention. We went about the task of responding to the requirements document, following the instructions exactly. We adopted the strategy of aligning our vision with UPeC. If the consortia really wanted to transform the e-book market, the most compelling way to do that would be to join forces with one of the largest and most successful aggregations of humanities and social sciences journals in the world. We presented a strong case to the UPeC Board in late January under the theme of 'One Vision'.

We were doing this for the community and were part of it. We committed to investing several million dollars to make this happen and to hiring 15 additional staff members at the outset. We developed the name the University Press Content Consortia (UPCC) to signal to the market that book and journal content together was only the beginning. In the future, we will transform the platform again to include reference works, datasets, multimedia, annotation, collaboration and commenting features.

After much discussion and follow-up, they selected us as their partner.

> There is enormous value in providing our students and faculty with an integrated discovery and access environment that includes not only an expanding database of university press monographs but also embraces the journals in Project MUSE. (James G. Neal, VP for Information Services and University Librarian, Columbia University)[5]

As I write this case study, 23,000 e-books from 83 publishers have been launched on a reinvented MUSE platform integrating book and journal content for the first time ever in the humanities and social sciences. With an ongoing commitment to improving our technology and expanding capacity, MUSE developed an RFP to find a suitable technology partner. MUSE has recently signed an agreement with HighWire as the hosting solution of the future for the book and journal content. Over the next five years our goal is to build the definitive research environment in the humanities and social sciences. That means adding services as well as content to our platform. We anticipate being able to offer readers increased customisation of the MUSE platform, allowing users to create personal libraries within the MUSE environment and for cataloguing and annotating their reading. We are looking to empower the individual scholar with the tools be able to make new discoveries and interpretations of texts.

The MUSE message: evolve, expand, engage and embrace the future

Today, the MUSE staff are actively engaged in:

- *evolving the platform* to embrace new forms of content and improve the user experience;
- *expanding the content* by offering and broadening access, driving usage and enhancing discoverability; and
- *engaging the MUSE community* of publishers, libraries and end-users through innovation and results-driven collaboration.

Key takeaways are the following:

- Adopt a commitment of continuous engagement with your communities (e.g. libraries, publishers, end-users).
- Commit to endless usability testing and market research.
- Develop the rationale for ongoing investment into the platform.
- Build a robust stable of key stakeholders from all communities.
- Listen to your customers and build relationships based on trust.
- Communicate extensively in person and one-on-one with partners.
- Know your readers, editors, authors, researchers, students and librarians.
- Embrace the digital chaos of tomorrow – do not fear it.
- Invest in your people.
- Commit to project management.

MUSE 2020

We see an exciting future for the expansion of content on the MUSE platform. We are fortunate to have strengthened our team with new

Associate Director Terry Ehling who is responsible for Content Development and Publisher Relations. We are exploring additional services for our publishers to help them realise their dreams. We see an opportunity to link from the primary document to the journal article to the e-book chapter to the YouTube lecture to the podcast to the commentary to the group collaboration in an endless cyclical endeavour of research and investigation.

Notes

1. *http://muse.jhu.edu/about/publishers/documents/niso_article_level_ enhancements.pdf*
2. M.B. Schaffner, J. Luther and O. Ivins (2005) 'Project MUSE's new pricing model: a case study in collaboration,' *Serials Review*, 31 (3): 192–9.
3. W. Mame (2006) 'Jack Goellner interview', *MUSE Oral History*. From Special Collections in the Eisenhower Library at JHU.
4. *http://muse.jhu.edu/about/librarians/fall10.pdf*
5. *http://www.libraryjournal.com/lj/home/889748-264/two_university_press_ ebook_initiatives.html.csp*

Case Study 3

Organic, symbiotic digital collection development

Jennifer A. Johnson and Kristi L. Palmer

Abstract. One of the critical success factors most evident in this project is cooperation and collaboration on a community-wide scale. While grants and internal resource allocations provided the necessary start-up funds, partnership working enabled the project leaders to lever additional funds from other sources. Success has bred success, with other partners wanting to participate as a result of initial achievement. Care needs to be taken, however, when there is multiple bidding for funds as a partner institution and clarity of role is required in applications.

Keywords: business models, costing models, economic models, financial models, funding models, pricing models

Introduction

The University Library at Indiana University-Purdue University Indianapolis[1] (IUPUI) has been creating digital collections since 2001. Several factors facilitated this library's early move towards digital cultural heritage collections, including: a university and library mission rooted in community collaboration; forward-thinking, flexible and innovation-valuing library leadership; and flexible, open-minded individuals on the staff, passionate about creating worldwide access to unique collections but also willing to think creatively about funding and workflow models. This case study will first provide background on the characteristics of the library that facilitated the digital collections' creation, then follow up with several specific, exemplary collections. Details will include project workload balance between collaborators and funding lines. Finally, there is a summary of lessons learned and thoughts on how to proceed with this community model in the future.

Introduction to the university and library

IUPUI is an urban university situated on the western edge of downtown Indianapolis. This location makes collaboration with geographically close businesses and cultural heritage institutions ideal and is recognised in IUPUI's mission and value statement: 'IUPUI provides for its constituents excellence in Civic Engagement, Locally, Nationally, and Globally,' and this is characterised by 'collaboration within and across disciplines and with the community.' The goal is for IUPUI students, faculty and staff to benefit from the expertise and hands-on experience of local community practitioners, while community members benefit from university groups providing cost-effective solutions from highly motivated individuals, recently trained in cutting-edge methodologies. This give-and-take mentality has lent itself well to the Digital Libraries Team of IUPUI University Library. As a fairly young institution (established in 1969) IUPUI has less archival/historical content than many of the university and college libraries doing digitisation work. While we have special collections and archives – and indeed our earliest collections began with (and continue to come from) our own archival collections – we have always had an eye on community institutions as the supplier of source material for digitisation. Our tag line early on was: 'We have the technology, they have the stuff.' A symbiotic relationship grew out of IUPUI University Library being able to provide technological support (both in terms of equipment and expertise) to cultural heritage institutions which had a plethora of historically significant documents, photographs, and artifacts but did not have the technological capabilities or funding streams to support digitisation projects. As with many symbiotic relationships, this university/ community connection was organic, developing over time in varied directions with a goal of providing wide, free access to local historical resources, but with an open mind on how best to reach this goal in terms of production and funding. The following project descriptions will exemplify this organic nature.

Digital collection community partnerships

Indiana Landmarks

The creation of community digital collections began in 2004 when an IUPUI Geography Department graduate who volunteered at Indiana Landmarks[2] connected the foundation with a fellow Geography graduate who was also a member of the IUPUI Digital Libraries Team. After reviewing the collection and needs, the two groups decided to pursue a Library Services Technology Act (LSTA) grant administered by the Indiana State Library. LSTA is part of the Institute of Museum and Library Services Act. This federal funding is used to increase the use of technology in libraries, foster sharing among libraries and target library services to special populations. LSTA funding has stipulations limiting which entities may apply. While Indiana Landmarks did not meet the institutional criteria, IUPUI did and a joint project allowed for a grant application. IUPUI University used the grant award to purchase slide digitisation technology and to create an hourly wage budget to cover digitisation of 3,000 slides. Technology included a slide scanner, portable laptop and an external hard drive.

IUPUI University Library staff members oversaw the digitisation process and uploaded images onto an external hard drive. Being the curator of the original collection, Indiana Landmarks was responsible for creating image metadata. Once the metadata was complete, the hard drive was returned to IUPUI University Library for uploading into the content management system CONTENTdm. Both institutions performed quality control measures. The initial collection contained 3,000 slides and metadata for each image.

While the initial project was grant funded, both institutions leveraged internal resources to increase collection content post-grant. Over the years, processes have been streamlined to accommodate the needs of each institution. Indiana Landmarks staff now have the network capacity to handle importing and uploading images. They also continue to create metadata for the digitised slides. IUPUI University Library sets aside a specific amount of time and money each year for the continuation of the Indiana Historic Architecture Slide Collection.

Conner Prairie Interactive History Park

As the IUPUI University Library digital libraries programme began to grow, there was a desire to extend the technology capabilities and explore the digitising of three-dimensional artifacts using digital cameras. The library administration was supportive of this idea and used internal funding for the purchase of camera equipment including: two professional cameras, backdrops, lighting, battery packs and small camera gadgets to simplify the processes. With minimal camera experience, Digital Libraries Team staff reached out to the Conner Prairie Interactive History Park professionals who were interested in capturing digital images of their quilt and coverlet collection.

Acknowledging the Digital Libraries Team need to develop expertise in the area of digital photography, Conner Prairie agreed to be the test case for the project and allowed the library to experiment with the new digital equipment. The digitisation process took place on location at Conner Prairie and curators from the museum prepared the physical materials to be digitised while the library worked with the new technology to create high-resolution images. The Digital Libraries Team members found proper lighting techniques to be the most significant challenge to digital photography work. We became very familiar with aperture, shutter speed and ISO (International Organization for Standardization). We also had the opportunity to experiment with various lenses including macro and wide-angle lenses. The digitisation took place over the course of five days with the successful completion of 62 digitised artifacts. A digital collection was created utilising the digital images and metadata exported from the Conner Prairie records database.

This quilt digitisation project demonstrates community partnerships fulfilling complementary needs and goals. The Conner Prairie Living History Museum had in its possession a deteriorating quilt and coverlet collection that was unable to be viewed by the public. Digital access to these fragile textile legacies has not only allowed this restricted collection to be viewed daily by a world-wide audience but also enhances the viewing experience with the ability to zoom in, beyond the capabilities of the naked eye. The Digital Libraries Team acquired much needed, hands-on testing of digital photography techniques. As the IUPUI University Library has become more experienced with digital photography, LSTA funding was awarded to work with Conner Prairie to create additional artifact collections, including historic clothing, arms making, blacksmithing and transfer ware.

Indianapolis Recorder Newspaper Archive

The *Indianapolis Recorder* is a historic African-American newspaper published in Indianapolis but of national significance as the fourth oldest, consecutively published African-American newspaper in the country. Dean David Lewis of the University Library reached out to the publishers, a local, well known, philanthropically minded Indianapolis family, and secured permission to digitise the full run of the newspaper, 1899–present. Gaining this permission was essential (though rarely granted by newspaper publishers), offering the library but also the newspaper a unique opportunity to be one of the few full-run newspapers made freely available online to a worldwide audience. The University Library sought funding from the Central Indiana Community Foundation (CICF), a community foundation committed to helping transform the lives of central Indiana residents. In 1989 an anonymous donor established a Library Fund to benefit designated public, academic and high-school libraries in Indianapolis. CICF was especially interested in the *Indianapolis Recorder* project because of its collaborative nature between digitisation expert (library) and long-time Indianapolis community member (newspaper), and because its content captured a unique historic view of the community CICF aims to support.

IUPUI University Library used internal funding to purchase the microfilm version (originally produced by the Indiana Historical Society) of the newspaper, but sought to outsource the microfilm's digitisation because the library's internal digitisation lab was not equipped with high-speed microfilm scanners. Again, leveraging the variety of funding resources available, digitisation was through Lyrasis.[3] Lyrasis is the nation's largest regional non-profit membership organisation serving libraries and since 2008 has been supported in part through a grant from the Alfred P. Sloan Foundation to provide cost-effective mass digitisation services. Indicative of a willingness to experiment, the University Library was approached by Lyrasis to test a new digitisation service provider. We were happy to oblige and were thoroughly pleased not only by the product provided by Creekside Digital but by the opportunity to lend our support to an important organisation like Lyrasis.

Once the digital files were transferred from Creekside Digital to the library, internal library staff were used to prepare the files (renamed and grouped into appropriate folders) for upload into CONTENTdm. When added to CONTENTdm, files undergo Optical Character Recognition (OCR) which creates a computer-generated transcript from the digital image. Once uploaded the OCRed transcripts of the images were also spot-checked by library staff. The grant through CICF supported the outsourced digitisation and internal file manipulation. Because of the national significance of this collection, the Digital Library Team partnered with the library's External Relations Team to plan and hold a community collection launch. Funded by CICF, the IUPUI University Library and an Indianapolis utility company, Citizens Energy Group, this two-hour event was open to the Indianapolis community and included a reception, a brief introduction to using the digital collection and a panel presentation on the significance of the newspaper from both a historical and a digital perspective. Ultimately, this collection received local and national attention because of its historical significance but also because university administrators and newspaper managers promoted the collection's launch. The digitisation of the *Indianapolis Recorder* is a highly successful example of a multi-faceted approach to workflow, funding and advertisement of new collections.

Insights for the future

Above are highlighted three of over 30 community-partnered digital projects led by the IUPUI University Library. Our success in these collaborations is a result of openness to thinking innovatively about digital collection creation and levels of ownership (a community partner owns the original but the IUPUI University Library supports the digital version). The fact that the IUPUI's mission is rooted in a connection to the local community makes these collaborations all the more relevant and our local partnerings increase the types of funding sources to which we have access. As with many digital library projects, our initial years were spent primarily looking for partners, promoting our services and building our technology core. Over time, we have become a sought after collaborator, with local cultural heritage institutions and for-profit entities (the Indianapolis Motor Speedway being the newest partner) seeking us out as a means of creating digital access to their valuable (often deteriorating) collections. Overall, our allowance of organic relationship development has been wildly beneficial.

One minor pitfall we encountered recently in connection with one of our regular funding agencies involved confusion over our participation in a multitude of grant applications filtering through their agency. We apply to this fund for our own projects but are also often named as a partner on other libraries' applications. The review board was concerned that funds were not being dispersed widely enough across new applicants. While our own and our partners' projects were funded, the board's comments have encouraged us to think about what is best for both our own funding lines and those of our partners. We continue to collaborate but are now more cognisant of how our partnership is described in grant applications. We fully anticipate experiencing more growing pains but are equally as confident that our culture of innovation and openness to experiment will pave the way to new partners with amazing collections to share with a world of researchers.

To access all collections mentioned in this case study, Google: IUPUI digital scholarship.

Notes

1. *http://www.iupui.edu/*
2. *http://www.indianalandmarks.org/Pages/default.aspx*
3. *http://www.lyrasis.org/*

Case Study 4

Developing a portal framework for humanities scholars

Joan A. Smith

Abstract. The study focuses on the decision-making points through the various stages of a project, all the time emphasising the importance and necessity of long-term sustainability.

Keywords: community, development tools, Emory University Library, humanities, portal, Southcomb, sustainability

Introduction

This case study concerns a three-year grant-funded investigation[1] conducted by Emory University Library to explore inter-institutional scholarly portal services supporting research in the humanities. Officially titled *A Cyberinfrastructure for Scholars*, a key goal of the research project was the development of a suite of software tools to create and maintain humanities-oriented search portals.[2] A portal is a user-configurable software interface that is typically used to integrate several tools together into one dashboard-like screen. An example of a popular portal is iGoogle,[3] which has numerous widgets (small applications) that can be custom-arranged into a screen layout that makes sense for the individual user (see Figure CS4.1). Another important feature of a portal is that other widgets can be built by community members at large. As such, it acts as a framework for the community to use and extend, evolving to meet the community's changing needs.

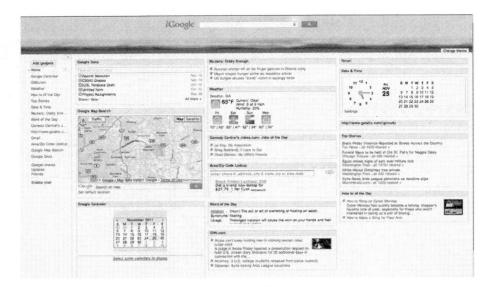

Figure CS4.1 An *iGoogle* portal page configured with a selection of widgets

The project team created a new humanities portal called 'SouthComb', designed to provide a comprehensive and faceted search across scholarly information sources. The tools that were developed in support of the SouthComb portal enabled harvesting, automatic classification and meta-searching for information originating across multiple resources including the World Wide Web, OAI-compliant Open Archives, various library catalogues and other digital information collections. Even though the source code for the portal was released as an open source project under *Google Code*,[4] the project did not attract sufficient community support to become self-sustaining and the principal website[5] has been in a static state since 2009. From an economic perspective, the institution felt there was insufficient return on investment (ROI) to maintain the software in-house, and website usage was too low to justify committing manpower to ongoing content development.

Project objectives (mission)

The project's primary mission was to improve the research process for humanities scholars by providing better technology tools and implementing a compelling, working example. Three objectives were established to achieve the mission:

1. *Build a sustainable combined search portal service.* This online community portal for the interdisciplinary field of Southern Studies includes a combined resource search system and various participatory services, and has been proposed as a low-cost subscription-based service. The key features demanded by scholars have been embedded in the open source software developed during the project, which was open-sourced via Google Code's (free) project hosting service. With a rich feature set in high demand by customers, the product could be sustainable through a modest mixed-revenue stream.

2. *Improve networked access to humanities collections of the US South.* The use of technology in humanities research is inconsistent, even at institutions like Emory University which has a well-established reputation in this area. In part the problem has been *accessibility* of materials via the usual discovery channels (web and catalogue searches). A key initiative of the portal project is improving the available tools and techniques for exposing, organising and discovering humanities collections. As a result, these features had the highest priority when planning the portal's development.

3. *Explore sustainable models for the advancement of scholarly Cyberinfrastructure.* Sustainability is a recognised issue for academic research projects, particularly those in the humanities. Our intent was to creatively address the sustainability challenges of our own production system, thereby advancing digital library project sustainability more broadly.

Users can add, delete and arrange the widgets in a way that makes personal, visual sense. The goal of the Cyberinfrastructure project was to create a portal for humanities scholars that would aggregate research resources (widgets) from across a broad spectrum of information sources.

As part of the project's mission, the Principal Investigators also sought answers to a number of questions common to research libraries today:

- Are there useful categories of services and functions that can serve to organise thinking about such projects during initial planning efforts?

- Can we identify effective strategies for institutionalising technology-based research services for long-term operations?
- Can we define a generalisable process for inter-institutional development of a complex engineering project?

These questions are especially applicable to humanities researchers, where there have so far been few tools to leverage technology's capabilities. Answers to these questions could help establish principles of practice applicable to the rapidly evolving digital humanities research setting.

Building the portal (experiences to date)

Technology and engineering considerations

The technical work of our project went through several different implementation phases, beginning with software evaluation, moving to prototype implementations and finally transitioning to a production phase during which we launched several staged releases of the SouthComb service. The technical requirements were established during the first year of the project and included the following core goals:

1. Be sustainable
2. Be easily manageable
3. Be easily reusable
4. Harvest OAI
5. Harvest web materials
6. Automatically classify records
7. Conduct meta-searching
8. Provide organised and uniform access to records

Goals 4 to 7 are geared toward the user community, intending to provide a 'value-added' component that would ideally drive up the user base, amortising the cost of overall development among a large number of users. Success in this dimension depends upon correctly targeting user needs and building a strong community. In contrast, the first three goals relate directly to the economic feasibility of any project, and can be significantly impacted by engineering decisions. For example, obscure development tools or environments can require a longer familiarisation timeline for new members coming into the development team. On the other hand, if the existing engineering staff come from non-traditional backgrounds, choosing enterprise-class technologies can extend development time beyond the funding lifecycle and greatly complicate long-term maintenance.

The portal team evaluated a variety of development environments and software tools (including crawlers and classifiers) that might contribute to achieving the goals. To improve overall productivity, we explored different development processes and methodologies, notably Waterfall and Agile, revising our original concept of a distributed engineering team in favour of a single in-house team to minimise communication complexity. We also sought to re-use software from our prior projects, but these proved unsatisfactory in part because that software had not been designed for a production-level environment.

Numerous engineering challenges arose throughout the course of product development. We prototyped the portal with popular products like jBoss, Jetspeed and uPortal, but found the implementations bulky and requiring areas of expertise not well aligned with that of our engineering staff. As a result, we went through several engineering restarts. Another consideration was that we wanted to use open source products, particularly those that did not have a licence fee. Eventually, it became clear that we needed to build the environment using established tools (Lucene, SOLR and others) rather than inventing our own, and to develop the portal using lightweight frameworks like Ruby on Rails which supports rapid application development. We also switched database engines, migrating from MySQL to PostgreSQL in order to improve XML integration. The final beta product was composed of five core elements:

- a front-end for the user application built with Rails;
- an administrative front-end to activate harvests, which was also built with Rails;
- the Java-based harvester to crawl and harvest content;
- a PostgreSQL database to store the content;
- the Lucene/Solr tools to perform searches and content indexing.

Project staffing and management

The project experienced many changes in staffing during the three-plus years of its existence, including a change in Principal Investigator during the final months. There were numerous technical staff changes as well. For example, a sequence of ten engineers worked on the code for periods ranging from five to 18 months, averaging less than one year per programmer. Every funded project role experienced at least one turnover during the performance period so that, by the end of the grant period, none of the original (first-year) project members remained. Given the typical approach to academic research projects, that is the lion's share of the work is accomplished by students, this is not unusual. Nonetheless, costs and sustainability are greatly impacted by so much turnover, due in part to the time required for new team members to become productive on the project and to the loss of 'project memory' with each team member's departure.

These were not the only major changes in project participants. We initially conducted user testing with Emory faculty, staff and students, all of whom volunteered their time. Numerous issues with the portal led us to shift user testing from this more random group to a set of targeted users, many from within our own library community, who could give more specific feedback on the portal. Community contributors carved time from their regular duties, which is yet another uncounted financial investment in the portal. The team retained an advisory board whose time was also unpaid, and held several conferences where scholars from other institutions provided helpful insights and suggestions for the project. All of this participatory effort represents a significant, unpriced investment in the project that does not appear on the balance sheet.

Deploying the portal

As each beta version of the product was deployed, performance issues and software problems were uncovered that needed to be addressed. Because portal components were built on different languages (notably Java and Rails) and depended on a variety of open source packages (Lucene, SOLR, Heritrix, Apache Web Server and others), deploying each release was a complex task of dependency analysis and version-conflict resolution. The lack of dedicated performance experts together with project code complexity made it harder to evaluate the source of performance bottlenecks exposed during beta user tests. In contrast, commercial groups typically invest a considerable proportion of the overall development cycle into deployment planning before the first release is in beta. Server capacity, performance tuning, security considerations and quality assurance are all exercised by performance engineering experts to determine the optimal configuration of the deployed product's environment, particularly if the company will host the software for its users (as we were doing for the SouthComb portal).

Continuous feature and user interface (UI) changes added complications, in part because with each UI change a new software development tool was added and/or the overall development environment was fundamentally modified. This practice adds to the cost of software development because the engineers need time to adapt to the changes and to determine whether there are cascading effects, that is if other parts of the software will be impacted by the change, or if the deployment server hardware will need upgrading.

This last aspect, the target deployment server(s), has economic implications that may be overlooked in the academic library. Server costs are typically expressed as one-time costs (X dollars to buy server brand ABC) with other considerations embedded in routine institution operating costs. For example, network bandwidth and power use add a predictable amount to the lifecycle cost of a server and are typically aggregated at the departmental budget level into a network provider monthly fee and the building's total electricity bill. But the real economic impact of each server is in the ongoing system administration time that it will require and consequences arising from such administration. For each deployed machine, system engineers need to apply operating system and software product patches, perform backup operations, manage user access and accounts, and – perhaps most importantly – monitor overall system security through the machine's logs, patterns of access and other security vulnerabilities. In many cases, addressing a security issue can create a problem with underlying software. One example seen in our institution's experience was the transition from PHP's[6] version 4.x series to the 5.x series where code written for PHP 4.x (which had a critical security issue) failed when the server was upgraded to the PHP 5.x version. Engineering costs accrue in the process of either reworking the broken code, rewriting the product from scratch or archiving (abandoning) the product altogether, but these are seldom accounted for in the budget.

Lessons learned

The project goals (as listed earlier) were at least superficially achieved with the deployment of the SouthComb web portal in 2007–8. We built a feature-rich, combined-search portal service, improved network access to various humanities collections of the southern United States and examined issues pertaining to sustaining a digital library portal. In retrospect, however, we did not fully meet the technology goals we set for the project, which contributed to a short 'shelf-life' for the portal. That is, the portal has not been maintained beyond its initial production version nor has a user community emerged to demand a new release. We learned several lessons from this experience that helped with subsequent projects:

- *True cost estimation.* According to our financial report to the grant agency, we were less than 1 per cent over our project budget at the conclusion of the award period. A lot of programming time was lost in the search for the optimal development environment, which equates to an unplanned increase in product development cost. We rewrote key portions of the code each time we switched our development tool set, and in some cases had to resolve bugs occurring from incompatible tool set versions.

- *Process management.* We erred in not matching our engineering process to our development process, spending about a third of the performance period using the Waterfall approach. Although we did change to an Agile methodology, it would have helped us to discuss and evaluate software process methodologies before we began the coding effort. We might have made more forward progress on the portal and had fewer code rewrites, thus getting a better return on our engineering investment.

- *Usability.* Feedback from target users is essential to creating a viable product. We had input from a wide range of users and user types, but maintaining a small core group of test users would have been more helpful. Another approach that would have helped is that of 'wireframing' the product. This gives the test user a sense of product flow before the actual software is written and can reduce total programming time by providing an approved 'spec' for the programmer to follow.

- *Deployability.* We integrated a wide variety of tools into the portal, including Lucene, SOLR, Heritrix, a PostgreSQL database server and

XML-based components. Such a complex deployment environment introduces potential versioning conflicts that can delay or even prevent releasing the product to the public. It also complicates the process of identifying sources of security breaches, adding to the maintenance cost over time. Finally, system administrators need to be very familiar with each of the installed components and understand how to tune the server for optimum performance of those tools without compromising other services. The time involved in the server administration functions should be included when planning the product's deployment.

- *Sustainability*. There are many factors involved in sustaining a digital library. From a simple budget perspective, the costs of keeping a server (electricity and bandwidth) are quickly calculated and the basic system administration cost is also predictable. What is not readily estimated is the maintenance factor. How much expertise is needed to keep the product running when underlying systems (OS, web server, compiler/interpreter and so on) are upgraded? Higher expertise typically costs more in annual salary and is also harder to replace in the case of staff turnover. Can the digital library coexist with other services, or does it require dedicated resources? Resource-friendly, low-demand digital libraries equate to lower costs. How large is the user base and/or how unique is the digital library? Ultimately, sustaining the digital library may be more a question of academic obligation than plain cost assessment but if the cost is high then other services offered by the institution may find themselves no longer sustainable in order to offset the higher cost of the mission-critical product.

Recommendations (key messages for other practitioners)

The following recommendations are geared toward organisations that are building new products intended for wide use in a production environment.

- *Know before you go*. Every software development language has both strengths and weaknesses. Recognise the pros and cons of each language and/or framework under consideration, then make a choice and stick with it through at least a full version 1.0 release. Where possible, use tools that have broad community acceptance so that: (a) you can leverage the web community for technical support; and (b) you will have a larger pool of programmer candidates from which to choose, should you need to augment the team.

- *Keep IT simple.* The target deployment environment (which includes web and database servers, compilers/interpreters and the system's operating system) should be as close to your institution's existing IT services as possible. This will simplify maintenance, make deployments easier to debug and improve long-term sustainability of the project.

- *Plan early, plan often.* Newer software process models like the Spiral and Agile methodologies are plan-oriented, calling for frequent team meetings where current status is reviewed, the software task list is re-prioritised, assigned and time estimated, and delivery dates are adjusted based on current progress. These planning-intensive methodologies can improve software development because (a) they give all team members frequent feedback on progress; (b) changes to the software design can occur incrementally; and (c) costs can be contained by modifying or eliminating planned features in a timely fashion.

- *Identify the minimum viable product (MVP).* The key benefit of custom software development (whatever features you want) is also a disadvantage, since it is difficult to predict user interest in each of the special features. Time and money might be spent on a feature that is rarely used rather than improving the highest-demand features. The MVP strategy deploys a fully operational core product together with features that are non-working links (typically during beta tests). Logs track user clicks on the non-operational items (which can have a 'coming soon' message, for example) and those that are frequently clicked can be implemented for the version 1.0 release. This approach can help resolve disagreements over which features will be important to users and allow the team to focus energy on those in highest demand.

- *Budget carefully.* Developing digital library software is expensive. Students can play a key role (thus reducing cost in some areas), but technical leadership and project management should be filled by the institution's permanent staff. If the project is likely to be widely used, sufficient in-house system administration time needs to be budgeted into the project ahead of the planned deployment date. Some time should also be allocated for ongoing, post-deployment product support.

- *Commit to a core team.* Successful digital library software development requires engineering expertise and a consistent vision. Every time the lead programmer or project manager changes, the vision for the product will change. This inevitably adds to the cost of the product since the new leader needs time to become familiar with the new role, even if already familiar with the product. Wherever possible, assign temporary members (student programmers, for example) to low-complexity tasks that have short ramp-up time in order to maximise their productivity.

- *Know your organisation's limitations.* Software requires long-term care, even if no further development is planned beyond the first production release. If your organisation experiences frequent changes in IT staffing, or if the IT staff are already overwhelmed with maintenance of the current in-house systems, the project is likely to have a short shelf-life. IT staff will have increasing difficulty keeping the product operational with each update to core system environments.

Conclusions

All software development projects go through the common phases of conceptualisation, implementation design, programming and deployment. In cases where the final project will have a very limited audience – whether because of limited public access or lack of broad appeal – it can often be fully realised with only a few in-house contributors or with rotating members such as students from the university's Computer Science Department. On the other hand, creating a robust, production-quality software framework is a complex engineering project which requires the full range of software engineering staff, including software quality assurance and security engineers, technical documenters and performance/capacity tuning engineers – in addition to the usual programmers, user interface designers, project managers and subject matter experts. Whether or not it is practical for the institution to devote this much manpower to a single project depends on its local mission and role in the larger academic world. Instead of calculating value solely on the size of the user community, a project's ROI can be calculated using critical academic impact factors such as collection uniqueness or institutional mission. From a practical perspective, project teams should plan to use their standard development tools for the majority of the software tasks, limiting experimental development to a manageable proportion so that coding delays or functionality limitations do not add to development costs or impact product deployment.

Notes

1. Funded by the Andrew W. Mellon Foundation from 2005 to 2009.
2. The original project proposal, implementation and development plan were created and managed by Katherine Skinner (now of Educopia) and Martin Halbert (now at the University of North Texas). The economic assessment and recommendations regarding the project's future were made by this author as Principal Investigator during the final term of the project.
3. *http://www.google.com/ig*
4. Source code for the project is available at: *http://code.google.com/p/southcomb.*
5. *http://southcomb.org*
6. A scripting language. See: *http://www.php.net/.*

Models and tools

Abstract. Chapter 3 considers the various types of model – business, costing, funding and pricing – that are relevant to the digital library. It aims to bring together the key themes from earlier chapters and case studies to provide a broader picture of digital library economic management in practice.

Keywords: business models, costing models, economic models, financial models, funding models, pricing models

Introduction

In this chapter we cover the various types of model – business (economic/financial), costing, funding, pricing – that are relevant to the digital library. We aim to provide a critique of the various models, drawing on practical examples and the case studies and categorising the models according to purpose and requirement. There are many different options for the digital library manager in terms of funding streams, and many of the case studies that accompany this chapter have been selected in order to give practical examples of the ways in which activity can be funded, particularly in the longer term.

Defining the different models

Business (economic, financial) model

There are many definitions of the terms 'economic (or financial) model' and 'business model' and the phrases are often used interchangeably, including in the case studies that form the bulk of this handbook. We regard them as different concepts, however, not least in the digital library context. For us, an *economic* model is a 'theoretical representation of economic reality showing the interrelationships between selected economic variables' (Alexander and Baden, 2000) characterised as 'a simplified framework designed to illustrate complex processes, often but not always using mathematical techniques'.[1] A *business* model provides 'a set of generic level descriptors of how a firm organises itself to create and distribute value in a profitable manner' (Baden-Fuller and Morgan, 2010). We regard a *financial* model[2,3] as being midway between an economic and a business model in that it describes mathematically the relationship between financial and operational aspects of a business and offers the opportunity to carry out 'what if' scenario planning and the likely financial impact of a particular set of decisions, thus enabling effective risk management to happen. Given the more practical approach of this book, we focus on business rather than economic or financial models for the most part.

Funding model

We regard a *funding* model as being 'a means of establishing an appropriate funding level for sustainment of the assets'[4] – in this context, collections, services or other digital library resources or activities. We also add to this definition the identification and management of the sources of funding. 'The requirements of ongoing sustainability demand at their base a source of reliable funding, necessary to ensure that the constant, albeit potentially low level, support ... can be maintained for as long as it is required' (Bradley, 2005). The Blue Ribbon Task Force commented:

> Funding models should be tailored to the norms and expectations of anticipated users. They should leverage economies of scale and scope whenever possible. Digital assets do not need to be treated as a public good in all cases. Market channels are often the most efficient means of allocating resources for preserving many types of digital content. (Blue Ribbon Task Force, 2010)

Costing model

We found the following definition of a costing model helpful and suggest that it is particularly appropriate for digital library work:

> In order to calculate the costs of providing services it is necessary to design and build a framework in which all costs can be recorded and allocated or apportioned to specific customers or other

activities. Such cost models can be developed to show, for example, the cost of each service, the cost for each customer or the cost for each location.[5]

Pricing model

A pricing model is 'a method for deciding what prices to charge for [an organisation's] products or services'.[6] We would add that the determination of pricing levels is likely to depend upon the overall business model chosen, the costs likely to be incurred, possible sources of funding, the outcome of any financial modelling and the level of risk to be entertained. Due account needs to be taken of what those being charged are willing and able to pay.

Business models

The Blue Ribbon Task Force (Blue Ribbon, 2008: Interim Report) defined a business model as

> a description of the ways in which an organization does its business to achieve its mission. A formal business model includes items such as the market being served, its product and service offerings, the perceived value delivered to the market, sources of revenue, financial and cost models that will support inflows and outflows of funds, and its strategic alignment, policies, and procedures. In general, however, business models are not formally expressed except at start-up, when funding bodies require proof that a coherent and sustainable plan does exist. Frequently, the term 'business model' is used in everyday parlance as a way to express a general intuition of the ways in which an organization raises its money to sustain itself.

On the other hand, Collier commented that:

> The term 'business model' is used for a broad range of informal and formal descriptions to represent core aspects of an organization, including purpose, offering, strategies, infrastructure, organizational structures, trading practices, and operational processes and policies. (Collier, 2010)

Halliday and Oppenheim (1999) undertook one of the first British studies attempting to develop business models (which they term 'economic models') – 'ancient history in terms of digital libraries' (Law, 2009). Since then, there has been a good deal of work on the economic aspects of digital publishing and, more recently, on digital preservation and content creation. Building on this previous work, Houghton (2009) looked at the costs and potential benefits of alternative models for scientific and scholarly publishing in three European countries. The work began in Australia in 2006 with a study of research communication costs, emerging opportunities and benefits (Houghton et al., 2006). This was followed by a major study of the economic implications of alternative scholarly publishing models for the Joint Information Systems Committee (JISC) in the UK (Houghton et al., 2009). In Case Study 7 Houghton comments on and updates this work.

The search for suitable business models in order to deliver sustainability continues to be a major theme (see, for example, Beagrie et al., 2008; Ayris, 2010; Knight, 2010; Beagrie et al., 2010). The Digital Preservation Coalition's *Preservation Management of Digital Material Handbook* (2006) also deals with the business model for the digital library, including the issues of benefit and value. It references approaches, such as the British Library's use of 'contingent valuation', to 'enumerate the value of collections and services which had previously appeared to be unquantifiable'.

Types of business model

In *Digital Library Economics* (Baker and Evans, 2009), we identified a number of potential business models for digital commerce. Table 3.1 summarises our findings. The choice of model will vary depending upon the particular circumstances (Knight, 2010).

Tanner (2009) notes that 'the business models most associated with Open Access (OA) are the article processing charge (APC) and the direct funding model. In the APC model a fee is levied for the cost of publication, paid generally by the author's funder or institution. In the direct funded model, a society, a foundation or a research organisation funds the publication as part of the mission of the organisation. The question remains whether the costs to digital libraries of maintaining access will be equitable in OA models against traditional journal publication.[7] In many cases there will be a range of possible business models that can be adopted and a hybrid approach may be the best way forward.

Table 3.1 Types of business model for digital commerce

Type	Comment
'Free'	The costs of set-up and maintenance are absorbed by the owner rather than passed onto the user. Such collections and services may suffer from poor quality, with the user needing to spend time searching to find the good ones.
Controlled circulation	The user registers and perhaps pays a membership fee to a 'society' or similar organisation which is signed up to access the content. Access and quality are perhaps more obviously monitored, with the costs of provision being associated with qualification for membership and then with user access and authenticity management processes.
Subscription	Access will normally be password based; costs will relate to the subscription charge for the users, and for the providers will relate to monitoring/authenticating users and security issues or content aggregators. There will be the potential for having personalised levels of subscription, ranging from a basic, cheaper, subscription for basic access, with premium services that cost more but which are more in-depth, more useful for the individual and perhaps therefore more exclusive.[1]
Advertising subsidised	Here, content is subsidised by a third party in exchange for advertising space, though experience suggests that it may be difficult to make such a deal attractive and cost-effective for the advertisers, especially because there is no standard model for pricing the advertising offer and 'ad hoc Web advertising pricing models will continue to hinder the sponsorship model as a legitimate revenue stream' (Kahin and Varian, 2000). There would seem to be a need for proper metrics and performance indicators to ensure pricing models are based on accurate and sustainable bases in this kind of environment.
Transactional or pay-per-view	There are potential cost-savings in this model because of efficiency through specificity, but the costs may be unpredictable with a high administrative overhead cost from administering payments.
Broadcast	User-created profiles trigger content being delivered to users' desktops. Most of the costs would seem to be fielded by advertisers but there are also fixed costs associated with establishing and running the push technologies.

Table 3.1 Types of business model for digital commerce (*cont'd*)

Bundling	Bundling has a number of advantages and disadvantages. The bundle may consist of a fixed list of titles for a number of years. If the purchaser does not have the funds to add new titles, this can lead to a lack of flexibility if some journals lose their attraction while new ones gain in value and relevance during the lifetime of a contract; however, bundling and lack of flexibility does provide budget predictability which is often required by libraries and public institutions (Baker and Evans, 2009).
Partnership provision	One way of engendering sustainability is to develop (public-private) partnerships, where the roles of content creators and revenue generators are shared, as for example with JSTOR (Case Study 1). Other, more hybrid, models have developed. In the case of the *18th Century Official Parliamentary Publications Portal 1688–1834*[2] at the University of Southampton, materials are served through different platforms.[3] Here, a percentage of the commercial publisher's revenues are shared among the consortia, which helps to maintain and develop the 'open access' eighteenth-century materials. Increasingly, consortia of research libraries[4] are contributing content to joint ventures where the production costs are lowered. Digitisation centres undertake digitisation for 'special collections' or are outsourced through vendors for less valuable objects and then delivered through either not-for-profit agencies such as JSTOR or via commercial partners – adding e-infrastructure and track records in the delivery of collections to various markets.
Versioning/ quality discrimination	'Consumers [will] … sort themselves into different groups according to their willingness to pay' (Kahin and Varian, 2000). There will be a need to find out what measures of 'quality' the customers are interested in. There is a fear that substandard information may be dangerous and that producers will seek to maximise profits by producing very low-quality products to those at that end of the spectrum. However, if a number of levels are provided, business models could be created that offer better quality at the higher 'levels', though the provider must ensure that added features and different elements can be offered so that versioning is possible in this environment.

Notes:

1. See, for example, Willinsky (2007).
2. *http://www.parl18c.soton.ac.uk/parl18c/digbib/home*
3. *http://www.il.proquest.com/pressroom/pressrelease/07/20071017.shtml*
4. UK examples include the Research Libraries UK nineteenth-century pamphlet project: *http://www.jisc.ac.uk/whatwedo/programmes/digitisation/pamphlets.aspx* and the Core e-Resource on Ireland: *http://www.jisc.ac.uk/whatwedo/programmes/digitisation/ireland.aspx*.

Types of funding model

The traditional funding model requires libraries to acquire their basic (digital) library services through the purchase of site licences, usually by annual subscription. Individual users then pay for any additional services such as printing and photocopying. Seer (2004) has analysed how the library budget can be stretched and highlights a number of basic approaches which are pertinent to all libraries in general. These approaches include:

- decision-making where fee based e-resources have similar content;
- negotiating with vendors and avoiding pressure to subscribe to an entire package where a subset of the package will actually satisfy the need;
- questioning individuals' purchasing of personal subscriptions;
- promoting resources and leading users to them;
- having a written acquisitions policy;
- having patience when facilitating the change process; and
- keeping the users 'on side'.

These are all areas the library should be engaging with but they take time and need to be handled methodically and sensitively.

A number of alternative funding models have been suggested. Institutions could continue to cover the full costs, as now, and as technology gets cheaper there are arguments that this model will itself become cheaper. Lesk (2004) considers other models, including funding by institutions, by authors, by user subscription and via advertising, as well as a number of other potential funding routes. Lesk also looks at the cost of a book in terms of digital space and storage and calculates that most of the cost of a library is in services such as cataloguing, reference, circulation and other related services, which implies not so much money will be saved by reducing the storage costs in favour of digitisation. 'If 80% of a library's cost is in services, even reducing the storage cost to zero leaves the library needing 80% of its budget.'

The report commissioned by the Strategic Content Alliance on *Sustainability and Revenue Models for Online Academic Resources* (Guthrie et al., 2008) listed the following types of funding model:

- subscription;
- pay-per-use;

- contributor pays;
- host organisation support;
- corporate support;
- advertising;
- philanthropic support;
- content licensing.

This list can be categorised into direct and indirect beneficiaries as payers:

- direct beneficiaries pay subscriptions/one-off payments/per use;
- contributors pay;
- indirect beneficiaries pay (for example, host institutions, sponsors, advertisers, philanthropists, content licensing).

Many fear the pay-per-use/transaction model less than a situation in which publishers cut out libraries completely and interact directly with users, which may restrict society's access to, and ownership of, information and will in turn reduce a library's interest in facilitating the preservation of information, possibly resulting in loss to future generations.

Charging, costing and pricing models

Charging for content and services is inextricably bound up with costing of the activities needed to provide the product. What to charge – the price – is also a fundamental part of the equation (see, for example, Lesk, 1997, 1999, 2005). In addition, libraries have to justify costs, especially where they increase. Can use justify cost? Methods need to be used to offer proper evaluation in order to answer this question (Koehn and Hawamdeh, 2010). If information is created by or for the public sector or with public-sector funding, should it be free? There is a risk that if 'the public' has to pay for it, the business model becomes in effect one of double charging – via taxes and then via direct charges. Should digital libraries, then, be supported and structured like traditional libraries, and provided free either to certain defined groups of users or, indeed, to all users? Some argue that public sector institutions should not automatically have to provide free, open access. Information needs to be treated as a valuable commodity, not a free public good, or it is a public good but it must have sufficient investment to protect its continued existence and quality. It is important to understand that e-information does not necessarily fit within the existing model of the free-market economy. The digital library offer therefore needs to be both attractive and potentially flexible. Although initial costs are higher than with other forms of library, if the digital library resource is used more frequently than others it should be a good investment. The challenge, then, is likely to relate to increasing usage to make sure that provision is as cost-effective as possible as quickly as possible.

However, as Lynne Brindley points out:

> There has been relatively little deep discussion of charging and pricing models ... with a general philosophy underpinning national site licence deals being that of 'free at the point of use' to all those in the scope of the community covered by the relevant deal ... In the twenty-first century, the emphasis has moved much more towards user driven models of economic value, with users wanting more personalized information systems and free access to an increasingly rich set of public domain software tools and content. They expect to experience these for free, albeit often with targeted advertising attached, as new business and service models emerge and begin to dominate. (Brindley, 2009)

We also noted in *Digital Library Economics* that:

> When first developing electronic access, many producers or publishers based their pricing models on those in use for hard-copy materials. A more appropriate model would have been to look to do new things and to make the services – and the prices – most attractive to the consumer. (Baker and Evans, 2009)

In this context, it is important to note that costs can be redistributed. While there may be costs associated with digital libraries that are not present in traditional library services, there will also be savings, as many of the case studies in this handbook point out, and these must be taken into account when looking at the overall business model.

> It is the role of foundations and government agencies to provide start-up capital for academic projects that are unlikely to generate commercial returns and are therefore unlikely to attract commercial

interest. Some foundations may be prepared to make repeated investments in projects that are critical to their own missions, and perhaps prepared to make recurring commitments to fund operating expenses. But in most cases, projects must regard initial funding as precisely that – start-up funding to bridge the organisation to other reliable, recurring, and diverse sources of support. Taking this approach is healthy because it forces projects to engage a variety of beneficiaries directly (users; commercial, governmental and non-profit beneficiaries), rather than working only to ensure that the primary funder continues to be satisfied with progress. (Guthrie et al., 2008)

Start-up costs will present a major challenge for digital libraries. Finding the resources to make the initial investment will require a strong business case to be made. Typically, as noted in Case Study 6, the single largest cost – recurrent as well as capital – will be staff time.

Hardy et al. (2001) researched into charging mechanisms for the delivery of digitised texts to students in the (UK) higher education sector and considered a number of possible pricing strategies in relation to the HERON (Higher Education Resources ON-demand) project that would be 'mutually acceptable' to all the key stakeholders. Hickox et al. (2006) describe how to carry out a variable cost analysis so that the total costs to the library can be determined, noting the need to predict future costs broken down according to key categories. Mayrhofer (2003) discusses the pricing of information goods with respect to the digital library. He notes that 'the cost structure ... is a special one'. The cost of production is dominated by the 'first-copy costs' which means that information is produced costly but reproduced cheaply. Hence the fixed costs are large but the variable costs of reproduction are small which is a typical case of substantial economies of scale. The Blue Ribbon Task Force (2010) described 'economies of scale' as referring to a situation where:

> The average cost of producing a good (or service) declines as the scale of production increases. This could happen, for instance, if a firm can buy in bulk, taking advantage of lower unit costs on its inputs, or by allowing more specialization of its workforce, allowing each worker to become more efficient. Economies of scale occur because the organization can spread its fixed costs over a larger and larger level of output as it expands in scale. If a particular industry experiences economies of scale, this suggests that one very large firm can produce the product at a lower average cost than a number of smaller firms could.

Maron and Loy (2011) comment that:

> The economies of scale needed to develop and deliver electronic resources do not favour the creation of many small, independent entities, each developing its own infrastructure and content to serve niche audiences. Even the most prestigious national collections with vast holdings to draw from ... actively develop content partnerships and continuously seek ways to achieve the scale they feel will provide value to their users and their customers. Smaller, niche collections surely have their work cut out for them.

Mayrhofer (2003) also considers different options of price discrimination and models of pricing – depending on type and status of user (individual, group, organisation, member/non-member), willingness and/or ability to pay and time of year/level of demand – were examined with special emphasis on the economics of bundling information goods. Bundling is a pricing tool primarily for monopoly suppliers and which 'not only guarantees payment in advance, but also secures payment for low use [materials]'. It also provides certainty – though not necessarily the greatest economy – to the subscriber. The PSLI (UK Pilot Site Licence Initiative) used bundling as a pricing mechanism, with the publishers involved gaining more revenue by offering all of their titles as a single product.[8]

The PEAK (Pricing Electronic Access to Knowledge) project at the University of Michigan[9] provided a production service-based opportunity to develop experimental pricing for journals available from Elsevier Science, to evaluate the effect of different schemes on users and producers and to look at the additional value that can be gained from the use of electronic resources and pricing schemes. Three types of bundling were offered:

- traditional – buy access to pre-designed journals;
- generalised – buy access to user-chosen articles in bundles of 120;
- per article – buy individual and unlimited access to articles.

Initially libraries saw 'the generalised subscription as a way of increasing the flexibility of their journal budgets and of tying purchasing more closely to actual use' (Bonn et al., 1999), though experience suggests that the majority of usage is clustered around a small number of articles. According to Mayrhofer's research, bundling is particularly apposite when there is a relatively broad range of demand for different products that therefore make bundling attractive to the producer, especially where economies of scale ensue because the added cost of providing material to subsidiary audiences is marginal or even zero. This is not always the case, especially where the cost of bringing bundles to widely disparate readerships results in significant additional cost in which case differential pricing – if feasible – has to be introduced. A number of interesting aspects of digital usage have emerged from bundled provision and these provide some of the reasons for developing new pricing schemes. The (digital) environment has changed in recent years and, at least in terms of academic publishing and usage, because the article or the chapter is the main transaction unit rather than the journal or the book (Baker, 2006), bundling in particular is arguably becoming less attractive than when electronic versions first appeared (Baker and Evans, 2009). Unbundling (that is, pay-per-unit or access/use rather than blanket subscription) may be a better option both for supplier and consumer. There are lots of options (based on variables such as access level, length of access and functionality) which are feasible in a digital library situation in a way in which they would not be with print-on-paper provision.

The importance of market research (as discussed in Chapter 2 and Case Studies 2, 10 and 12) is stressed in much of the relevant literature, as is the need to be clear about the actual costs of production and delivery. The prices set should be realistic in the context of actual expenditure, target income and surplus levels. Similarly, products and services need to be developed that are not only attractive to the relevant markets but are also likely to attract a sufficient share of those markets to command a sufficient degree of 'market power', as Mayrhofer (2003) puts it. Price discrimination can be difficult when there is limited market differentiation (that is, most of the potential customers are in a similar position – students, for example, with limited disposable income). As already suggested, the likely outcome in more complex environments (highly differentiated education sectors, for example) is a hybrid approach to pricing, such as 'a mixed bundling strategy, which offers a menu of different bundles at different prices' (Kahin and Varian, 2000) to satisfy the different needs of customers. This is unlikely to work well if there is 'leakage' between the different sub-sectors and/or the pricing model becomes too complex for users to understand easily.

Bia (2006) looks at estimating digitisation costs in digital libraries using software engineering methods. The estimate of web-content production costs is a very difficult task. It is difficult to make exact predictions due to the great quantity of unknown factors. However, digitisation projects need to have a precise idea of the economic costs and the times involved in the development of their contents. Kejser et al. (2009) describe a project funded by the Danish Ministry of Culture to set up a model for costing the preservation of digital materials held by national cultural heritage institutions. The overall objective of the project was to provide a basis for comparing and estimating future financial requirements for digital preservation and to increase the cost-effectiveness of digital preservation activities. In this study they describe an activity-based costing methodology for digital preservation based on the OAIS Reference Model. In order to estimate the cost of digital migrations they identified cost-critical activities by analysing the OAIS model and supplemented this analysis with findings from other models, literature and their own experience. The study found that the OAIS model provides a sound overall framework for cost breakdown, but that some functions, especially when it comes to performing and evaluating the actual migration, need additional detailing in order to cost activities accurately.

Wright et al. (2009) focus on modelling costs and risks. As storage costs drop, storage is becoming the lowest cost in a digital repository – and the biggest risk. They examined current modelling of costs and risks in digital preservation, concentrating on the total cost of risk when using digital storage systems for preserving audiovisual material.

Focusing on digital reference services, Gross et al. (2006) present three measures isolated by project participants as being most useful for their immediate needs: total cost of providing digital reference services; the cost of digital reference services as a percentage of the total reference budget; the cost of reference as a percentage of the total library or organisational budget. Bia et al. (2010) stress that estimating digitisation costs is a very difficult task, despite the fact that digitisation projects need to have a precise idea of the economic costs and the times involved in the development of their contents. Based on 'methods used in Software Engineering for software development cost prediction ... and using historical data gathered during five years at the Miguel de Cervantes Digital Library during the digitization of more than 12,000 books', they developed a method for time and cost estimates named DiCoMo (Digitization Costs Model) for digital content production in general. This method can be adapted to different production processes. 'The accuracy of the estimates improve with time, since the algorithms can be optimized by making adjustments based on historical data gathered from previous tasks.'

Case studies

The next set of case studies – while exploring all the major themes outlined in the first two chapters of the handbook – have a particular focus on the topics discussed in this chapter.

Case Study 5

The approach adopted by accessCeramics is a common one, where the project is funded by a 'parent' or 'host' institution that is prepared to resource the activity because it brings (largely) non-financial benefits. The case study thus provides an interesting perspective on cost and benefit and return on investment. The 'altruism' seemingly evident in the project is possible because of the low marginal cost involved in provision, the ability to reinforce core resource provision and the opportunities provided for significant staff development (particularly in managing other digital projects). However, some of the benefits (for example, improved student recruitment) must remain intangible in terms of the lack of robust evidence for a direct correlation between the presence of accessCeramics in the institution and its standing and well-being, whether this be financial or otherwise. The sorts of methods and metrics discussed and analysed in Case Study 10 could be useful here on top of the cost comparisons actually used by the College. The overall business model is worth further study, based as it is on artist participation and funding and a strong emphasis on cooperative and collaborative working as stressed elsewhere in the handbook and – once the start-up phase had been completed – on cost saving, notably in terms of staffing. But other models that aim to monetise the growing value of accessCeramics as a saleable product are considered for the longer term, and include:

- further collaborations;
- subscriptions;
- sponsorships;
- donations;
- endowment;
- advertising;
- fundraising through a related business venture.

This reinforces the options referred to earlier in this chapter. The authors note, however, that some approaches – such as, for example, a subscription model – may well run counter to the spirit and core objectives of the project as it was set up: in this case 'broad open access'. A membership model – supported by some of the other options listed here – might be more appropriate in such circumstances. As always, there is a delicate balance that needs to be achieved between volume, demand, cost (including an acceptable level of overhead), price and willingness to buy.

Case Study 6

The theme of longer-term sustainability (what to do after the initial funding has run out) is further discussed in relation to the Chronopolis project. The case study usefully focuses on the economic challenges associated with digital preservation (in this instance on a very large scale) and ways in which the significant opportunities and advantages of digital libraries can best be utilised and exploited. Once again, collaboration is very much in evidence. The project management narrowed down longer-term funding sources into four types:

- subscriptions;
- research funding partners;
- grant funding;
- institutional support from host or partner organisations.

None of these options were seen as ensuring long-term sustainability other than when combined in a layered funding approach (see Case Study 6, Figure CS6.1) and a distributed model where risk and responsibility are shared. Experience shows that sustainability needs to be built in from the start and partnership arrangements need to be properly formalised from the beginning.

Case Study 7

Open access is a major tool in the drive to increase both efficiency and effectiveness in the digital library as well as (academic) digital publishing more generally. Indeed, there are those who would see the adoption of open access models as the end of traditional libraries and the publications that they store and organise.[10] As noted by Derek Law in Chapter 4, John Houghton's work has been of considerable importance in ensuring that the economic and financial implications of new models of publishing are well calculated, understood and considered. All the evidence produced by Houghton's studies – and similar work by others – points to the significant cost-benefit and return on investment over time of open access to digital content as opposed to other (more traditional) models, and also as compared with print-on-paper provision. This case is especially useful, though, for the insight that it gives into the various techniques used to evaluate the various options (based on a lifecycle approach), and notably:

- process mapping;
- activity costing;
- macro-economic modelling.

Case Study 8

The not-for-profit business model is exemplified by Portico and the case study describes the move from grant funding to self-sustaining activity on the basis of well-balanced cooperation between the key stakeholders with their diverse (if not divergent) interests. As the Blue Ribbon Task Force stressed (Blue Ribbon Task Force, 2010) there is often no single stakeholder group on which digital library managers can focus:

> Stakeholders for digital materials are often diffuse across different communities. The interests of future users are poorly represented in selecting materials to preserve. Trusted public institutions – libraries, archives, museums, professional organisations and others – can play important roles as proxy organisations to represent the demands of their stakeholders over generations.

Economies of scale and diversity of revenue base were also critical to sustainability, though understanding the partners' needs – and satisfying them in a transparent way – was the key factor. One major challenge for digital libraries (and their sustainability) is the free rider problem.

> There is a particular risk of 'free riding' with digital materials because the cost of preservation may be borne by one organisation but the benefits accrue to many. Effective governance mechanisms

are needed to aggregate the collective interest into an effective preservation strategy that ensures that the effort and cost of preservation are appropriately apportioned. (Blue Ribbon Task Force, 2010)

This is a major challenge particularly in a digital preservation project because of the non-rival nature of the entity created and its potential availability to those who have not provided funding. Conversely, the need to invest in digital preservation may not be immediately obvious, with benefits only being realised in the longer term. Flexibility – as identified earlier in this handbook – is the key to developing and maintaining buy-in on an ongoing basis. Ultimately, the ability to evolve business models appropriate to dynamic environments and changing requirements provides the best chance of success.

Case Study 9

The application of preferred business models requires funding decisions, as evinced by many of the case studies in this handbook. As we stressed in *Digital Library Economics* (Baker and Evans, 2009) calculating the return on investment (ROI) is a fundamental part of effective decision-making in the digital library, though the key challenge is to calculate what this is in the context of the particular environment in which content and services are being provided. Closely linked to ROI is the whole question of value for money. 'In e-terms, value for money also means systems and services that are capable of effective, widespread, deep, relevant and malleable usage' (Baker, 2005).

But there are difficulties. As Dempster and Grout (2009) point out, 'the evidence on which any future attempt to predict [cost] may be based is useful but fragmentary. Perhaps this is because assessment of cost really depends on notions of value and what might be considered an adequate return on investment.' How is cost-effectiveness measured? Hulme (2006) seeks to describe the key elements of cost-effectiveness analysis and to demonstrate how such analysis may be used in the library environment. The extent to which there is a 'return' on the investment is also likely to be the key factor in resource allocation. The greater the return the increased chance there will be of long-term sustainability because those investing in the initial activities associated with the project will be attracted into further investment, and so on. Relative cost and value need to be compared in order to provide possible preferred options. As much definition and information as possible should be gathered and analysed in order to ensure cost-effective decision-making that will lead to sustainable solutions and conclusions. This case study distils experience and knowledge of many of the techniques and associated metrics that can be used to calculate ROI in a range of environments and as appropriate to different types of library.

Case Study 10

As already noted, pricing plans form an integral part of many digital library business models and are likely to become ever more prominent in future environments where grant aid is less forthcoming. The process of determining the when, where, why, what, to whom and how of charging for digital activities, content and services can prove to be valuable in a wide range and variety of circumstances, not least because, in order to carry out this work, the core offer has to be defined, all relevant costs have to be identified and the market for the offer has to be studied. Only then can an appropriate pricing model be identified, developed and applied.

This case study looks at sustaining a service through cost recovery via charging users. In order to do this, the four key steps just described were taken. Building on significant prior experience and a robust pre-existing user base, the leaders of EZID were able to harness key groups and advisers to produce a sustainable service. It is clear from the author's experience, however, that one 'size' of pricing model is unlikely to fit all markets. Continuing and continuous renewal and enhancement of the offer provide the best chance of success in the longer term.

Case Study 11

Much digital library provision is within what could broadly be described as the public sector, that is, typically, organisations that are funded at least in part by government (local, regional, national) to provide collections and services for the common good. However, as is evident from previous chapters and many of the case studies within this handbook, major change is happening within such public services as a result of significant financial pressures and funding constraints. More 'commercial' approaches are therefore being embraced, as noted, for example, in Case Study 10. Case Study 11 was therefore commissioned in order to look at the development of costing and pricing models from a private-sector viewpoint. One key message from the study is the need for ongoing improvements in provision, leading to high perceptions of added value by those paying for services rendered, especially in the context of what other providers could offer and at what price. The study also reinforces the conclusion reached in Case Study 10 – the importance of good market research as the basis of delivery of what customers want and need, and, particularly in a tight financial climate, a good return on investment and significant opportunities to reduce costs while adding value.

Case Study 12

This case study also takes a publisher perspective on digital economics. The ability to offer digital products at marginal cost provided an important incentive to publishers in the early years of development. But, here again, thorough market research enabled the formulation of business models that facilitated a move from add-on to mainstream.

Case Study 13

Taking risks is an inevitable element in digital library management. This is especially the case where a project needs to develop into a service. As a project, grant aid is likely to be available, but almost inevitably this will be finite. As noted earlier in this handbook, in order to achieve long-term sustainability, other sources of income have to be found, with clear justification as to why there should be investment in the proposed service, whether it be reduced costs or increased benefits, or preferably both. In order to do this, it is crucial to ensure that all activities have been fully and properly costed (including both direct and indirect costs) within an overarching framework where the vision and the mission are clearly articulated.

Case Study 14

Digital library economics has a number of key facets, as described throughout the handbook. This case study brings together many of the main themes discussed, in particular: sustainability, resource allocation, the main costs associated with digital library service provision and cost-effective decision-making in order to ensure the best possible deployment and use of resources to meet stated aims and objectives.

Conclusion

This chapter has focused on finance-based models for the digital library, and in particular on business models and their constituent parts and techniques as well as the key associated tools, while aiming also to bring together the key themes from earlier chapters and case studies to provide a broader picture of digital library economic management in practice. Chapter 4 aims to provide a further, fuller summary.

Notes

1. *http://en.wikipedia.org/wiki/Economic_model*
2. *http://www.businessdictionary.com/definition/financial-model.html#ixzz22 snpcKcD*
3. *http://financial-dictionary.thefreedictionary.com/Financial+model*
4. *http://www.assetinsights.net/Glossary/G_Funding_Model.html*
5. *http://www.knowledgetransfer.net/dictionary/ITIL/en/Cost_Model.htm*
6. *http://dictionary.cambridge.org/dictionary/business-english/pricing-model*
7. See, for example, *http://www.nls.uk/media/808985/future-national-libraries.pdf.*
8. Also see SPARC (Scholarly Publishing and Academic Resources Coalition) which aims at facilitating the publication of affordable journals at: *http://www.lib.utexas.edu/ejour/SPARC.html?*
9. See, for example, *http://www.dlib.org/dlib/june99/06bonn.html*
10. *http://www.uk.sagepub.com/repository/binaries/pdf/Library-OAReport.pdf*

References

Alexander, P. and Baden, S. (2000) *Glossary on Macroeconomics from a Gender Perspective.* Institute of Development Studies, University of Sussex.

Ayris, P. (2010) 'The status of digitisation in Europe: extensive summary of the second LIBER-EBLIDA workshop on the digitisation of library materials in Europe', *LIBER Quarterly*, 19 (3/4): 193–226. Online at: *http://discovery.ucl.ac.uk/19078/1/19078.pdf.*

Baden-Fuller, C. and Morgan, M.S. (2010) 'Business models as models', *Long Range Planning*, 43: 156–71. Online at: *http://www.cassknowledge.com/sites/default/files/article-attachments/517~~business_models_as_models.pdf.*

Baker, D. (2005) 'Digital Library Development to 2010', unpublished Final Report and Routemap. Bristol: JISC.

Baker, D. (2006) 'Digital library futures: a UK HE and FE perspective', *Interlending and Document Supply*, 34 (1): 4–8.

Baker, D. and Evans, W. (eds) (2009) *Digital Library Economics: An Academic Perspective*. Oxford: Chandos Publishing.

Beagrie, N., Chruszcz, J. and Lavoie, B. (2008) *Keeping Research Data Safe – A Cost Model and Guidance for UK Universities*. JISC. Online at: *http://www.jisc.ac.uk/publications/publications/keepingresearchdatasafe.aspx*.

Beagrie, N., Lavoie, B. and Woollard, M. (2010) *Keeping Research Data Safe 2*. JISC. Online at: *http://www.jisc.ac.uk/media/documents/publications/reports/2010/keepingresearchdatasafe2.pdf*.

Bia, A. (2006) *Estimating Digitization Costs in Digital Libraries Using Software-Engineering Methods*. Centro de Investigación Operativa, Universidad Miguel Hernández de Elche. Online at: *http://cio.umh.es/ES/publicaciones/ficheros/CIO_2006_04.pdf*.

Bia, A., Murioz, R. and Gomez, J. (2010) 'Estimating digitization costs in digital libraries using DiCoMo', *Research and Advanced Technology for Digital Libraries*, 6273: 136–47.

Blue Ribbon Task Force (2008) *Sustaining the Digital Investment Issues and Challenges of Economically Sustainable Digital Preservation. Interim Report of the Blue Ribbon Task Force on Sustainable Digital Preservation and Access*. Online at: *http://brtf.sdsc.edu/biblio/BRTF_Interim_Report.pdf*.

Blue Ribbon Task Force (2010) *Sustainable Economics for a Digital Planet: Ensuring Long-Term Access to Digital Information. Final Report of the Blue Ribbon Task Force on Sustainable Digital Preservation and Access*. Online at: *http://brtf.sdsc.edu/biblio/BRTF_Final_Report.pdf*.

Bonn, M., Lougee, W., MacKie-Mason, J. and Riveros, J. (1999) 'A report on the PEAK experiment', *D-Lib Magazine*, 5 (6). Online at: *http://www.dlib.org/dlib/june99/06bonn.html*.

Bradley, K. (2005) *APSR Sustainability Issues Discussion Paper*. Australian Partnership for Sustainable Repositories, January. Online at: *https://digitalcollections.anu.edu.au/bitstream/1885/46653/5/APSR_Sustainability_Issues_Paper.pdf*.

Brindley, L. (2009) 'Foreword: Digital library economics: an introduction', in D. Baker and W. Evans (eds), *Digital Library Economics: An Academic Perspective*. Oxford: Chandos Publishing.

Collier, M. (ed.) (2010) *Business Planning for Digital Libraries*. Leuven: Leuven University Press.

Dempster, S. and Grout, C. (2009) 'Digitisation – trends in the economics of retro-conversion', in D. Baker and W. Evans (eds), *Digital Library Economics: An Academic Perspective*. Oxford: Chandos Publishing.

Digital Preservation Coalition (2006) *Preservation Management of Digital Material Handbook*, Section 3.7: Costs and Business Modelling. Online at: *http://www.dpconline.org/component/docman/doc_download/299*.

Gross, M., McClure, C. and Lankes, R.D. (2006) 'Costing reference: issues, approaches, and directions for research', *Reference Librarian*, 46 (95/96): 173–86.

Guthrie, K., Griffiths, R. and Maron, N. (2008) *Sustainability and Revenue Models for Online Academic Resources.* Ithaka. Online at: *http://sca. jiscinvolve.org/files/2008/06/sca_ithaka_sustainability_report-final.pdf.*

Halliday, L. and Oppenheim, C. (1999) *Economic Models of the Digital Library.* Loughborough: Loughborough University.

Hardy, R., Oppenheim, C. and Rubbert, I. (2001) 'Pricing strategies and models for the provision of digitized texts in higher education', *Journal of Information Science,* 28 (2): 97–110.

Hickox, C., Jackson, R., Markham, G. and Cox, C. (2006) 'Going broke, going digital: a preliminary cost analysis of building a digital library', *Internet Reference Services Quarterly,* 11 (1): 51–66.

Houghton, J. (2009) *Open Access: What Are the Economic Benefits? A Comparison of the United Kingdom, Netherlands and Denmark.* Knowledge Exchange. Online at: *http://ssrn.com/abstract=1492578.*

Houghton, J.W., Steele, C. and Sheehan, P.J. (2006) *Research Communication Costs in Australia: Emerging Opportunities and Benefits.* Department of Education, Science and Training, Canberra. Online at: *http://dspace.anu.edu. au/handle/1885/44485.*

Houghton, J.W., Rasmussen, B., Sheehan, P.J., Oppenheim, C., Morris, A., Creaser, C., Greenwood, H., Summers, M. and Gourlay, A. (2009) *Economic Implications of Alternative Scholarly Publishing Models: Exploring the Costs and Benefits.* Bristol: JISC. Online at: *http://www.cfses.com/EI-ASPM/.*

Hulme, C. (2006) 'Using cost effectiveness analysis: a beginner's guide', *Evidence-Based Library and Information Practice,* 1 (4): 17–29. Online at: *http:// ejournals.library.ualberta.ca/index.php/EBLIP/article/view/92/183.*

Kahin, B. and Varian, H. (eds) (2000) *Internet Publishing and Beyond – The Economics of Digital Information and Intellectual Property.* Cambridge, MA: MIT Press.

Kejser, U., Nielsen, A. and Thirifays, A. (2009) 'Cost model for digital curation: cost of digital migration', *iPRES 2009: The Sixth International Conference on Preservation of Digital Objects,* California Digital Library, UC Office of the President, 5–6 October. Online at: *http://escholarship.org/uc/item/ 4d09c0bb;jsessionid=43E95E8C4EF8D3B32AD15D351BF24993#page-4.*

Knight, S. (2010) 'Early learnings from the National Library of New Zealand's National Digital Heritage Archive project', *Program: Electronic Library and Information Systems,* 44 (2): 85–97.

Koehn, S. and Hawamdeh, S. (2010) 'The acquisition and management of electronic resources: can use justify cost?', *Library Quarterly,* 80 (2): 161–74.

Law, D. (2009) 'Digital library economics: aspects and prospects', in D. Baker and W. Evans (eds), *Digital Library Economics: An Academic Perspective.* Oxford: Chandos Publishing.

Lesk, M. (1997) *Practical Digital Libraries: Books, Bytes and Bucks.* San Francisco: Morgan Kaufman.

Lesk, M. (1999) 'The organisation of digital libraries', *Science and Technology Libraries,* 17 (3–4): 9–25.

Lesk, M. (2004) 'How to pay for digital libraries', in J. Andrews and D. Law (eds), *Digital Libraries.* Aldershot: Ashgate.

Lesk, M. (2005) *Understanding Digital Libraries*, 2nd edn. San Francisco: Morgan Kaufman.

Maron, N. and Loy, M. (2011) *Revenue, Recession, Reliance: Revisiting the SCA/Ithaka S+R Case Studies in Sustainability*. Bristol: JISC.

Mayrhofer, M. (2003) *Research Findings of Pricing Information Goods for Digital Libraries: Development of a Pricing Strategy*. Online at: *http:// michael.hahsler.net/SE/SS2003/Mayrhofer/pricing_finalversion.pdf*.

Seer, G. (2004) 'No pain, no gain: stretching the library dollar', *The Bottom Line: Managing Library Finances*, 17 (1): 10–14.

Tanner, S. (2009) 'The economic future for digital libraries: a 2020 vision', in D. Baker and W. Evans (eds), *Digital Library Economics: An Academic Perspective*. Oxford: Chandos Publishing.

Willinsky, J. (2007) *Scholarly Associations and the Economic Viability of Open Access Publishing*. Online at: *http://journals.tdl.org/Jodi/article/view/Article/ Jodi-117/103*.

Wright, R., Miller, A. and Addis, M. (2009) 'The significance of storage in the "cost of risk" of digital preservation', *International Journal of Digital Curation*, 4 (3). Online at: *http://www.ijdc.net/index.php/ijdc/article/viewFile/ 138/173*.

accessCeramics: building and sustaining a global resource for arts education

Mark Dahl

Abstract. The case study concerns a sponsorship-type model where an institution funds the activity ostensibly for the greater good but, in consequence, enjoys non-financial benefits – not least increased prestige – that justify the resource allocation, though the actual level is at a low marginal cost add-on to the institution's own core activity. Collaboration is much in evidence – in this case through artist participation and funding – and a flexible approach has enabled the sponsoring institution to respond to financial challenges, including by means of cost reduction. The case study looks at the ways in which comparative cost and benefit might best be calculated and explores alternative funding models for digital library collections and services.

Keywords: accessCeramics, arts education, benefits, collaboration, costs, future, revenue models, sponsorship type model, sustainability

Introduction

accessCeramics[1] is a growing collection of images of contemporary ceramic art created to support arts education. It fills a gap in art image collections on the Web, and uses an innovative user-contributed collection-building model. accessCeramics is an example of an online academic resource whose costs are borne largely by its sponsoring institution but whose benefits are enjoyed by a much broader community.

The resource benefits its sponsoring institution through its educational value to students, through the professional development opportunities that it provides for faculty and staff, and by enhancing institutional visibility and prestige. The educational, research and artistic value that it provides to the wider community comes at a low marginal cost to its sponsoring institution. But its sponsoring institution might consider a range of business models that would allow it to capture some of the value it provides to the wider community. These models include: collaborations, subscriptions, sponsorships, donations, endowment, advertising and fundraising through a related business venture.

Background

Created in 2008 by the Watzek Library and the Department of Art at Lewis & Clark College, accessCeramics is an innovative online collection of contemporary ceramic art images. Designed to support arts education, accessCeramics fills a gap in artistic image collections on the Web by providing high-quality images of contemporary ceramic art suitable for an instructional environment. Since its inception, accessCeramics has grown to 4,852 images representing 352 artists from six continents. Visitors to the site increased 46 per cent in 2009–10, 50 per cent in 2010–11 and 44 per cent in 2011–12, which saw a total of 76,205 site visits from 124 countries.

accessCeramics uses a collaborative collection-building model in which artists submit and catalogue their own work using the social photo sharing software Flickr.[2] A five-member curatorial board solicits and reviews artists' submissions based on quality of work, professional status and contribution to the field. The accessCeramics model, which has drawn international attention, provides opportunities for learning, inspiration and easy access to contemporary ceramic arts images to a global audience.

Lewis & Clark College,[3] a small, selective, private liberal arts college that enrolls approximately 2,000 undergraduates, hosts the project. accessCeramics is a collaboration between librarians and an art faculty member at the College. The librarians handle the logistics of the project, including the development of the website, management of collection metadata, grant writing and other logistical support. Ted Vogel, Associate Professor of Art and Programme Head of Ceramics at Lewis & Clark, heads the curatorial board and sets the broad direction of the project. Together, Vogel and library staff members make up the accessCeramics team.

Costs

accessCeramics has been a front-loaded project with its largest cost consistently being staff time of team members at the project's host institution, Lewis & Clark. In early 2008, the accessCeramics team spent considerable hours conceiving the project's idea and scope, creating a prototype website and seeding it with an initial collection. In the 2008–9 academic year, the project team redesigned the website, recruited initial artist participants, and marketed the project with support from a grant from the National Institute for Technology in Liberal Education.[4] With a website and a submissions system in place, a grant from the National Endowment for the Arts[5] for the 2009–10 academic year provided funds for a submissions coordinator who recruited prospective artists and assisted the curatorial board with voting. Following the end of grant support in June 2010, the project team reconfigured the project to be less labour-intensive by putting in place an automated voting system for artist review by the curatorial board. During the 2010–11 academic year the accessCeramics team moved the project into more of a maintenance mode with staff time only devoted to occasional fixes and adjustments. This less time-intensive state proved successful as the size of the collection and its use continued to grow during the period.

Staff working on the project spend time on grant writing, software development, metadata management, marketing, workflow design and coordination of submissions. The College's sponsored research officer has also contributed a significant amount of time to grant writing for the project. Other costs associated with running the site are minor or incidental. The project runs on a server that is already a sunk cost for the College and utilises a Flickr Pro account that costs $25 per year. One could argue that the project distributes many of what would be costs in a traditional library digital project or art publication to participating artists. The artists in accessCeramics must bear the cost of photographing their work and are responsible for uploading and cataloguing the images that populate the collection. In summer of 2011, the project team submitted a second grant application to the National Endowment for the Arts that would support institutional collaborations. Under the proposed project, arts institutions such as the American Museum of Contemporary Craft will contribute their own collections and take part in artist recruitment and training for accessCeramics, thus bearing some of the costs of expanding the collection. The proposal was not funded, however.

Benefits

The accessCeramics project benefits its host institution in a few different ways. Chiefly, it provides educational resources for Lewis & Clark's studio art programme that would not otherwise be available. Students in ceramics courses consult accessCeramics on a regular basis as they study the work of other artists and develop ideas for their own work. Student employees supporting the project have had the opportunity to learn more about classification of art and to develop relationships with artists. In these ways, accessCeramics contributes directly to the educational mission of Watzek Library and the broader College of Arts and Sciences at Lewis & Clark, which the library supports. Lewis & Clark College supports professional development for its faculty and accessCeramics provides an aspect of this for its curator, Ted Vogel. accessCeramics builds connections between Vogel and fellow ceramicists and this enhances his own creative work. Furthermore, Vogel's curation of the accessCeramics collection is an intellectual and creative endeavour in its own right.

Among the library staff, accessCeramics has served to inspire and influence other digital projects. The digital services coordinator has modified and re-used the underlying software for a couple of other projects, including Oregon Poetic Voices, which collects recorded poetry in a similarly distributed way. The project has provided the visual resources coordinator with an opportunity to develop a new approach to visual resources collection building, which she has shared widely among colleagues and applied to at least one other project. Overall, the project has honed the library's capacity to manage compelling academic digital projects and secure funding for them.

Economists have argued that non-profit colleges and universities are motivated to maximise institutional prestige (James, 1990). A prestigious institution is able to attract high-quality faculty and students and accrue more financial resources, all of which contribute to its educational mission. The academic library literature identifies special collections and grants as ways that academic libraries can contribute to institutional prestige and reputation (Oakleaf, 2010). Indeed, accessCeramics could be considered a special collection of Watzek Library. The high artistic quality of the artwork represented in accessCeramics and its global reach serve to increase the visibility and prestige of Lewis & Clark. Beyond their nominal value, grants in support of accessCeramics draw attention to Lewis & Clark's academic excellence, especially that of its art programme.

Alignment of benefits and costs

Given these costs and benefits, the question arises as to whether the accessCeramics project is a worthwhile endeavour for its host institution, Lewis & Clark College. Because the collection is supported primarily by the library, whose mission is to support the academic activities of the College with resources and services, one way to gauge this is to determine whether or not accessCeramics provides educational benefits in proportion to other expenditures on resources and services made by the library.

During its first two academic years of existence, it is hard to make the case that the benefits that accessCeramics provided to Lewis & Clark students as an educational resource were anywhere close to the costs of the project. During those two years, the collection was small and growing and the web interface was immature. Usage by Lewis & Clark students was light, with an estimated 99 visits in the first year and 407 visits in the second year. Even with grant support for assistance with web design and the submissions coordinator position, three library staff members devoted approximately ten percent of their College-funded work time to the project during this time.

The year 2011/12 might be described as accessCeramics' first production year. The collection had reached a critical mass of almost 4,000 images and 200 artists and the procedures and systems for maintaining and growing the collection were basically in place. During that year, the project cost approximately $5,280 (0.08 full-time equivalent (FTE)) in library staff time and $2,751 (0.03 FTE) in faculty time for a total cost of $8,031. Over that time, there were approximately 1,056 visits to the site by Lewis & Clark students. When accessCeramics is viewed as a benefit only to this population, each visit to the site by a student cost approximately $7.60, a cost almost five times higher than the $1.60 cost of a visit to ARTstor,[6] an academic image database to which Watzek Library subscribes. By another measure, if one compares visits to the accessCeramics site with access to full-text articles provided by a popular science journal vendor at $15.40 each, the accessCeramics costs look more moderate. When the project is viewed in terms of its aggregate usage (at Lewis & Clark and beyond), the cost of each of the 53,909 visits in the 2010–11 academic year drops to $14/visit.

Clearly, to make the case that accessCeramics is cost-effective for its host institution, more factors need to be brought to bear than its direct educational benefits to Lewis & Clark students. This is especially the case in its initial start-up years, when the project brought fairly minimal benefits to the educational mission of the College. A 2008 report by Ithaka on approaches to sustaining online academic resources identifies one category of revenue model as a situation where the host institution, as an indirect beneficiary, supports the project. The report notes that this is a common approach and that it works best when the resource is key to the reputation or mission of the institution. The report identifies several indirect benefits that are applicable to the accessCeramics project including reputation enhancement, the creation of 'skills, expertise and opportunities that are valuable elsewhere in the organization' and the establishment of models of collaboration (Maron et al., 2008).

The professional development benefits of accessCeramics to its team members and faculty leader were clearly high during the start-up phase of the project, which was a creative period during which new models and systems were developed. This was also a period when grant support was the highest, offsetting at least some of the start-up costs. accessCeramics' contribution to the College's global profile is clearly another benefit of the project. This benefit was high during the start-up phase as the project won publicly visible grants and as the team publicised the project at professional conferences in the art, library and visual resources fields. As the project's base of artists and art images has grown, its popularity and influence within the artistic community has increased and the overall success of the project continues to raise the College's global profile. While in production mode the accessCeramics project can stand on its own as a somewhat expensive and specialised educational resource for Lewis & Clark students. But to justify its start-up costs one must invoke some of the indirect benefits that are harder to quantify: professional development of faculty and staff, its value as a model for other projects and greater visibility and prestige for the host institution.

Revenue models

To make accessCeramics more sustainable and cost-effective, it is worth considering ways that the project could bring in further revenue to offset its costs. With nearly 54,000 visits to the site last academic year, clearly accessCeramics is of tremendous utility to populations beyond Lewis & Clark. There may be some potential to monetise that utility. The Ithaka report notes that subscription-based models are common for many online academic resources, particularly online journals (Maron et al., 2008). The accessCeramics team has shied away from any such models chiefly because the growth and the usefulness of the resource hinges on broad open access. To recruit more artists for the project the site must be as visible and accessible on the Web as possible. Much of the activity on the contemporary Internet depends on the ability to freely link to content, and many businesses distributing information on the Internet, including news organisations, operate under a model in which all or at least some of their content is available for free for these reasons (Anderson, 2008).

A variant on the subscription-based model could be a 'freemium' approach, common among Internet content businesses in which basic access to the site is free but a fee is required to access certain content such as high-resolution images. The basic problem with even this limited approach to the subscription model is that it would hinder accessCeramics' mission of broad educational use. Furthermore, given accessCeramics' current size, it is questionable whether it has a critical mass of content to warrant packaging it and charging for it. Another variation on the subscription idea could be an institutional membership model, where arts and educational organisations pay a membership fee and in return have acknowledgement on the website and some say in the direction of the project. The arXiv.org[7] project is currently pursuing a similar model (Rieger and Warner, 2010). As arts and educational organisations with the most potential interest in accessCeramics have limited financial resources, however, securing any amount of significance through these means might be prohibitive.

The Ithaka report cites an endowment as a means of having indirect beneficiaries support the project over the long term. This concept is attractive, but it would require raising a large amount of capital, a significant obstacle in a college fundraising environment where there are many priorities more directly associated with the institution's core mission. It is possible that a gift targeted at the accessCeramics project could support a small revenue stream for the project (Maron et al., 2008).

Online advertising is a common revenue-generation strategy for online media, though it is almost non-existent in the world of online academic resources. The accessCeramics team has discussed the possibility and come down against having search adverts or display advertising embedded in the main content of the site as this would compromise its educational feel. The team has discussed the idea of corporate sponsorship in which affiliated businesses or institutions would make an annual pledge to accessCeramics in exchange for a visible acknowledgement on the site similar to public television in the United States. accessCeramics provides visibility to artists who may be actively selling their artwork, and there may be a possibility of monetising this value. A variation on the advertising model would be the development of an online art store that uses the accessCeramics name and is linked from accessCeramics. The accessCeramics group could contract someone to set up an online store using Etsy[8] or a similar sales platform to sell artwork from accessCeramics artists, dividing the revenues between the artists, the store contractor and the accessCeramics project. This would appear to be an attractive option that merits further scrutiny, especially as accessCeramics grows larger. The viability of this approach would depend highly on artists' willingness to participate, sales volume and the overall administrative costs. This model is probably not widely applicable to other academic digital projects as most do not contain content that is a surrogate of items for sale so in that sense it may be a unique opportunity.

Contingencies for the future

With a growing collection and user base, a strong faculty sponsor, a vibrant ceramics programme and a library committed to digital projects and visual resources, accessCeramics has a secure home at Lewis & Clark for the foreseeable future. As already noted, the accessCeramics team has a plan to grow and expand the collection in collaboration with partner institutions. But what if this constellation of circumstances should change? What if a new, more compelling destination for contemporary ceramic art emerges on the Web? What if the library changes focus away from digital initiatives or the faculty leader moves to another institution?

One possible future for accessCeramics could be migration to a new home where the collection would continue to grow and evolve. At some point, the accessCeramics team might find that the project would be better carried forward by another organisation such as one that supports a larger artistic digital collection. Merging and absorption of various online enterprises is normal in the business world and certainly could make sense in this non-profit endeavour. Another future scenario could be to wind down the growth of the project and move it into a read-only mode. It would be a fairly inexpensive prospect to continue to make the images and metadata of the project available online at some level if the current highly customised site was not sustainable. The content could be hosted on Flickr, a larger-scale art image collection such as ARTstor or through a generic digital collections platform at Lewis & Clark. In any event, preserving the artistic content of the project into the future should be possible at minimal expense.

Lessons learned

As reflected by continued growth in artist participation and usage, accessCeramics fills a global gap in artistic image collections on the Web. Identifying this gap was possible through the initial insights of the accessCeramics founders at the inception of the project. Any digital project should undertake a careful assessment of the potential needs that it will fulfil before beginning. The project has demonstrated a tremendous synergy between a faculty member and an academic library. It has fused a faculty member's expertise in the art world with the library's competencies in digital technologies and visual resources. This relationship has resulted in an excellent end product and has also strengthened the faculty leader's connections in the art world, increased the library's capacity for digital projects and developed a model for faculty–library collaboration that can be exploited in other contexts. Though this project was labour-intensive in its initial stages, it was really a breakthrough in terms of what is possible in the area of faculty–library collaboration.

In the context of Watzek Library, the project might be termed a flagship digital project, one that sets an example for success and whose indirect benefits exceed its direct benefits. Having one or two such projects is certainly possible given Watzek Library's capacity, but having several is clearly cost-prohibitive. Watzek Library is building on accessCeramics by developing smaller-scale digital projects that are more directly targeted at supporting the educational mission of Lewis & Clark rather than serving a larger audience. These projects have attracted positive attention to the library (Meyer and Sykes, 2010). An example of this is the Spiders of Lewis & Clark project[9] for which introductory biology students captured samples of spider species in the area and developed a web resource that documents and classifies the spider species collected. Other examples include projects connected to Lewis & Clark's off-campus programmes, including one in which students documented graffiti art in New York City[10] and another (currently in progress) in which students studying in India document architecture, monuments and daily life.

accessCeramics' broad impact on an external community may be an exception among digital projects supported by Watzek Library, but that impact has excited and invigorated those that work on the project. The accessCeramics team is extremely gratified when it looks at a map that displays the growing global audience for the site. accessCeramics' success has inspired library staff to take a more ambitious approach to digital initiatives and this approach is paying off in projects beyond accessCeramics.

Notes

1. *http://www.accessceramics.org*
2. *http://www.flickr.com*
3. *http://www.lclark.edu/*
4. *http://www.nitle.org/*
5. *http://www.nea.gov/*
6. *http://www.artstor.org/*
7. *http://arxiv.org/*
8. *http://www.etsy.com/*
9. *http://library.lclark.edu/projects/spiders/*
10. *http://library.lclark.edu/projects/graffiti/*

References

Anderson, C. (2008) 'Free! Why $0.00 is the future of business', *Wired Magazine*, 16 (3). Online at: *http://www.wired.com/techbiz/it/magazine/16-03/ff_free*.

James, E. (1990) 'Decision processes and priorities in higher education', in S.A. Hoenack and E.L. Collins (eds), *The Economics of American Universities*. Buffalo, NY: State University of New York Press.

Maron, N.L., Guthrie, K. and Griffiths, R. (2008) *Sustainability and Revenue Models for Online Academic Resources. An ITHAKA Report*. Online at: *http://www.sr.ithaka.org/research-publications/sustainability-and-revenue-models-online-academic-resources*.

Meyer, S. and Sykes, C. (2010) 'Digital shift', *Lewis & Clark Chronicle*, Spring. Online at: *http://www.lclark.edu/chronicle/2011/spring/features/11959-digital-shift*.

Oakleaf, M. (2010) *The Value of Academic Libraries: A Comprehensive Research Review and Report*. Chicago: Association of College and Research Libraries.

Rieger, O. and Warner, S. (2010) 'Developing sustainability strategies for arXiv', *Information Standards Quarterly*, 22 (4): 17–18. Online at: *http://www.niso.org/publications/isq/free/OP_Rieger_Warner_arXiv_isqv22no4.pdf*.

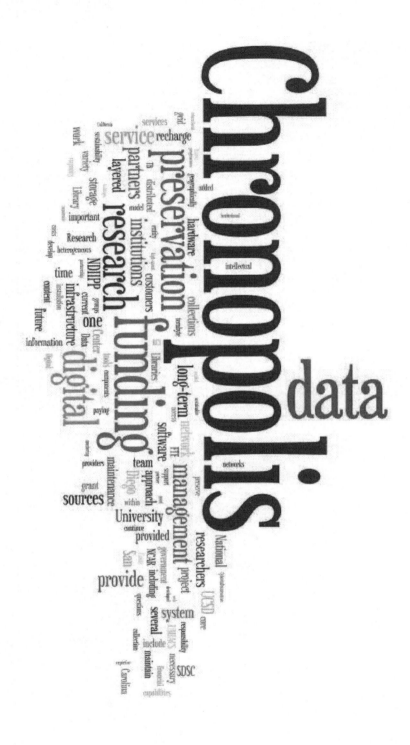

Case Study 6

The Chronopolis digital network: the economics of long-term preservation

David Minor and Ardys Kozbial

Abstract. The case study describes the experience of the Chronopolis Digital Network after the initial funding was exhausted and considers the various funding models that are most likely to enable the activity to achieve sustainability in the longer term. A layered funding approach is seen as the most appropriate way forward.

Keywords: Chronopolis Digital network, economics, funding models, preservation, sustainability

About Chronopolis – digital preservation across space and time

Spanning academic institutions and disciplines, the Chronopolis digital preservation network provides services for the long-term preservation and curation of digital materials. Because of the ephemeral nature of digital information, it is critical to organise and preserve the digital assets that represent society's intellectual capital – the core seeds of knowledge that are the basis of future research and education.

The San Diego Supercomputer Center (SDSC) and University of California San Diego (UCSD) Libraries, with the National Center for Atmospheric Research (NCAR) and the University of Maryland Institute for Advanced Computer Studies (UMIACS), have created Chronopolis to address these issues. Originally funded by the Library of Congress, the Chronopolis digital preservation network has the capacity to preserve hundreds of terabytes (TB) of digital materials – data of any type or size, with minimal requirements on the data provider. The project leverages high-speed networks, mass-scale storage capabilities and the expertise of its partners to provide a geographically distributed, heterogeneous, highly redundant archive system. Features of the project include:

- three geographically distributed copies of all data;
- curatorial audit reporting;
- development of best practices for data packaging and sharing.

'Chronopolis is part of a new breed of distributed digital preservation programs,' says Brian E.C. Schottlaender, a Principal Investigator for Chronopolis and the Audrey Geisel University Librarian at UCSD. 'We are using a virtual organizational structure in order to assemble the best expertise and framework to provide data longevity, durability and access well into the next century.'[1]

Chronopolis in depth

Chronopolis is a digital preservation data grid framework developed by the San Diego Supercomputer Center at UCSD, the UC San Diego Libraries and their partners at the National Center for Atmospheric Research (NCAR) in Colorado and the University of Maryland's Institute for Advanced Computer Studies (UMIACS). The Chronopolis network provides cross-domain collection management for long-term preservation. Using existing high-speed educational and research networks and mass-scale storage infrastructure investments, the network leverages the data storage capabilities at SDSC, NCAR and UMIACS to provide a preservation data grid that emphasises heterogeneous and highly redundant data storage systems. Each

Chronopolis member organisation operates a grid node containing at least 250 TB of storage capacity for digital collections. For reference, just one terabyte of information would use up all the paper made from about 50,000 trees. The Chronopolis data grid provides a minimum of three geographically distributed copies of its data collections, while enabling curatorial audit reporting and access for preservation clients. The key underlying technology for managing data within Chronopolis is the integrated Rule-Oriented Data System (iRODS), a preservation middleware software package that allows for robust management of data.[2] The Chronopolis partnership is also developing best practices for the worldwide preservation community for data packaging and transmission among heterogeneous digital archive systems.

Chronopolis has concentrated on housing a wide range of content that is not tied to a single community. Currently, there are five significant collections housed in Chronopolis:

1. Data from the North Carolina Geospatial Data Archiving Project, a joint project of the North Carolina State University Libraries and the North Carolina Center for Geographic Information and Analysis. It is focused on the collection and preservation of digital geospatial data resources from state and local government agencies in North Carolina.

2. Scripps Institution of Oceanography at UC San Diego (SIO) has one of the largest academic research fleets in the world, with four research vessels and the research platform FLIP. Since 1907, Scripps oceanographic vessels have played a critical role in the exploration of our planet, conducting important research in all the world's oceans. SIO houses data from several decades of data from its cruises.

3. The California Digital Library (CDL) is storing content from its 'Web-at-Risk' collections. Web-at-Risk is a multi-year effort led by CDL to develop tools that enable librarians and archivists to capture, curate, preserve and provide access to web-based government and political information. The primary focus of the collection housed in Chronopolis is state and local government information, but may include web documents from federal and international government as well as non-profit sources.

4. The UCSD Libraries Digital Library has recently added its complete holdings to Chronopolis and plans to continue to add more content

as it becomes available. This content is a full backup of its digital library holdings, representing many decades of important cultural artifacts.

5. The UCSD Research Cyberinfrastructure Curation Program[3] will be adding more than 150 TB of curation research datasets into Chronopolis. These are data that have been determined to be scientifically important for the intellectual future of the University. Chronopolis will form the preservation environment for this programme.

Initial funding

As has been noted, Chronopolis began as a grant-funded programme under the auspices of the Library of Congress's National Digital Information Infrastructure and Preservation Program (NDIIPP).[4] This initial funding, which totalled more than $2 million over approximately three years, provided the seed funding that allowed Chronopolis to purchase and install the hardware infrastructure, install and configure the software and middleware components, ingest data from a variety of providers, and maintain and update all components as necessary. This funding also provided the necessary staffing for all of the above work, including management of the system. As with all NDIIPP projects, this work was intended to benefit NDIIPP and its partners. Thus the initial collections housed in Chronopolis came from NDIIPP partners. The approximate breakdown of responsibility among the Chronopolis partners was:

- *SDSC* provided project management, hardware and software installation and maintenance, financial management of the system: 5 full-time equivalent (FTE).

- *NCAR* provided hardware and software installation and maintenance, aided in the development of user-facing services, including a web portal and ingest tools: 1 FTE.

- *UMIACS* provided hardware and software installation and maintenance, and developed two of the core tools used in the Chronopolis network for moving and monitoring data: 1 FTE.

Funding: the next generation

It was always explicit during the NDIIPP funding period that one day Chronopolis would need to stand on its own: to look for its own funding and customers. NDIIPP funding for Chronopolis began to wind down in the first half of 2011. The Chronopolis partners had already begun the process of looking for new sources of funding, as this transition had been expected. The Chronopolis management team identified several possible sources:

- work with paying customers – that is, customers who would pay an annual fee, likely per terabyte, that would maintain the Chronopolis costs;
- work with researchers or research groups to prepare them to enter Chronopolis into their current and future research programmes;
- continue to look for grant funding, from a variety of sources;
- seek long-term institutional support from at least one of the Chronopolis home institutions.

Work with paying customers

SDSC, the financial management arm of the Chronopolis team, worked for several months to develop a recharge model. This model, based on a per terabyte per year charge, was designed to offset the costs for the basic maintenance of the Chronopolis infrastructure. This financial model has many components, including:

- FTE necessary at the three Chronopolis partner sites;
- costs to continue maintenance of current hardware infrastructure as well as costs to upgrade it on a reasonable time schedule;
- costs to cover adding infrastructure in a timely manner if the capacity of the system demands it;
- costs if necessary are added for 'overhead', which is required in the university setting.

Work with researchers or research groups to prepare them to enter Chronopolis into their current and research programmes

Another closely related customer opportunity comes in the form of individual researchers, or research groups, writing Chronopolis as their designated preservation environment into grants and long-term data management planning. The need for this kind of service has become particularly relevant because several large funding agencies in the United States, including the National Institute of Health and the National Science Foundation, are requiring these kinds of services be added into the narrative of all grants. Using the recharge described above, Chronopolis can provide a ready-made infrastructure that researchers wouldn't have to develop or maintain on their own.

Continue to look for grant funding, from a variety of sources

In order to keep the recharge amount at the most reasonable level, it was decided that it would not include funding for research within the Chronopolis team. This research has always been one of the core pieces of the enterprise. In order to fund this, Chronopolis will be investigating and applying for its own grant funding from a variety of services. This will provide a layered approached to funding in the future. Options appropriate for grant funding would include activities such as: further enhancement of the digital object monitoring capabilities, further enhancement of high-speed research networks and examination of new data management tools. Grants of this type would allow the production system to continue running on stable software with a stable work flow. At the same time, the Chronopolis team would be able to experiment and research without compromising current data that are under Chronopolis care.

Seek long-term institutional support from at least one of the Chronopolis home institutions

Finally, and perhaps most importantly, all of the above funding scenarios are short term, that is they provide the funding needed to maintain Chronopolis for finite amounts of time. They do not address the central question of long-term sustainability. In order to address this issue, Chronopolis has sought the support of an institution which itself is committed to long-term existence. In the spring of 2011, Chronopolis achieved this level of funding when it was chosen as the preservation service for UCSD's new Research Cyberinfrastructure (RCI) Data Curation service. This service is funded from central campus funds, because it is designated as a core service that the campus needs to supply in order to protect and enhance its intellectual capital. The RCI programme offers UC San Diego researchers computing, network and staffing to create, manage and share data. Campus researchers are encouraged to use the campus's RCI in addressing federal sponsors' existing and new data management requirements.

Funding: a layered approach

Given the funding sources outlined above, Chronopolis now has a layered approach to funding which can be represented roughly as in Figure CS6.1. Note that while the sizes of the pyramid sections above are indicative of scale, they are not themselves to scale.

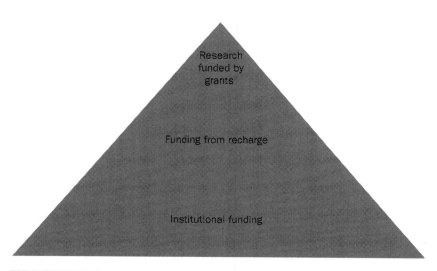

Figure CS6.1 Chronopolis – layered approach to funding

This layered approach represents Chronopolis's long-term economic strategy. It is important to note that the specific layers listed do not represent specific institutions, organisations or customers. Nor are they exclusive: it should be the case that no one institution provides the base funding; instead, a more sustainable operation requires a mix of institutions dedicated to maintaining digital preservation.

Lessons learned

The Chronopolis team has learned several lessons in the half-decade of development and service.

- *Begin work on planning for sustainability as soon as possible.* There are many practical concerns regarding sustainable funding that may not be immediately apparent. For example, for Chronopolis, the proof of concept and start-up phases were well within the mission of all of its partners. However, once Chronopolis began seeking paying data providers, it became more like a vendor, an entity that provides a service for a price. Is this service provider role included in any of the partners' missions? Fortunately for Chronopolis, providing service at a recharge rate is in SDSC's mission. This may not be true for many educational institutions.

- *Begin work on service level agreements (SLAs) and memoranda of understanding (MOUs) early.* Executing written partnership agreements, such as MOUs, among institutions can take significant amounts of time to complete, especially when the legal departments of the institutions must get involved. SLAs, such as those that Chronopolis has with its data providers, pose issues of responsibility and money-taking. Which entity takes responsibility for the data? Which partner entity can receive recharge payments? Don't wait until the concept has been proved to begin asking these questions.

In sum, the Chronopolis digital preservation system was founded with a strong belief that technology could be harnessed to provide long-term archiving solutions. This belief has been demonstrated to be true. The economic sustainability of the project requires at least as much attention as the technical, however. It has many more open questions in both the present and the future. Chronopolis has sought to answer these questions using a layered approach to funding sources.

Notes

1. *http://chronopolis.sdsc.edu*
2. *https://www.irods.org*
3. *http://rci.ucsd.edu*
4. *http://www.digitalpreservation.gov*

Case Study 7

Economic implications of alternative scholarly publishing models

John W. Houghton

Abstract. Financial pressures – reducing budgets and increasing prices – have been one of the key drivers in the search for alternative, open-access-based publishing models, particularly in the higher education sector. Houghton's case study describes the ways in which he used lifecycle and costing techniques in a macro-economic modelling approach to test the extent to which new methods of publishing were more cost-beneficial to research and development activity than existing ones. He found that there was a significant return on investment especially through cost-savings over a transitional period of 20 years in all the countries studied, and for research libraries in particular, even though there was a degree of variation as a result of regional factors. He describes and discusses the methodology used, which incorporated process mapping, activity costing and macro-economic modelling using a modified version of the Solow-Swan model. There remain questions of sustainability, though archiving policies, as described by Houghton, should do much to improve the likelihood of long-term viability, especially if projected savings can be achieved.

Keywords: alternative scholarly publication models, higher education, macro-economic modelling, open access, publishing models, research libraries, self-archiving, subscriptions, sustainability, viability

Introduction

This case study examines the findings of a series of studies that have explored the implications of alternative scholarly publishing models for researchers and research libraries, especially those in higher education institutions (HEIs).The primary study was funded by the UK Joint Information Systems Committee[1] (JISC) and looked at the costs and benefits of alternative publishing models for the UK in general and UK HEIs in particular (Houghton et al., 2009a). That study generated a good deal of interest and there have been a number of follow-on projects, including national studies in the Netherlands and Denmark (Houghton et al., 2009b; Houghton, 2009a), and a three-country comparison of the UK, the Netherlands and Denmark that sought to compare the potential impacts of open access publishing models in one of the larger, a mid-sized and one of the smaller European countries (Houghton, 2009b).

During 2010 and 2011, there were four further projects. The first focused on Germany and brought the German National Licensing Programme (NLP)[2] into the mix of alternative publishing and distribution models (forthcoming). The second was conducted by Alma Swan of Key Perspectives and used the online cost model developed for the original JISC study to examine the cost implications for a sample of UK universities (Swan, 2010). The third significantly extended one aspect of the method used in the original study to explore the return on investment implications of the proposed US Federal Research Public Access Act (FRPAA) (Houghton et al., 2010). The fourth project approached it from the user perspective, exploring the information needs and access levels of small high-technology firms in Denmark (Houghton et al., 2011).

All of these projects have examined the potential impacts of alternative publishing models on the costs faced by various stakeholders, and the potential direct and wider benefits of more open access to the findings of publicly funded research. Looking at the publishing models as alternatives, they suggest that:

- Open access (OA) publishing models are likely to lead to cost savings and substantial wider benefits arising from increased access to research findings and efficiency gains in the performance of research activities.

- Self-archiving alternatives (such as Green Open Access) appear to be the more cost-effective, although whether or not self-archiving in parallel with subscription publishing is sustainable over the longer term is open to debate.

- Open access publishing might bring substantial activity cost savings in research libraries, as well as subscription cost savings, helping to free resources that could be used in meeting new needs and taking on new responsibilities.

Alternative publishing models

The UK, Dutch and Danish studies all focused on three alternative models for scholarly publishing, namely:

- traditional *subscription or toll access publishing*, using individual subscriptions or the so-called Big Deal, where institutional subscribers pay for access to online aggregations of journal titles through consortial or site licensing arrangements;
- *open access publishing*, using the 'author-pays' model, where publication costs are paid from the author's side rather than by readers;
- *open access 'self-archiving'*, where authors deposit their work in open access repositories, making it freely available to anyone with Internet access.

Of itself, self-archiving does not constitute formal publication, so analysis focused on two publishing models in which self-archiving is supplemented by the peer review and production activities necessary for formal publishing, namely:

- 'Green OA' self-archiving operating in parallel with subscription publishing;
- the 'deconstructed' or 'overlay journals' model in which self-archiving provides the foundation for overlay journals and services (Smith, 1999, 2005; Van de Sompel et al., 2004; Simboli, 2005; Houghton, 2005).

Hence, each of the publishing models explored includes all of the key functions of scholarly publishing, including peer review and quality control.

Method

The approach taken to the three national studies involved a combination of process mapping, activity costing and macro-economic modelling, and the research involved four main steps.

Process mapping

To provide a solid foundation for the identification of activity costs we adopted a formal process modelling approach using the Integration DEFinition (IDEFO) modelling standard,[3] which is often used in business process re-engineering. It is a development of the lifecycle model created by Björk (2007), which we extended to include five main activity elements:

- Fund research and research communication.
- Perform research and communicate the results.
- Publish scientific and scholarly works.
- Facilitate dissemination, retrieval and preservation.
- Study publications and apply the knowledge (see Figure CS7.1).

Each of these activities is further subdivided into a detailed description of the activities, inputs, outputs, controls and supporting mechanisms involved, creating an activity model with some 53 diagrams and around 200 activities. The process model[4] is available online.

Activity costing

This formal process model provided the foundation for detailed activity costing, using a spreadsheet-based cost model that included all of the elements in the lifecycle model, as well as the base data necessary for the study (relating to research and scholarly communications activities at the national and higher education levels). The costings relied primarily on existing sources and the collation of activity cost information from the wide-ranging literature on scholarly communication and publishing. Where necessary, these sources were supplemented by informal consultation with experts in the field. For the UK national and higher education data, we relied on national and international sources on research and development (R&D) expenditure and personnel by activity and sector, expenditure and employment trends. Detailed data on

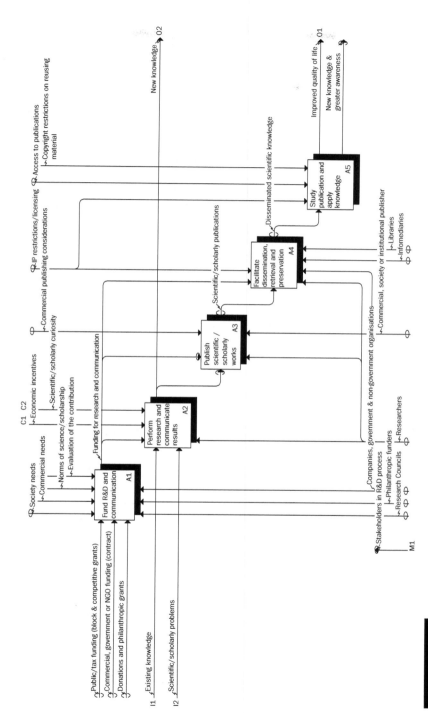

Figure CS7.1 The scholarly communication lifecycle process

Source: Houghton et al. (2009a).

higher education were sourced from such agencies as the Society of College, National and University Libraries (SCONUL) and the Higher Education Statistical Agency (HESA). The resulting activity cost model included more than two thousand data elements.

Macro-economic modelling

To measure the impacts of alternative scholarly publishing models on returns to R&D expenditure, we modified the standard Solow-Swan model. The standard approach makes some key simplifying assumptions, including that all R&D generates knowledge that is useful in economic or social terms (*the efficiency of R&D*), and all knowledge is equally accessible to all entities that could make productive use of it (*the accessibility of knowledge*). Addressing the fact that these assumptions are not realistic, we introduced *accessibility* and *efficiency* into the standard model as negative or friction variables, to reflect the fact that there are barriers to access and limits to efficiency. Then we explored the impact on returns to R&D of changes in accessibility and efficiency (Houghton and Sheehan, 2006, 2009; Houghton et al., 2009a).

A step-wise approach

As noted, there were four main steps in the research process. In the first, we produced a detailed costing of all of the activities identified in the scholarly communication lifecycle model, focusing on areas where there were likely to be activity and, therefore, cost differences between the alternative publishing models. In the second, we summed the costs of the three publishing models through the main phases of the scholarly communication lifecycle, so we could explore potential system-wide cost differences between the alternative publishing models. In the third step, we used the modified Solow-Swan model to estimate the impact of changes in accessibility and efficiency on returns to R&D. The final step was to compare costs and benefits, for which we used the three elements outlined:

- the direct costs associated with each of the models;
- the associated indirect system-wide costs and cost savings;
- the benefits accruing from increases in returns to R&D resulting from increases in accessibility and efficiency. Because the returns to R&D lag expenditure and accrue over a number of years, the cost-benefit comparisons were made over a 20-year transitional period.

Main findings

The analysis of the potential benefits of more open access to research findings suggested that open access could have substantial net benefits in the longer term, and while net benefits may be lower during a transitional period, they are likely to be positive for both open access publishing and overlay services alternatives (*Gold OA*) and for parallel subscription publishing and self-archiving (*Green OA*). For example, during a transitional period of 20 years we estimated that in an open access world:

- the combined cost savings and benefits from increased returns to R&D resulting from open access publishing all journal articles produced in UK universities using an author-pays model (*Gold OA*) might be around three times the costs;
- the combined cost savings and benefits from open access self-archiving in parallel with subscription publishing (*Green OA*) might be around seven times the costs;
- the combined cost savings and benefits from an alternative open access self-archiving model with overlay production and review services (*overlay services*) might be around four times the costs.

While the benefits from unilateral national adoption of open access alternatives would be lower, they would be substantial – ranging from two to four times the costs.

In exploring the potential impacts of alternative publishing models in the Netherlands and Denmark, differences in the modelling were kept to a minimum, although some minor adjustments of the basic model were necessary to fit different national circumstances (Houghton, 2009b). Nevertheless, there are a number of factors that can affect the benefit/cost estimates for different countries. As modelled, these included such things as:

- the number and size of universities and research institutions;
- the implied number of institutional and other repositories, each with substantial fixed costs and relatively low variable costs;
- the ratios of publicly funded and higher education research spending to gross national expenditure on R&D;
- historical and projected rates of growth of R&D spending by sector;
- relative national and sectoral publication productivity;

- historical and projected growth in publication output;
- the mix of publication types.

There were also inherent data limitations that varied somewhat between the countries. For example, in addition to cost differences between the countries, there were minor differences in the official national methods used to estimate the full cost of researcher activities.

Despite these influences, the different national studies produced very similar results and exhibited broadly similar patterns within the results. The cost-benefits of the open access 'author-pays' publishing model were similar across the three countries. In terms of estimated cost-benefits over a transitional period of 20 years, open access publishing all articles produced in universities in 2007 would have produced benefits of two to three times the costs in all cases.

One observable difference related to scale and the impacts of unilateral national adoption of open access, with the benefits of worldwide adoption being relatively larger for smaller countries as they produce a smaller share of the world's journal articles. However, the most obvious difference between the results related to the 'Green OA' self-archiving and repositories model, which did not look quite as good in the Netherlands as in the UK and nothing like as good as it did in Denmark. This was due to the implied number of repositories, each with operational overheads. As modelled, the number of institutional repositories required in each country related to the number of institutions, and their operational overheads were shared across the number of articles produced and archived. For example, under the modelled assumptions, for 2007 outputs, the Netherlands' 86 higher education institutional repositories might have housed around 26,000 articles (an average of 302 each from that year), the UK's 168 higher education institutional repositories might have housed around 100,000 articles (an average of 595 each from that year) and Denmark's eight universities' repositories might have housed around 14,000 articles (an average of 1,750 each from that year). As modelled, these differences materially affected the implied per article cost of self-archiving. Of course, had we used an averaged per article lifecycle costing, these differences would not have been apparent.

Notwithstanding these differences, the modelling suggested that open access alternatives would be likely to be more cost-effective in a wide range of countries (large and small), with 'Gold OA' or author-pays publishing, the deconstructed or overlay journals model of self-archiving with overlay production and review services, and 'Green OA' self-archiving in parallel with subscription publishing being progressively more cost-effective.

Given the potential benefits identified in the three countries, we recommended a policy focus on creating a level playing field by reducing the barriers to innovation in scholarly publishing and raising awareness of the opportunities. We suggested that this might involve, perhaps above all else, ensuring that research evaluation is not a barrier to innovation by developing metrics that support innovation in scholarly publishing rather than relying on traditional evaluation metrics that tend to reinforce traditional publishing models and reward traditional behaviours. It might also involve:

- ensuring that there is funding for author-side fees by encouraging funders to make specific provision for publication charges;
- encouraging – and perhaps funding – OA repositories to enable self-archiving should authors choose;
- supporting advocacy initiatives to inform all stakeholders about the potential costs and benefits of alternative publishing models.

Extensions and developments

The general approach used in the three national studies has been further developed and extended in recent work in Germany, the UK, the US and Denmark.

Germany

As a part of a much larger project, funded by the Deutsche Forschungsgemeinschaft (DFG), we worked with colleagues at Goethe University in Frankfurt on a study that brings the German National Licensing Programme (NLP) into the mix of alternative publication and dissemination models, and compares the NLP with the subscription and open access alternatives.

The German NLP provides enhanced access for researchers in Germany through an extended form of consortial purchasing and licensing. While it centralises a number of activities in the lifecycle process relating to facilitating dissemination, retrieval and preservation (for example, negotiation and licensing), the NLP does not fundamentally change the activities performed. However, the NLP does impact a number of activities in the scholarly communication lifecycle, thereby affecting costs.

There is one important difference between the comparisons in the German study and those in the previous studies. Subscription and open access publishing perform very different roles. To the limits of affordability, subscription publishing seeks to provide an institution's researchers with access to the worldwide research literature whereas open access seeks to provide worldwide access to an institution's research output. These are very different things, but to compare cost-effectiveness it is necessary to compare like with like. It is also important to note that subscriptions do *not* cover the cost of subscription publishing. There is also revenue from advertising and reprints, page and plate charges, membership and other subsidies to subscription journals. So, despite the fact that it is what most people do, it is not always correct to compare open access publishing costs with subscription expenditures. In the JISC study, we compared the costs associated with publishing UK article output under different models, including subscription. In contrast, the German study compares the costs of operating within alternative models. This does not compare the cost of using alternative models to achieve a comparable task. Rather, it compares the cost implications of alternative models for a particular actor, in this case for Germany.

We found that the benefits of open access publishing are likely to outweigh the costs in Germany, as elsewhere. Interestingly, the NLP returned the second highest benefit/cost ratio during a transitional period – after 'Green OA' self-archiving. However, the NLP is a long-term commitment, and there is a risk that new developments in publishing models may change the relative cost-benefit of the NLP over time.

The United Kingdom

Alma Swan, of Key Perspectives,[5] undertook another follow-on study for JISC in which she applied the online cost model produced as a part of the original study to an examination of the cost and benefit implications of alternative publishing models for a small sample of UK universities (Swan, 2010). As in the German study, Swan compared the costs of operating within alternative models, in this case for a sample of universities, by setting the cost of publishing UK articles under alternative publishing models against the costs of access to that share of worldwide articles to which the institutions currently subscribed.

Swan showed how universities could compare the impacts of alternative publishing models for themselves, and that by looking at whole-of-system costs we can start to question the somewhat simplistic arguments that suggest that in research-intensive universities author-pays fees may be higher than current subscription expenditures. While that may be true in some cases, it is also apparent from this study that the potential savings in research time, library handling costs and so on that could arise from more open access would also be greatest in the more research-intensive universities. To understand institutional cost impacts, we need to take a fuller account of system-wide costs than has been typical to date.

The United States

During 2010, the Scholarly Publishing and Academic Resources Coalition (SPARC) supported a feasibility study that sought to outline one possible approach to measuring the impacts of the proposed US Federal Research Public Access Act (FRPAA) on returns to public investment in R&D (Houghton et al., 2010). The aim of the study was to define and scope the data collection requirements and further model developments necessary for a robust estimate of the likely impacts of the proposed FRPAA archiving mandate.

The project involved a major shift from previous studies in that its focus was on the modified Solow-Swan model rather than the scholarly communication lifecycle model or the associated activity cost model. That focus enabled further development and refinement of the modified model, particularly in relation to the most appropriate lag and distribution over time of returns to R&D, the most appropriate depreciation rate for the underlying stock of R&D knowledge arising from federally funded R&D, and metrics to measure potential changes in accessibility and efficiency. To establish plausible base case values for these parameters we drew on the extensive literature on returns to R&D (Salter and Martin, 2001; Martin and Tang, 2007; Sveikauskas, 2007; Hall et al., 2009).

The other piece of the puzzle is the input data required for the modelling. These include the implied archiving costs, the volume of federally funded research outputs (such as journal articles) and the levels of federal research funding and expenditure trends. For the purposes of preliminary analysis we used publicly available sources and published estimates. Data relating to federal research funding, activities and outputs were taken from the National Science Board *Science and Engineering Indicators 2010* (NSB, 2010), and we explored three sources for archiving costs: the LIFE[2] Project lifecycle costs (Ayris et al., 2008) and submission equivalent costings from arXiv (such as the former Ginsparg Archive at Cornell) and the National Institutes of Health PubMed archive (arXiv, 2010; NIH, 2008).

Preliminary modelling suggested that over a transitional period of 30 years, the potential *incremental* benefits of the proposed FRPAA archiving mandate for all federally funded R&D might be worth around four times the estimated cost using the higher-end LIFE[2] lifecycle costing, eight times the cost using the NIH costing, which is likely to be the best guide, and as much as twenty times the cost using the historical arXiv costing. Perhaps two-thirds of these benefits would accrue within the US, with the remainder spilling over to other countries. Hence, the US national benefits might be of the order of five times the costs and be worth more than $1 billion a year.

Exploring sensitivities in the model in order to prioritise areas for further data collection and model development, we found that the benefits exceed the costs over a wide range of values. Indeed, in the US model, and in the other national models, it is difficult to imagine any plausible values for the input data and model parameters that would lead to a fundamentally different answer.

Denmark

In a study funded by the Danish Ministry of Culture and Ministry of Science, Technology and Innovation, we approached the issue from the user side and explored access to, and use of, academic research among small high-technology firms in Denmark (Houghton et al., 2011). It was a small, non-random sample: we received 98 usable responses to an online survey and conducted 23 in-depth interviews. Nevertheless, we found that:

- the firms make substantial use of academic research;
- they are experiencing access difficulties;
- they do use open access material.

Comparing responses on the importance and ease of access suggests that the things that are both important and difficult to access include research articles and market survey research and reports (and, for some firms, patents):

- 48 per cent rated articles very or extremely important;
- 38 per cent said they always or frequently had difficulty getting the articles they needed; and
- a further 41 per cent said they sometimes had difficulties.

Among the researchers:

- 72 per cent reported using institutional or subject repositories;
- 56 per cent used open access journals on a monthly or more regular basis.

Asked how long they spent trying to access the last article they had difficulties accessing, the average among researchers was 63 minutes, and an average of 17 articles presented access difficulties during the last year. So, access difficulties could be costing around DKK 540 million a year among specialist researchers in Denmark alone.

Looking at the value of academic research for the firms, we found that an average of 27 per cent of the products and 19 per cent of the processes developed or introduced during the last three years would have been delayed or abandoned without access to academic research. The value of academic research to sales was around DKK 16 million per firm per year and the value to cost savings around DKK 95,000 per firm per year. So, on a simple pro rata basis, academic research is directly contributing the equivalent of around 12 per cent of sales revenue.

Implications for research libraries

Throughout these studies, analysis of the potential benefits of more open access to research findings suggested that open access could have substantial net benefits in the longer term, and while net benefits may be lower during a transitional period, they are likely to be positive for both open access publishing and overlay services alternatives (*Gold OA*) and for parallel subscription publishing and self-archiving (*Green OA*).

Given a capacity to enhance access at very little cost, self-archiving alternatives appear to be the more cost-effective. Although whether or not self-archiving in parallel with subscriptions is a sustainable model over the longer term is, perhaps, debatable, nevertheless the evidence from these studies suggests that archiving policies and mandates, be they at the national, sectoral, funder or institutional levels, can enhance accessibility and improve efficiency at relatively little cost, and with no immediate disruptive change to scholarly publishing practices and traditions.

With an increasing number of policy directives and funder and institutional mandates calling for more open access to the findings of publicly funded research, it seems inevitable that the share of material available in open access will increase. The most recent count suggested that more than 20 per cent of the journal articles produced during 2008 were already freely available online the following year (Björk et al., 2010). So, open access is already a reality and an increasingly important part of the access landscape.

At the same time, of course, traditional publishing models live on, and the mix of access and publishing models increases. This has brought, and is likely to continue to bring, a shift in research library activities and responsibilities, adding the operation of institutional or subject repositories and a new role in the dissemination of the institution's research publications (and data) to existing and increasingly challenging duties to assist in information literacy and access. These shifts also bring a wider range of users to research libraries, as users outside the traditional subscription world can and do seek open access materials – be they open access journals that may be supported and hosted through a research library or open access articles and other materials produced by the institution and hosted on an institutional repository.

While the studies reported in this case study suggest that open access might bring substantial subscription and activity cost savings for research libraries (such as in negotiation and licensing, library handling and access control and so on) there are also new challenges to be met. The savings that might be realised in some areas may release resources to address the new challenges (curating and sharing data, improving information literacy, building tools to enable researchers to do their work better and more efficiently, and do new kinds of work based on text mining, data mining, complex research workflows and so on). The benefits of being able to address some of these challenges with the resources released by open access and, of course, the shift toward electronic-only holdings could be considerable.

Acknowledgements

The author would like to acknowledge the support of the UK Joint Information Systems Committee (JISC) in the development of the modelling approach underpinning the studies reported, the SURF Foundation and Denmark's Electronic Research Library (DEFF) for enabling its application in the Netherlands and Denmark, SPARC for enabling its further development and application in the US, and DfG for extending the work in Germany. Thanks are due to the research team from the original JISC project, including principal collaborator Charles Oppenheim of Loughborough University, Bruce Rasmussen and Peter Sheehan of Victoria University in Melbourne, and Anne Morris, Claire Creaser, Helen Greenwood, Mark Summers and Adrian Gourlay of Loughborough University, as well as members of the project advisory group. Thanks are also due to the research teams for the Netherlands project, including Jos de Jonge and Marcia van Oploo of EIM/Research voor Beleid and to the many people who assisted in both the Dutch and Danish studies, Bruce Rasmussen and Peter Sheehan of Victoria University in Melbourne, Alma Swan and Sheridan Brown of Key Perspective, and Wolfgang König, Berndt Dugall, Matthias Hanauske, Julia Krönung and Steffen Bernius of the Goethe University in Frankfurt.

Notes

1. *http://www.jisc.ac.uk/*
2. *http://www.dfg.de/en/research_funding/programmes/infrastructure/lis/ digital_information/library_licenses/index.html#micro1653861*
3. *http://www.idef.com/IDEF0.htm*
4. *http://www.cfses.com/EI-ASPM/SCLCM-V7/*
5. *http://www.keyperspectives.co.uk/*

References

arXiv.org (2010) *arXiv Business Model White Paper*. Cornell University. Online at: *http://arxiv.org/help/support/whitepaper*.

Ayris, P., Davies, R., McLeod, R., Miao, R., Shenton, H. and Wheatley, P. (2008) *The LIFE² Final Report*. Bristol: JISC. Online at: *http://discovery.ucl.ac. uk/11758/*.

Björk, B.-C. (2007) 'A model of scientific communication as a global distributed information system', *Information Research*, 12 (2): 307.

Björk, B.-C., Welling, P., Laakso, M., Majlender, P. and Hedlund, T. (2010) 'Open access to the scientific journal literature: situation 2009', *PLOS ONE*, 5 (6): e11273. Online at: *http://www.plosone.org/article/info:doi/10.1371/journal. pone.0011273.*

Hall, B.H., Mairesse, J. and Mohnen, P. (2009) *Measuring the Returns to R&D*, NBER Working Paper 15622. Cambridge, MA: NBER.

Houghton, J.W. (2005) 'Economics of publishing and the future of scholarly communication', in G.E. Gorman and F. Rowland (eds), *International Year Book of Library and Information Management 2004–2005: Scholarly Publishing in an Electronic Era*. London: Facet Publishing.

Houghton, J.W. (2009a) *Costs and Benefits of Alternative Publishing Models: Denmark*. Copenhagen: DEFF. Online at: *http://www.knowledge-exchange. info/Admin/Public/DWSDownload.aspx?File=%2fFiles%2fFiler%2fdownloads %2fDK_Costs_and_benefits_of_alternative_publishing_models.pdf.*

Houghton, J.W. (2009b) *Open Access: What Are the Economic Benefits? A Comparison of the United Kingdom, Netherlands and Denmark*. Brussels: Knowledge Exchange (June). Online at: *http://knowledge-exchange.info/ Default.aspx?ID=316.*

Houghton, J.W. and Sheehan, P.J. (2006) *The Economic Impact of Enhanced Access to Research Findings*, CSES Working Paper No. 23. Melbourne: Victoria University (July). Online at: *http://www.cfses.com/documents/wp23. pdf.*

Houghton, J.W. and Sheehan, P. (2009) 'Estimating the potential impacts of open access to research findings', *Economic Analysis and Policy*, 39 (1): 127–42.

Houghton, J.W., de Jonge, J. and van Oploo, M. (2009b) *Costs and Benefits of Research Communication: The Dutch Situation*. Utrecht: SURF Foundation (June). Online at: *http://www.surf.nl/en/publicaties/Pages/CostsandBenefitsof OpenAccessPublicationlTheDutchSituation.aspx.*

Houghton, J.W., Rasmussen, B. and Sheehan, P. (2010) *Economic and Social Returns on Investment in Open Archiving Publicly Funded Research Outputs*. Washington, DC: SPARC. Online at: *http://www.arl.org/sparc/publications/ papers/vuFRPAA/index.shtml.*

Houghton, J.W., Swan, A. and Brown, S. (2011) *Access to Research and Technical Information in Denmark: Report to the Danish Agency for Science, Technology and Innovation (FI) and Denmark's Electronic Research Library*. Copenhagen: Forsknings- og Innovationsstyrelsen and Denmark's Electronic Research Library. Online at: *http://eprints.soton.ac.uk/272603/.*

Houghton, J.W., Rasmussen, B., Sheehan, P.J., Oppenheim, C., Morris, A., Creaser, C., Greenwood, H., Summers, M. and Gourlay, A. (2009a) *Economic Implications of Alternative Scholarly Publishing Models: Exploring the Costs and Benefits*. Bristol: JISC. Online at: *http://www.cfses.com/EI-ASPM/.*

Martin, B.R. and Tang, P. (2007) *The Benefits of Publicly Funded Research*, SWEPS Paper No. 161. Brighton: Science Policy Research Unit. Online at: *https:// www.sussex.ac.uk/webteam/gateway/file.php?name=sewp161&site=25.*

National Institutes of Health (NIH) (2008) *Analysis of Comments and Implementation of the NIH Public Access Policy.* Washington, DC: NIH. Online at: *http://publicaccess.nih.gov/analysis_of_comments_nih_public_access_policy.pdf.*

National Science Board (NSB) (2010) *Science and Engineering Indicators 2010.* Arlington, VA: National Science Foundation (NSB 10-01). Online at: *http://www.nsf.gov/statistics/.*

Salter, A.J. and Martin, B.R. (2001) 'The economic benefits of publicly funded basic research: a critical review', *Research Policy*, 30 (3): 509–32.

Simboli, B. (2005) *Subscription Subsidized Open Access and the Crisis in Scholarly Communication.* Bethlehem, PA: Lehigh University.

Smith, J.W.T. (1999) 'The deconstructed journal, a new model for academic publishing', *Learned Publishing*, 12 (2): 79–91.

Smith, J.W.T. (2005) 'Open access publishing models: reinventing journal publishing', *Research Information*, May–June. Online at: *http://www.researchinformation.info/features/feature.php?feature_id=79.*

Sveikauskas, L. (2007) *R&D and Productivity Growth: A Review of the Literature.* Washington, DC: Bureau of Labor Statistics Working Paper 408. Online at: *http://www.bls.gov/osmr/pdf/ec070070.pdf.*

Swan, A. (2010) *Modelling Scholarly Communication Options: Costs and Benefits for Universities.* Bristol: JISC. Online at: *http://ie-repository.jisc.ac.uk/442/.*

Van de Sompel, H., Payette, S., Erickson, J., Lagoze, C. and Warner, S. (2004) 'Rethinking scholarly communication: building the system that scholars deserve', *D-Lib Magazine*, 10 (9). Online at: *http://www.dlib.org/dlib/september04/vandesompel/09vandesompel.html.*

Sustainable economic models: Portico

Amy Kirchhoff and Kate Wittenberg

Abstract. Portico, like many of the other projects referred to in this handbook – and the case studies in particular – relies on cooperation and balance between the key stakeholders to work. Sustainable projects need to take account of the free-rider problem and this case study shows one way of doing this. The emphasis is on flexibility with particular reference to the business models chosen, which differ depending upon the product or service.

Keywords: community, content, economic model development, electronic book preservation, electronic journal preservation, Ithaka, Portico, preservation, sustainability

Introduction

Portico[1] is a not-for-profit digital preservation service and is among the largest community-supported digital archives in the world. In 2010, Portico became the first preservation service to be independently audited by the Center for Research Libraries (CRL) and certified as a trusted, reliable digital preservation solution that serves the needs of the library community. Working with libraries, publishers and funders, Portico preserves e-journals, e-books and other digital scholarly content to ensure researchers and students will have access to these resources in the future. Portico is a service of Ithaka,[2] a not-for-profit organisation dedicated to helping the academic community use digital technologies to preserve the scholarly record and to advance research and teaching in sustainable ways.

As of December 2012, Portico was preserving more than 19 million journal articles, nearly 28,000 books and nearly 2.4 million items from digitised historical collections (d-collections, for example digitised newspapers of the eighteenth century). Portico's approach to preserving this content addresses the key goals of digital preservation:

- *usability* – the intellectual content of the item must remain usable via the delivery mechanism of current technology;
- *authenticity* – the provenance of the content must be proven and the content an authentic replica of the original;
- *discoverability* – the content must have logical bibliographic metadata so that the content can be found by end users through time; and
- *accessibility* – the content must be available for use to the appropriate community.

Portico meets the rigour of these goals through a migration-based strategy; Portico will migrate or transform preserved content from one file format to another as technology changes. Portico supplements and supports this migration policy by preserving the original source files along with the migrated versions. In addition, Portico has developed a technology and application independent archive (for example, the Portico archive can be exported into a standard file system with all the information necessary to understand the contents of the archive in organised files).

History of Portico

Since the 1990s, digital publications have become an increasingly important component of scholarly communications, as evidenced by the increasing percentage of the university membership of the Association of Research Libraries (ARL) expenditures on digital resources (see Figure CS8.1).

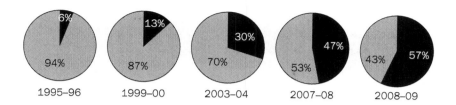

1995–96 1999–00 2003–04 2007–08 2008–09

⬤ ARL university non-e-resource expenditures
● ARL university e-resource expenditures

Figure CS8.1 ARL university library materials expenditures

Source: Kyrillidou and Morris (2011: 20–1).

From the beginning of digital publication, the academic community expressed the need for reliable long-term preservation of these new publications (Garrett and Waters, 1996) and specifically stressed the need for preservation of electronic journals (Waters, 2005). Without a reliable system for preservation, neither publishers nor libraries would be able to transform into modern organisations with full reliance on the digital format – a format often preferred by students and scholars for its ease of access and use. Without effective preservation, both publishers and libraries were locked into a dual-format world with all the expense that duplication imposed.

In 2002, JSTOR[3] established the Electronic Archiving Initiative ('E-Archive') with a grant from the Andrew W. Mellon Foundation (see Figure CS8.2). The purpose of the initiative was to further Mellon's

2002
Launch of Electronic Archiving Initiative by JSTOR

2006
Portico ingests initial e-journal content into the archive

2009
Portico ingests initial e-book content into the archive

2009
CRL audit of Portico begins

2005
Portico launched

2007
Portico makes first trigger title available

2009
Portico fulfils first PCA claim

2010
Portico ingests initial d-collection content

Figure CS8.2 Portico history

seminal E-Journal Archiving Program by developing the organisational and technical infrastructure needed to ensure the long-term preservation of and access to electronic scholarly resources. The E-Archive team worked with publishers and libraries to develop an approach that balanced the needs of each group while creating a sustainable digital preservation model. In 2005, Portico was officially launched as a result of these efforts with support from JSTOR, Ithaka, the Andrew W. Mellon Foundation, the Library of Congress and numerous library and publisher participants. Portico's initial focus was on e-journal preservation.

As of 2011, Portico offers three separate preservation services to the academic community: e-journal preservation, e-book preservation and d-collection preservation. The economic models supporting each service differ. The Portico e-journal preservation service and the Portico e-book preservation service are financially supported by publishers and libraries. The Portico d-collection preservation service is financially supported by publishers only.

Economic model development – electronic journal preservation

In early 2002, when JSTOR launched E-Archive, existing market mechanisms had failed to produce a preservation approach for e-journals that garnered the support of a wide range of publishers and libraries, and this suggested a not-for-profit approach was needed. Any reliable preservation mechanism would need wide uptake to secure the economies of scale and diversity of revenue base required to ensure long-term sustainability of the preservation service. Portico took a system-wide view that included the perspectives of large and small commercial and university presses, and a variety of large and small US and international libraries.

In 2002, digital preservation was not well understood, but it was recognised as an important issue to be addressed. With print publications, libraries traditionally held the responsibility for archiving the scholarly record. With the advent of digital scholarly communications, publishers took on preservation responsibilities because the digital files remain in their custody rather than on the library's shelves. In order to develop the e-journal preservation service, Portico staff worked with publishers and libraries to identify and understand the technological and business issues. These issues informed the development of the e-journal preservation business model as Portico strove to make certain it served the needs of the entire academic community.

The infrastructure required for digital preservation is extensive and carries significant costs. E-journals are particularly expensive to preserve because of the wide variety of formats used in the content and variety of packaging schemes implemented – it is simply expensive to transform and preserve e-journals in a manner that ensures their future usability. We realised early on that both publishers and libraries must be invested in a preservation solution to make it sustainable. We needed cooperation from publishers to secure the preservation rights and to ensure the timely deposit of content. Initially, publishers had significant concerns about placing their content in the care of a third party. Portico overcame this concern with careful stewardship of the content and transparency about archival policies, and third-party preservation is now widely seen as a best practice for creators of digital publications.

Libraries wanted assurance that when they needed access, the preserved content would be available. Libraries also needed the ability to audit and verify the integrity of the preserved content. Portico took an approach that balanced the needs of libraries and publishers: access to the content for scholarly use at an institution is only gained when special circumstances or trigger events occur, and participating libraries have access to an audit site for verification purposes. In addition, publishers have the option to allow Portico to fulfil post-cancellation or perpetual access requests to preserved content. Libraries and publishers make an annual contribution to the e-journal digital preservation service, sharing in the cost of the infrastructure required to preserve this content.

One of the ongoing concerns for any digital preservation entity is that of the free-rider problem:

> Preserved digital assets are non-rival in consumption because once one party preserves the assets, they are for all intents and purposes preserved for all. In these circumstances, the incentive for any single party to incur the cost of preservation is weakened, since the other parties can free ride on the benefits. (Blue Ribbon, 2010)

Institutions may not recognise the need to contribute to digital preservation as the long-term benefit may not be immediate and is for the future academic community. Portico addressed this reality in the e-journal preservation business model by including trigger event and post-cancellation access, whereby only library participants in Portico gain access to the content. In addition, early library adopters of the Portico e-journal preservation service were given a founders discount on their annual fees.

Libraries and publishers join Portico for three-year terms. The agreements automatically renew at the end of the term unless Portico is otherwise alerted. A three-year term gives Portico the flexibility to make changes in the pricing model (for example increasing or decreasing annual fees) should it need to do so in the future. Should a publisher choose to leave Portico, all content deposited remains in the archive with the existing trigger and post-cancellation access mechanisms in place for the preserved content. Portico currently has 376 US and 375 international library participants in its e-journal preservation service, with 173 publisher participants.

Economic model development – electronic book preservation

E-books are increasingly important vehicles for scholarly research and personal enjoyment. By December 2010, e-books made up '9 to 10 percent of trade-book sales' (Bosman, 2010) and as seen in the statistics gathered by the Association of American Publishers and International Digital Publishing Forum, trade retail e-book sales growth increased dramatically over 2009 and 2010 and is set to continue with exponential growth (International Digital Publishing Forum, 2011). Indeed, on 19 May 2011 Amazon 'announced that since April [2011], it sold more e-books for the Kindle than it has print books – by a ratio of 105 Kindle books to 100 print books – and that's both hardcover and softcover combined' (Knapp, 2011). This dramatic growth in the trade e-book market is mirrored in the academic market where in 2010 'almost all academic libraries ... say they currently offer e-books to users' (Library Journal and School Library Journal, 2010).

In the face of this demand for e-book access, the need for preservation of this content is rapidly increasing. Indeed, the urgency around the preservation of e-books in today's world is greater than the urgency around preservation of e-journals in yesterday's world because, by-and-large, libraries are not purchasing books in both print and electronic form.[4] In response to this increasing need for preservation, Portico preserved the first e-books in the archive in 2009 and formally launched an e-book preservation service in 2011. As with the e-journal preservation service, Portico invested a considerable amount of time working with the library and publisher communities to discuss the need for e-book preservation and develop an appropriate business model. Defining the term 'e-book' proved particularly difficult (Portico eventually settled on a definition that includes any book in digital format, whether born-digital or digitised). Much like e-journals, e-books are published by a wide variety of large and small, commercial and university presses, and licensed and purchased by a diverse group of large and small, US and international libraries. Thus it was logical to extend the dual support model of e-journal preservation to the Portico e-book preservation service, with the same trigger access and post-cancellation or perpetual access models in place.

There are several notable differences between Portico's e-book and e-journal preservation services. One difference is that the cost to libraries for e-books is reduced because Portico is able to leverage the infrastructure already developed for processing e-journals in the preservation of e-books. Another difference is that in addition to an annual fee, publishers must also pay an initial set-up fee that varies based upon the complexity and consistency of their e-book content, packaging and metadata. Through working with e-journal content, Portico learned that the effort involved with preserving content varies tremendously based upon the consistency of the supplied data, and we concluded that e-book publishers must pay a variable set-up fee to defray the costs of the initial tool development targeted specifically to their content. As with the e-journal preservation service, Portico offers a founders discount for early adopters of the e-book preservation service.

Economic model development – digitised historical collection preservation

The next frontier in the digital preservation of scholarly content for Portico was developing an economic model to support the preservation of digitised historical collections. Digitised historical collections, or d-collections, are different from e-books and e-journals in a number of significant ways. D-collections are typically sold, not licensed, to libraries. Libraries purchase these collections with a substantial up-front fee and then pay the publisher an annual access fee to provide their users with access to the publisher's web interface to the content. Many libraries also receive physical copies of the content on tape or DVD. Another differentiator from e-books and e-journals is that, given the expense of individual d-collections, the number of libraries purchasing a d-collection is much smaller than the number of libraries that might license or purchase any given e-journal or e-book. In addition to the differences in how d-collection content is licensed and sold, the actual content and metadata in a d-collection is typically straightforward and consistent (which is quite different from e-journals and e-books).

When Portico began developing an economic model to support the preservation of d-collections, we followed the same development process we had with previous services, including extensive discussions with a variety of publishers of digitised historical collections and libraries that purchased these collections. The resulting business plan has some similarities with the e-book and e-journal preservation services, but also some significant differences.

As with the other preservation services, d-collection preservation includes trigger event and post-cancellation access. And, as with the e-book preservation service, publishers are charged an initial set-up fee that is based upon the complexity and consistency of their e-book content, packaging and metadata. As we discussed d-collection preservation with publishers of d-collections, libraries that purchased d-collections and libraries that had not purchased d-collections, we began to understand that the original models by which libraries purchase d-collections were significantly different from how libraries license e-journals and how they license or purchase e-books. This necessitated a new preservation business model.

With the d-collection preservation service, only the publisher pays an annual fee and trigger event or post-cancellation access will be provided only to those libraries which purchased the collection from the original publisher (and that access will be provided regardless of the library institution's participation in Portico). The d-collection preservation model allows the publisher to have a single preservation plan for their content that meets the needs of all of the owners of the collection – not just those owners that are also Portico participants – and accommodates the reality that the vast majority of libraries will never purchase this content.

Lessons learned

Portico has developed and implemented three preservation services over the course of nine years. As a result of this experience, we have learned a number of lessons that are broadly applicable to others developing business models:

- *Lesson one*. The first business model developed for a digital library service is unlikely to be the final one, and it is important for the preservation agency and its constituents to respond to changes in the needs and expectations of libraries and publishers – expect to iterate during the business development phase and even beyond.
- *Lesson two*. The constituents, participants or customers of the digital library service must be involved in the development of the business model.
- *Lesson three*. A single organisation or agency may need to implement different business models to meet the requirements of different content types and stakeholders.

The future

The academic community relies on an increasing amount and diversity of digital content, much of which is in need of digital preservation. While robust preservation options are now in place for traditional forms of scholarly materials, the community is collectively working to resolve the long-term preservation of many other content types, including datasets, materials digitised locally by a library or scholar, reference databases, collaborative works, informal forms of scholarly communications (such as blogs, working papers, twitter feeds and so on) and work that includes multimedia elements. Portico is exploring future approaches and services that will respond to these new preservation needs. We are also exploring the connections among preservation entities – independent archives like Portico, national libraries and specialised digital repositories – that might be useful and what form those collaborations might take.

Notes

1. *http://www.portico.org*
2. *http://www.ithaka.org*
3. *http://www.jstor.org/*
4. *http://www.ebrary.com/corp/collateral/en/Survey/ebrary_eBook_survey_2007.pdf*

References

Blue Ribbon Task Force on Sustainable Digital Preservation and Access (2010) *Sustainable Economics for a Digital Planet: Ensuring Long-Term Access to Digital Information*, Final Report, February. Online at: *http://www.jisc.ac.uk/media/documents/publications/reports/2010/brtffinalreport.pdf*.

Bosman, J. (2010), 'Christmas gifts may help e-books take root', *New York Times*, 23 December. Online at: *http://www.nytimes.com/2010/12/24/books/24publishing.html?_r=0*.

Garrett, J. and Waters, D. (1996) *Preserving Digital Information: Report of the Task Force on Archiving of Digital Information*, Task Force on Archiving of Digital Information, 1 May. Online at: *http://www.clir.org/pubs/reports/pub63watersgarrett.pdf*.

International Digital Publishing Forum (2011) *Industry Statistics*. Online at: *http://idpf.org/about-us/industry-statistics*.

Knapp, A. (2011) 'What do Amazon's e-book sales mean for the future of books?', *Forbes*, 19 May. Online at: *http://blogs.forbes.com/alexknapp/2011/05/19/what-do-amazons-e-book-sales-mean-for-the-future-of-books/*.

Kyrillidou, M. and Morris, S. (2011) *ARL Statistics 2008–2009*. Association of Research Libraries. Online at: *http://www.arl.org/bm~doc/arlstat09.pdf*.

Library Journal and School Library Journal (2010) 'Survey of ebook penetration and use in U.S. academic libraries: executive summary', *Library Journal and School Library Journal*, November. Online at: *http://www.libraryjournal.com/csp/cms/sites/LJ/info/Reportpurchase.csp/a/li*.

Waters, D. (2005) *Urgent Action Needed to Preserve Scholarly Electronic Journals*, 15 October. Online at: *http://www.arl.org/bm~doc/ejournalpreservation_final.pdf*.

Methods and metrics for assessing the return on investment of public, academic and special libraries

José-Marie Griffiths and Donald W. King

Abstract. Griffiths and King describe their significant experience over many years of calculating the return on investment (ROI) in different types of library and using a range of techniques appropriate to the particular circumstances. The critical incident method is discussed as a particularly effective tool with which to study users and non-users. Cost analysis methods are also described in detail. The key element of ROI work, however, is return metrics, which are reviewed, along with value definitions and measures, and notably contingent valuation. ROI calculations are a major tool in digital library decision-making and library management more generally, not only because they provide assessments of relative value but also because they enable library managers to determine how best and where best to target resources.

Keywords: contingent valuation, cost analysis methods, investment metrics, return metrics, return on investment, ROI, use value

Introduction

Over the past 30 years we have conducted well over 100 studies of the various aspects of return on investment (ROI) of public, academic and special library services. These studies relied on specific methods and metrics, developed by us over time, and were substantially different for each of the three types of libraries. These differences may not be apparent to the casual observer. Below we try to describe these differences, recognising that there are many other approaches to assessing ROI which have merit (see, for example, Oakleaf, 2010). This chapter deals only with our experience and should not be considered a review of all ROI methods and metrics.

Specific experience for the ROI assessments described here is based on a large number of individual public library and state-wide library consortia studies performed in the United States during the 1980s and early 1990s (for example, Griffiths and King, 1982, 1989, 1991b, 1991c; Griffiths et al., 1986), two state-wide ROI studies in 2004 and 2006 (Griffiths et al., 2004, 2006) and national telephone interview studies performed for the Institute of Museum and Library Services (IMLS) in 2008. The latter public library studies are summarised in Griffiths and King (2011). Academic ROI studies were conducted on academic journal collections at the University of Pittsburgh (King et al., 2004a, 2004b) and Drexel University in 2002 (Montgomery and King, 2002a, 2002b). In-depth cost studies were also conducted on 11 academic libraries (Schonfeld et al., 2004a, 2004b) and a large number of value (that is the return component of ROI) studies have been performed with Carol Tenopir and colleagues at the University of Tennessee since 1993 (for example, Tenopir et al., 2009, 2010a, 2010b; King et al., 2009). The investment portion of these studies included only the collection purchase and user costs. Tenopir is currently co-principal investigator of a large IMLS grant dealing with ROI of academic libraries called LibValue.[1] Part of this grant includes a comprehensive ROI assessment of all 77 library services at Bryant University in Rhode Island and Drexel University in Philadelphia. Finally, a total of about 80 special libraries were evaluated for ROI in the 1980s and early 1990s which were summarised by Griffiths and King (1993). Tenopir and King also did a study of the Oak Ridge National Laboratory's journal collection in 2001 (Tenopir et al., 2001).

Framework for assessing ROI

The framework begins by describing the audiences of ROI assessments. These include funders as well as library administration and staff, and users who find aspects of ROI results of interest as well. The metrics that go into ROI calculations are often used for decision-making and planning. Library users are interested in how libraries are used by others and whether there are better ways for them to take advantage of library services. Presentations are often made to communities, universities and special library organisations which are well attended by both users and library staff, and summary reports of use, value and ROI are made available to them.

The population served by libraries is identified as including both users and non-users of the services. The general populations served by the three types of libraries are substantially different and therefore require different survey methods. The surveys always include actual users but also non-users to provide a context on use and highlight other sources of services and information and reasons for their selection. The population served by public libraries is generally divided into adults 18 and over and children under 18 years of age, and particular attention is also paid to the non-English-speaking population. Since public libraries serve other types of libraries the user surveys also include school, university, corporate, government and non-profit libraries. The populations served by academic libraries include faculty and professional staff, undergraduate and graduate students, and non-university users. Special libraries primarily serve professionals (that is researchers, lawyers, medical staff, administrators, and so on), often located in different departments and at multiple sites. Academic and special libraries also serve other libraries through library consortia, but rarely survey them.

The ROI assessments vary a great deal depending on the specific services involved. Public library services include online access during in-person visits to the library, remote online access and other in-library services. The amount of use of each service, who uses them and outcomes from use vary a great deal among the types of services. Academic library services have changed in recent years with declining in-person use by faculty and staff resulting from increased remote access to electronic collections and databases in offices, labs and other locations. While students also rely on remote access to services, they do continue to use their library as a place to meet and study, to use computers, to access the library's electronic network and to gain access to the physical collection. Many academic libraries also provide access to equipment (such as laptops, tablets) and other materials. They also provide access to special collections ranging from historical documents to artistic collections, non-US publications and artifacts. While a complete range of special library services were assessed earlier in time, a recent study of one special library's journal collection showed similar use of the collection as that observed for academic faculty and staff users (Tenopir et al., 2001).

Survey methods

There are two basic methods involved in assessing ROI. The 'return' component of ROI is addressed through user surveys that focus on the amount of use of services, the reasons and purposes for which services are used, and the value or outcomes of service use. The 'investment' portion includes the identification of sources and amounts of funds or revenues generated and library service costs including both direct and indirect costs and depreciated expenditures. Academic and special library surveys determine the time their users spend obtaining services, since the cost of this time is a component of the parent organisation's costs/investment in the libraries.

Critical incident method

Our surveys of library users rely heavily on the critical incident method (Griffiths and King, 1991a) where the critical incident is the last visit, last use of a service (for example, circulation, reference and access to other materials, workstations, space and so on) or last reading of a publication (i.e. article, book or other publication). From this point we reference only a visit or use of a specified service. Survey questions include the number of visits made by the user within a specified time period, such as the previous month (30 days). That number represents a 'cluster' of visits. Subsequent questions deal specifically with the last visit made during that month, such as how much time was spent during that visit and which services were used. When focusing on the critical incident, in a sense, the survey population shifts from people to visits and other activities. Total visits are estimated by multiplying the average number of visits per respondent made in a month times the surveyed population total and then projected to a year total (as, for example, times 12). Thus estimates of total visits are based on the population of visitors (and non-visitors). However, when estimates concern the critical incident of the last visit, the population observed becomes all visits of the population surveyed.

This is a powerful tool because one can develop observations from multiple cross-classifications, say from the last reading of an article. Questions about the last reading observed may include how the article was identified, where it was obtained, its format, the purpose for the reading and outcomes resulting from reading. The critical incident method can produce combinations of observations such as the age of articles identified through an online search, obtained from a library and used for research, or one could compare articles read from library sources versus other sources (such as personal subscription or a colleague), in print versus electronic, the respective time spent reading and outcomes of the reading by source (King et al., 2009).

There are two ways of estimating the total time spent visiting a library, for example. One way is to multiply the number of visits in a respondent cluster (such as 10 visits in a month by a respondent) by the time spent visiting (for example 30 minutes) to obtain a total time for that respondent (e.g. 30 × 10 = 300 minutes). This total time can be averaged across all respondents and multiplied by the total number of persons in the population to estimate total time (e.g. 300 × 1,000 = 300,000 minutes or 5,000 hours). The problem is that this method assumes that the time of the last visit (i.e. 30 minutes) is the same for all visits made by a respondent in the past month (i.e. 10 visits). Thirty minutes is treated as an 'average' of the respondent cluster of times which will sometimes be low and sometimes high for actual visits made.

Another way of estimating total time spent visiting is to calculate the average time per visit across all respondents (i.e. 30 minutes per visit per respondent). This number is multiplied by the population total number of visits (i.e. 10 visits per respondent × 1,000 respondents = 10,000 visits). Thus the total time is 30 × 10,000 = 300,000 minutes or 5,000 hours. This approach is subject to bias because visit time might be correlated to the number of visits of respondents. That is, those who visit frequently might tend to spend less time per visit. This bias can be minimised by stratifying by number of visits. The latter approach is most commonly used by us. It is noted that the 5,000 hours is an indication of the 'value' placed by users on library visits.

Survey estimates should be 'accurate', which means estimates represent the 'true value' of the population. Poor accuracy can occur because of a bias, as mentioned above, or because a respondent does not respond truthfully or misunderstands the question. Survey estimates should also be 'precise', which means that estimates do not deviate much from the 'true value' if repeated many times over again. The sample size determines 'precision', which is measured by 'standard errors' incorporated in confidence intervals. The first estimate of total time above is more accurate but less precise than the second method of estimation. These statistical aspects of the survey methods used in library surveys are discussed in detail in Griffiths and King (1991a). The survey methods used for the three types of libraries are discussed below.

Surveys of public library users

Surveys of public library users include adults aged 18 and over and other types of libraries. Adults are surveyed in libraries by self-administered questionnaires collected on exit or by random household telephone interviews. Each survey method has its flaws. For example, surveys in libraries are biased because users who visit frequently are more likely than less frequent users to be surveyed and their responses may be different from those of adults who visit infrequently. Information about remote visits (by the Internet or telephone) may also be biased and some who visit remotely may not visit in person and, therefore, information about remote use can be likely to be biased. The telephone surveys focus on the number of in-person and remote visits made in the past year, providing a population of visits to which critical incidents can be projected. Parents are asked questions about library visits made by their children, as surveys of children under the age of 18 require special permission and processing through Institutional Review Boards. Telephone interviews are sampled by random digit dialling but are becoming increasingly difficult because of survey fatigue, over-saturation of surveys and the increase in caller-id, voicemail and use of cell phones and Voice-over-IP, mostly unlisted in directories. Such households will therefore be excluded from the survey. Further, telephone interviews tend to result in inflated estimates of the number of visits, although estimates of visits and use can be adjusted from known data such as gate counts, circulation and similar data collection methods. These adjustments are known as 'ratio estimation' when the adjustments are extended to other types of uses. For example, gate counts should be accurate indicators of number of visits. If the estimate of number of visits is somewhat higher than the gate count one should use the gate count. Related estimates such as use of workstations, reference searches and so on would expect to be high as well and adjusted accordingly. On the other hand, telephone interviews include both users and non-users from which reasons for non-use can be determined. Academic, school, special and other public libraries are surveyed about the extent of use and consequences of use of public library services.

Surveys of academic faculty and staff

Surveys of academic faculty and staff are conducted from random samples using either paper-based or web-based instruments. Many universities have multiple sites or departments that must be addressed. Samples from these locations are treated as strata, which are weighted appropriately by the population in each site. Many universities have special libraries or collections that are surveyed as part of the samples discussed above or surveyed separately in each. Recent surveys of reading of publications have been conducted in three other countries (the UK, Australia and Finland) by the University of Tennessee (Tenopir et al., 2010b). The response rates for these surveys range from about 15 to 40 per cent among universities. Students are notoriously poor survey responders with about five per cent response rates not uncommon. Sometimes undergraduate and graduate students are surveyed separately. Student surveys often encourage response through an incentive such as participation in a raffle. Faculty are sometimes asked to set aside ten minutes at the end of class for students to complete surveys, resulting in much higher numbers of responses. This latter approach requires weighting of 'clusters' of responses from each class.

Special library surveys

Special library surveys include random samples of professionals in companies and government agencies. Just as in universities, these organisations often have libraries located at multiple sites or within departments. Response rates tend to be higher than in universities because faculty tends to be bombarded with surveys. Special library response rates tend to be in the 40 to 60 per cent range depending on the level of support by administration. That is, sometimes a vice president or director will support the survey, which encourages response.

Cost analysis methods

In-depth cost analysis for services of all three types of libraries is essentially done the same way, although recent ROI studies of public libraries have tended to rely on the entire public library budget and only the cost of some limited resources. The objective of cost analysis is to estimate the total cost of principal services to compare the investment to the values or return on this investment. The cost analysis not only gives a basis for investment, but also provides evidence of the cost per use of services, the relative costs of different publications and print and electronic formats, the productivity and cost per output of specific activities and the potential effect on costs of changes such as in the population of students and faculty served. In this way, the results provide sound evidence for decision-making and/or planning. Some basic steps used in cost analysis are to establish:

- principal services provided by the library; and
- resources such as staff, space, equipment, shelving, furniture, supplies that are used to provide the services.

With this knowledge one can estimate the costs of each resource in providing the service and sum the costs of the resources to obtain the total cost of each service. The library staff costs require information about each staff member such as work status (part-time vs. full-time, temporary or permanent) which has a bearing on fringe benefits, number of hours worked (e.g. 40 or 35 per week), compensated time not spent at work (e.g. vacation, sick leave, holidays), and since professionals often work more hours than in a normal working week the annual amount of this non-compensated work time and amount of time as paid overtime. Altogether, this provides estimates of the total hours worked by each staff member. Total compensation includes salaries or wages, fringe benefit compensation (insurance, pension and so on), overtime payment and bonuses. These data provide an estimate of the average cost per hour for each staff member. Staff are also asked to estimate the proportion of time they spend on relevant activities such as service-related activities (e.g. circulation, reference services, inter-library borrowing), administration (e.g. budgeting, personnel management, record-keeping) and non-service-processing activities (e.g. attending meetings, tea and coffee breaks, education). The number of activities in a typical library ranges from 80 to 120. The proportion of time spent is converted to number of hours spent by each staff member and multiplied by the cost per hour to estimate the total time and therefore the total staff cost of each activity. The activity costs are summed over all staff to establish staff costs of each service. The other resource costs (e.g. collection, space, furniture) are also allocated to each service and added to staff cost to estimate the total 'direct' costs of services.

In addition, there are 'indirect' costs that are allocated to services such as parent organisation administration or overhead costs. For public libraries this sometimes includes central IT services, human resource/personnel processing, payroll processing, legal backup, financing, licence/contract negotiation, marketing/public relations, fundraising and so on. For academic and special libraries the organisation overhead sometimes includes some of the same activities as with public libraries, depending on the size of the library staff. The organisations will often provide this as a percentage (typically 20 to 45 per cent of library costs). Sometimes fringe benefits are included in the organisation overhead.

The library administration costs that need to be allocated include activities performed in the library such as computer or other systems administration, finance, budgeting and accounting, personnel management, facilities management, policies and procedures, record-keeping and statistics, and so on. These costs include all resources involved including staff, space, furniture and purchases. Finally, some activities do not directly contribute to service processing such as attending internal staff and other meetings, professional development and training (e.g. internal training, workshops, society meetings) and tea or coffee breaks and lunch. These costs are also allocated as well. The allocation is determined by dividing total cost by the total cost minus the administration cost (or non-contributing cost). This calculation produces a factor which tends to range from 1.05 to 1.20 for library administration overhead and 1.20 to 1.30 for non-contributing activities. This factor is multiplied by the remaining activity cost (or one could merely add 5 to 20 per cent or 20 to 30 per cent). Once all the indirect costs are allocated to the resource costs a valid estimate of the total cost of each service is provided.

Return metrics

The return on investment is the total 'value' of services as observed from user surveys. The principal return metrics are the:

- amount of use of each service;
- reasons why library services were chosen from among many possible sources;
- purposes of use or needs satisfied by services;
- value of services, including what users pay for services in terms of their time and money and the outcomes from use of the services.

These metrics are described for public, academic and special libraries below.

Amount of use metrics

Amount of use is an important metric because estimates of both total return and total investment are dependent on it. Total use is estimated for the number of visits and the amount of use of each service. Since use is observed as a critical incident, the estimated averages observed on an incident are projected to the total use. For example, average time spent using a service is multiplied by total use of the service to provide an estimate of total time (and cost to the user). The total cost of using a service is then compared with the total library cost to provide the service based on the cost analysis. User time is one's most valuable resource and is generally used judiciously. A choice to use this time to use a library service is an indicator of the 'value' placed on the service. Typically this value totalled across all services is three to ten times the cost to the library in all three types of libraries but towards the lower end for public libraries.

For public libraries, the critical incident observations are projected to estimates of the number of in-person and remote visits derived from telephone interviews. Total service uses from in-person visits include: use and check-out of various materials, use of the catalogue and other reference materials, asking a librarian for help, attending a meeting, various types of instruction and a number of uses of workstations. Remote use includes obtaining information or requesting in-library services from a librarian, using a search engine, viewing or downloading electronic publications, viewing various websites and using e-mail. Children are estimated to visit libraries for use of materials, programmes, aftercare or after-school services, studying and so on. Public library visits and some services increase sharply during recessions and remain high following them. Also service provision shifts to services that help during recessions such as support for job hunting, access to government information and other activities (Griffiths and King, 2011).

Academic and special libraries focus much more on access to publications since reading is essential to both faculty and students. Here the critical incident of use is the last reading of an article, book, etc. A distinction is made between number of readings and number of articles read because an article can be read multiple times by a user. A 'reading' is carefully defined in the surveys. Information about a reading is found for how the reader became aware of the publication read, where it was obtained, including the library, age of read publication, purpose of reading and so on. For example, in academic and special library settings, library-provided articles tend to be identified more often by online search, are older and are read for research and less for current awareness than articles obtained from other sources. These questions provide a 'context' for comparing the use of materials provided by libraries with those from other sources such as personal subscriptions. Other academic library services include reference services, librarians serving as a participant in research, librarian assistance, instruction and access to workstations, workspace, equipment and other materials, duplication, and so on. In addition to the above, special librarians devote more time than academic librarians to conducting online searching of databases for their users.

Reasons and purposes of using library services

Public library users give many reasons for using library services such as having found libraries to be convenient or easy to use at a low cost in time and/or money, to be the best source of information and to provide information that can be trusted. The purposes of use of public library services include:

- recreation or entertainment (for example by reading, listening to music, attending a lecture, etc.);
- education needs as teachers (e.g. preparing a lecture, continued learning) or students (e.g. as a place to study when on an assignment) and for lifelong learning (as adults, retirees and young children);
- personal or family needs (e.g. learning about health or wellness, personal finances, news or current events, job-related information, day-to-day issues, hobbies or how to fix something); and
- work-related needs by users from organisations (e.g. research, legal issues, finance, how to start a business).

The purpose of using academic libraries by faculty and staff includes research, teaching, administration, writing, presentations, current awareness and other related activities. Students use the library to study or to look up information required for class, to prepare a paper or dissertation, to keep up with the literature, to work with other students and so on. The purpose of use of special library services is much like faculty and depends on the type of professional users such as researchers, medical staff or lawyers.

Value of library services

Economists define two types of 'value' of products and services (Machlup, 1979):

- *purchase or exchange value* – what one pays in time and/or money for use of a product or service;
- *use value* – the favourable consequences derived from use of a product or service.

The *purchase value* paid by users includes the time and/or money spent by them in obtaining and using library services. Griffiths (1982) provides an entire range of perspectives of value including a logic interpretation.

The *use value* of library services includes such consequences of use as the 'importance' of the service in achieving the purpose of use, positive ways in which the service affected the purpose and outcomes from use. One important value is what users would do to obtain services (or information) if there were no library. This indicator of value is known as 'contingent valuation' and is a method of evaluating non-priced goods and services. Contingent valuation is assessed by asking the following questions:

> If the service had not been available from the library, from where would you have obtained the service/information?
>
> (a) I would not bother getting the service/information (skip out).
>
> (b) I need the service/information but do not know where to get it (skip out).
>
> (c) I would obtain the service/information from another source. Please specify source _____.
>
> If (c) is checked:
>
> In order to obtain the same service/information, if the library were not available, I would expect to spend _____ minutes or _____ hours and/or $ _____.

Examples of values observed for the three types of libraries are indicators of the 'return' component of ROI.

Public library *purchase value* includes user time and transportation costs (i.e. mileage, parking, public transportation) of getting to and from the library. It also includes the time spent using the service and any in-library costs such as photocopying. Reading library publications includes time spent identifying, obtaining and reading the publication. The purchase value of remote visits includes an allocated cost of equipment and Internet connection costs as well as time spent using the remote services. Typical purchase value is about $21.00 per in-person visit (in 2011 dollars) and $17.00 per remote visit. The cost of time is based on reported salaries or wages. The purchase value depends on the purpose of visits ranging from $6.00 for student purposes to about $37.00 for work-related purposes.

Use value includes determination of the degree to which needed information was obtained (e.g. got all, some or did not get needed information), rating of importance of how well the service addresses user needs and whether a favourable outcome was achieved. Ratings are made of the quality, completeness, timeliness and trustworthiness of information obtained from critical incidents of use. Users indicate how the service/information helped achieve recreation or entertainment needs (e.g. encouraged further reading, helped learn something new, broadened perspective on life, led to other interests). Users rate the importance of the service in meeting specific needs. Use of service/ information often leads to other sources of information such as museums, government agencies and so on.

The survey of other types of libraries addresses a range of services provided to them by a public library including borrowing materials, reference services and use of public library meeting rooms. Value questions include number of uses (for example, 96 average times per year by school libraries, 58 by academic libraries and 81 by special libraries). Reasons for using public libraries were the unique items in the collection, ease of use, depth of the collection, low cost and so on. Contingent valuation questions revealed average annual savings of $4,900 for academic libraries, $1,100 for special libraries and $900 for school libraries which used public libraries (Griffiths and King, 2011).

Access to publications provided by academic libraries occupies a substantial amount of user time and purchase value. For example, faculty and staff spend about 72 hours annually reading articles from libraries versus 53 hours from other sources. This time includes browsing or searching for articles, books or other publications. Since browsing or searching can result in looking through multiple articles, the time for the critical incident of the most recently read publication is estimated by dividing the total time spent browsing or searching by the number of items read or planned to be read. Time might also include such activities as obtaining, requesting, receiving, downloading and displaying, photocopying, scanning or printing the publication. By far the greatest amount of time is spent reading. Faculty and staff cost of time is determined either by university overall average salaries or wages or by an average determined by position divided by 2,200 hours (which is an average annual time observed elsewhere). The cost of student time is the cost of tuition divided by reported hours spent in class, studying (in the library and elsewhere) and in other university activities (e.g. participating in or attending a scheduled event, co-curricular activities, recreational activities, athletic event, volunteer efforts).

Time spent using other services (e.g. workstations, workspace) also determines their purchase value. Four examples of the purchase value observed in the Bryant University assessment are as follows:[2]

- The purchase value of articles provided by the library includes faculty purchase value of $361,000 or 7.4 times the allocated library cost of $48,600 and $3,027,000 student purchase value or 6.0 times the library cost of $501,000.

- The purchase value of reference services for faculty is $29,900 or 5.8 times the library cost and $258,000 for students or 1.6 times the library cost of $156,500.

- Faculty and student purchase value of library workstations is $8,616,000 or 45 times the library cost of $192,100.

- Faculty and student value of workspace is $6,224,000 or 22 times the library cost of $278,200.

It is abundantly clear that purchase values of academic library services far exceed library costs.

Use value includes how important the service/information is in achieving the purpose of use and how the service/information affected the purpose of use (e.g. improved result, narrowed/broadened/changed the focus, inspired new thinking/ideas, resulted in collaboration, faster completion, saved time or other resources). These values are also found for most special library services.

All citizens and taxpayers, users or not, benefit from public libraries through the libraries' contribution to education, the economy, tourism, quality of life and so on. All of this would be lost if there were no public libraries. Users pay for public libraries through their taxes (which is an investment), but even more so through time and money expended going to the library and using the services. However, there are other contingent valuation aspects of public libraries including:

- It would cost users more to obtain needed or desired information from other sources (net benefit) – about $30.00 per visit.

- Library users would lose the favourable outcomes of information by not knowing where to go to obtain needed information – $2.00 per visit.

- Library wages and salaries would be lost to local and regional economies – $5.00 per visit.

- Purchases of library resources from gift shops would also be lost – $2.00 per visit.

- Library users often use local shops, restaurants, movie theatres and other services before and after their trip to the library. (Note that such other use is shared with the purchase value/costs of public libraries.) Based on a study in the UK, about 23 per cent of the total revenue is likely to be lost to local communities – $3.00 per visit.

(Proctor et al., 1997)

In the two state-wide studies an economic input–output model (REMI) was used to estimate the ripple effect of public libraries on other economic sectors over time (Griffiths et al., 2004, 2006). Contingent valuations of academic and special library services are found using the user surveys of services. For example, it would cost faculty about $25.00 more per article read from the library with similar results for a special library.

Investment metrics

Investment is considered differently by public libraries and academic and special libraries. Two state-wide studies (Griffiths et al., 2004 and 2006) address the 'taxpayer' return on investment, including local, state and federal taxes. The total investment in public libraries includes other sources of revenue such as grants, fees, fines and sales. The state-wide studies also acknowledged the investment by the state and others in library networks/cooperatives. The proportion of investment sources (revenue) changes dramatically during recessions in that state and federal revenue tends to decline and local revenue makes up for the decline or also decreases (Griffiths and King, 2011).

Investment in academic library services includes all direct and indirect costs of the library services such as access to the use of journal collections (Schonfeld et al., 2004a, 2004b). Two studies include the cost of using the services for ROI assessment of scholarly journal collections (King et al., 2004a, 2004b; Montgomery and King, 2002a, 2002b). The Bryant University investment in providing access to scholarly journals to faculty is $133,900 (that is, $85,300 in the cost to faculty and $48,600 in library cost) for 11,600 readings or $11.50 per reading, and $3,852,000 ($3,351,000 student cost and $501,000 library cost) for 247,400 readings or $15.60 per reading. Investment in providing reference services to faculty is $35,100 ($29,000 faculty cost and $5,200 library cost) for 712 uses or $49.30 per use and for students is $414,600 ($258,100 student cost and $156,500 library cost) for 21,580 uses or $19.20 per use. Much more time is spent per use with faculty than students (73 versus 17 minutes) and the hourly rate of faculty is much higher ($56.20 versus $34.60). Special library investment includes the library direct and indirect costs and professional user costs.

Return on investment

The return component of ROI includes all values and dollar indicators of the net benefit from contingent valuation. The dollar ROI in public libraries ranges from about 5.5 to 6.5 to 1. Application of the REMI economic model resulted in about 3.7 to 5.0 to 1. REMI statements concerning the ripple effect are that for every dollar of taxpayer support for public libraries:

- gross regional product increases by $9.08
- income (wages) increases by $12.66

and for every $6,488 of support, one job is created (Griffiths et al., 2004).

Two examples of return on investment are given from several observed at Bryant University: faculty access to scholarly journals and faculty and student use of reference services. ROI is calculated by the net difference between the cost of using alternative sources if the library were not available (contingent value) and the current cost to users. This amount is the dollar return which is then divided by the university investment for services to yield the ROI. The contingent value of faculty access to articles is $334,700 and the current cost to faculty is $85,300 so that the net difference is $249,400 return to the university. Since the cost to the library is $48,600 the ROI is 5.1 to 1. That is, the library investment saves $249,400 in faculty costs.

The same assessment of faculty use of reference services yields a net savings of $110,500 from a library budget of $5,200 or an ROI of 21 to 1. Students save $563,300 and the library cost is $156,500 so that ROI is 3.6 to 1.

Averaged across about 80 special libraries the ROI is 2.9 to 1. In all instances, libraries provide a positive and substantial return on investment of between 2.9 to 1 and 6.5 to 1.

Notes

1. *http://libvalue.cci.utk.edu/*
2. Results from the Bryant University report 'Demonstration of Methods to Assess the Use, Value and ROI of All Academic Library Services'. Online at: *http://libvalue.cci.utk.edu/sites/default/files/Demonstration%20of%20metho ds%20to%20assess%20the%20use%20value%20and%20ROI%20of%20all% 20academic%20library%20services.pdf*.

References

Griffiths, J.-M. (1982) 'The value of information and related systems, products, and services', *Annual Review of Information Science and Technology*, 17: 269–84.

Griffiths, J.-M. and King, D.W. (1982) *North Carolina Library Networking Feasibility Study*. Raleigh, NC: Division of State Library, North Carolina Department of Culture Resources.

Griffiths, J.-M. and King, D.W. (1989) *Library Systems in New York State*. Albany, NY: New York State Library, Division of Library Development.

Griffiths, J.-M. and King, D.W. (1991a) *A Manual on the Evaluation of Information Centers and Services*, No. 310. New York: American Institute of Aeronautics and Astronautics.

Griffiths, J.-M. and King, D.W. (1991b) *Massachusetts Libraries: An Alliance for the Future (Final Report)*. Boston: Massachusetts Board of Library Commissioners.

Griffiths, J.-M. and King, D.W. (1991c) *Management Review of the Brighton Memorial Library: For the Town of Brighton*. Brighton: King Research.

Griffiths, J.-M. and King, D.W. (1993) *Special Libraries: Increasing the Information Edge*. Washington, DC: Special Libraries Association.

Griffiths, J.-M. and King, D.W. (2011) *A Strong Future for Public Library Use and Employment*. Chicago: American Library Association.

Griffiths, J.-M., King, D.W., Lenox, C.L. and Lannom, L.W. (1986) *Alexandria Needs Assessment Final Report*. Alexandria, Virginia Public Library.

Griffiths, J.-M., King, D.W., Tomer, C., Lynch, T. and Harrington, J. (2004) *Taxpayer Return on Investment in Florida Public Libraries*. Florida Department of State, Division of Library and Information Services.

Griffiths, J.-M., King, D.W., Beach, S., Briem, C., Schlarb, J., Aerni, S., Choemprayong, C. and McClatchey, K. (2006) *Taxpayer Return on Investment (ROI) in Pennsylvania*. Commonwealth of Pennsylvania, Office of Commonwealth Libraries.

King, D.W., Tenopir, C., Choemprayong, S. and Wu, L. (2009) 'Scholarly journal information-seeking and reading patterns of faculty at five US universities', *Learned Publishing*, 22 (2): 126–44.

King, D.W., Aerni, S., Brody, F., Herbison, M. and Kohberger, P. (2004a) *A Comparative Cost of the University of Pittsburgh Electronic and Print Library Collections*. Online at: *http://scholar.cci.utk.edu/carol-tenopir/files/Pitt_Cost_Final.pdf*.

King, D.W., Aerni, S., Brody, F., Herbison, M. and Knapp, A. (2004b) *The Use and Outcomes of University of Pittsburg Print and Electronic Collections*. Online at: *http://web.utk.edu/~tenopir/research/pitts/Pitt_Use_Final.pdf*.

Machlup, F. (1979) 'Uses, value, and benefits of knowledge', *Knowledge: Creation, Diffusion, Utilization*, 14 (4): 448–62.

Montgomery, C.H. and King, D.W. (2002a) 'Comparing library and user-related costs of print and electronic journal collections', *D-Lib Magazine*, 8 (10): 1–14.

Montgomery, C.H. and King, D.W. (2002b) 'After migration to electronic journal collection: impact on faculty and doctoral students', *D-Lib Magazine*, 8 (12).

Oakleaf, M. (2010) *The Value of Academic Libraries: A Comprehensive Research Review and Report*. Chicago: Association of Research Libraries.

Proctor, R., Usherwood, B. and Sobczyk, G. (1997) 'What happens when a public library service closes down?', *Library Management*, 18 (1): 59–64.

Schonfeld, R.C., King, D.W., Okerson, A. and Fenton, E.G. (2004a) 'Library periodicals expenses: comparison of non-subscription costs of print and electronic formats on a life-cycle basis', *D-Lib Magazine*, 10 (1).

Schonfeld, R.C., King, D.W., Okerson, A. and Fenton, E.G. (2004b) *The Non-subscription Side of Periodicals: Changes in Library Operations and Cost*

Between Print and Electronic Formats. Washington, DC: Council on Library and Information Resources.

Tenopir, C., King, D.W., Edwards, S. and Wu, L. (2009) 'Electronic journals and changes in scholarly article seeking and reading patterns', *Aslib Proceedings: New Information Perspectives*, 61 (1): 5–32.

Tenopir, C., King, D.W., Hoffman, R., McSween, E., Ryland, C. and Smith, E. (2001) 'Scientists' use of journals: differences (and similarities) between print and electronic', in *Proceedings of the 22nd National Online Meeting*. Medford, NJ: Information Today, pp. 469–81.

Tenopir, C., King, D.W., Mays, R., Wu, L. and Baer, A. (2010a) 'Measuring value and return-on-investment of academic libraries', *Serials*, 23 (3): 182–90.

Tenopir, C., Wilson, C.W., Vakkari, P., Talja, S. and King, D.W. (2010b) 'Scholarly e-journal reading patterns in Australia, Finland and the United States: a cross-country comparison', *Australian Academic and Research Libraries*, 41 (1): 26–41.

Case Study 10

EZID: a digital library data management service
Joan Starr

Abstract. In order to pursue a cost recovery approach for its EZID service, the California Digital Library (CDL) service developed a pricing plan based on an annual subscription fee-for-service. The case study describes the four-part process of: service definition, cost identification, market study and creation of the pricing model.

Keywords: California Digital Library, digital content, EZID, persistent identifiers, pricing plan, sustainability

Introducing EZID

EZID ('easy-eye-dee') is a service offered by the California Digital Library[1] (CDL) to simplify the process of obtaining and managing long-term (or 'persistent') identifiers for digital content. An identifier is an alphanumeric combination assigned to an object, and if the assignment is managed and the object is made available over time, the identifier becomes a highly reliable way of keeping track of the object. EZID makes creating and managing identifiers easy. EZID has both a user interface[2] (UI) and an application programming interface[3] (API), which means that it can fit seamlessly into an automated data management workflow. CDL introduced EZID to the University of California (UC) campuses in the fall of 2010 and opened the service to outside organisations a few months later.

EZID supports two globally unique, persistent identifier schemes: Digital Object Identifiers (DOIs) and Archival Resource Keys (ARKs), and will add other schemes over time, including academic domain-specific schemes such as Life Science Resource Names (LSRNs).[4] DOIs are identifiers originating from the publishing world and are in widespread use for journal articles. CDL is able to offer DOIs by virtue of being a founding member of DataCite,[5] an international consortium established to provide easier access to scientific research data on the Internet. ARKs are identifiers originating from the library, archive and museum community. ARKs have certain features distinct from DOIs that make them an attractive option for unpublished materials as well as datasets that researchers want to cite at an extremely granular level.[6] Researchers may want to take advantage of both identifier schemes at different points in the lifecycle of the dataset, and EZID makes this possible.

The CDL and DataCite missions

As suggested above, DataCite's purpose is to facilitate dataset citation. By promoting the use of DOIs for datasets, DataCite hopes to extend to datasets the kind of recognition and exposure that scholarly journal articles have achieved. There are direct benefits to researchers from this exposure. They can look for increased citations[7] and a positive impact on tenure and promotion processes. Moreover, there is evidence showing that data sharing enables new discoveries[8] and greatly increases the number of publications tied to research data.[9]

Beyond CDL's participation in the DataCite mission, with EZID, it has a separate and specific calling to serve the UC libraries, which are facing two new pressures in today's climate. First, the concept of the scholarly record is expanding to include datasets, which means that librarians are required to gain new skills and engage with clients at a new level. Second, US funding agencies and major philanthropic organisations are issuing mandates for data management plans,[10] so university research offices look for a campus entity to meet this need. It makes sense for libraries to fill this role because it is an extension of their historic charge as stewards of institutional assets. Data management tools such as EZID are part of a portfolio of services that research libraries can now provide to their patrons.

Development of the EZID pricing plan

To sustain a data management service portfolio at CDL, the organisation has pursued a cost recovery strategy. For EZID, this has taken the form of an annual subscription fee-for-service. Development of the fee model took several months and involved four basic steps: definition of the service offering, identification of costs, study of the market and, finally, creation of the pricing model itself.

Service definition was the first task, because it meant looking at the system as a *product* in a market or markets and not simply as a library service. The desired outcome was an explicit statement of EZID's features and benefits, with special focus on any unique offerings. The reader has seen a version of EZID's service definition at the beginning of this study. A brief recapitulation aimed at the researcher client is as follows:

> EZID is a service that makes it simple for researchers and others to obtain and manage long-term identifiers (both DOIs and ARKs) for their digital content. With EZID, you can assign identifiers to anything: scientific datasets, technical reports, audio files, and digital photographs, for example. EZID helps you to take control of the management and distribution of your research, share and get credit for it, and build your reputation through its collection and documentation. EZID is available to individuals, groups and institutions, and can be a valuable tool for data management throughout the research life cycle.

The next step, capturing cost information, began with a scoping statement. It was decided that the EZID revenue model should cover operational expenses, as distinct from development costs.[11] This meant collecting estimates of salaries and benefits, supplies and expenses, and technological infrastructure costs at the expected levels for full operation. The category of 'supplies and expenses' included project supplies, telephone charges, general liability, employee practices liability and DataCite membership.

The last step prior to working on the pricing itself was to understand the market for the service or product. There were two aspects to this: identifying the target clientele and understanding the alternatives they may have to meet their needs. The primary EZID clients were (and are) the UC campus libraries and the researchers they serve. CDL has multi-channelled communications with the campuses, from representation on the Council of University Librarians[12] and numerous committees to status updates via newsletters and listservs. In connection with data management issues and services including EZID, CDL maintains a network of identified data management liaison contacts at each campus for information exchange and service support.

In addition to the UC clients, fellow partners in DataONE,[13] an international network supported by the US National Science Foundation, were also considered for early adoption, and one such partner, Dryad,[14] became the earliest user. There was additional interest in the possibility of offering the service even more broadly over time. Not only does CDL have other network-level relationships as a collaboration-based organisation, but also a broad client base would increase the likelihood of recovering costs.

The potential library clients do have an alternative source for DOIs: CrossRef,[15] a publisher-run organisation which has been offering DOI services since 2000, mostly for scholarly publications. In the last eleven years, CrossRef has built a large client-base from among its member publishers and can afford to offer inexpensive accounts to libraries. Originally, CrossRef did not issue DOIs for datasets but has recently moved into this market. Clearly, EZID could not compete with CrossRef on price, so the response would have to be feature-based, in that EZID offers more than DOIs. The inclusion of ARKs and other identifier schemes introduce an opportunity to support the full lifecycle of research.

Libraries and other cultural organisations also have an alternative for ARKs, although it is neither an off-the-shelf nor a hosted option. Any cultural memory organisation can become a registered ARK assignment authority[16] and then establish and operate a server[17] to generate and support the ARKs themselves. This is a group of tasks that requires a certain level of technical resource capacity. The EZID response to this option would be to emphasise the technical complexity and responsibility of managing a full identifier service.

The conclusions drawn from the market analysis were multiple:

- The primary client targets are the UC campus libraries and the researchers they serve.

- A secondary target group is comprised of the partners in networks of which CDL is a member.

- There is value in offering EZID more broadly. Because EZID accounts are available to non-profit organisations, for-profit commercial businesses and governmental agencies, there are clearly potential clients that do not have viable alternatives for creating and maintaining persistent identifiers.

When all the pieces were in place for the development of the pricing model itself, it was time to consider if the expertise was available in-house. The team concluded that outside assistance would be very helpful and contacted the UC Office of the President, Chief Financial Officer's Division. Lisa Baird, Associate Director, Strategic

Initiatives, took the service and market definitions and the cost information and created a working pro forma.[18] It showed five prospective years of cash flow with a particular, yet configurable, pricing scheme. Various other inputs, including staffing and expense costs, were also configurable. This made for an extremely flexible tool that could be used as a scenario planner and price model tester.

During the following three months, two changes to the environment occurred which caused the price model tester to be used repeatedly. First, the original pricing plan had been to charge on a per-identifier basis, consistent with the fees imposed by the International DOI Federation (IDF)[19] and following CrossRef's model. There would be volume-based bands with price breaks at certain levels. When the IDF announced, in the late fall of 2010, an intended policy change rejecting per-identifier fees, CDL management felt that it would be inappropriate to base charges on a non-existent price pressure. So, an entirely new approach had to be imagined and then tested using the pro forma mechanism. The new model was keyed to organisation size and level of research, based on the notion that larger effort is required to support more active research endeavours. The plan also built in a consortial discount arrangement. Fellow DataCite partner Purdue University[20] and CDL worked out parallel pricing categories using a very simplified version of the Carnegie Classifications for educational institutions.[21]

The second change was the addition to DataCite of a third member in the US. As noted, the original founding members included two US institutions: CDL and Purdue University Libraries. In 2011, the Office of Strategic and Technical Information,[22] US Department of Energy (OSTI) also joined. It was clear that a mutual understanding was needed for operational concerns. Some of the joint agreements have already been described. In addition, a relatively common challenge arises when a prospective client does not make an initial contact directly to one of the three partners, but instead contacts the DataCite central organisation first. It was decided that the following factors would help determine which partner takes the initiative: geographic location, existence of prior relationship with the prospective client and client type. (CDL is the only DataCite partner that works with commercial clients.)

Early experiences

Prior to gaining approval of the EZID business proposal, CDL invited organisations to try EZID free of charge, with the understanding that a payment plan would be imposed at some point in the future. UC researchers, UC campus libraries, several non-profit entities, as well as a few government research teams and one commercial venture took advantage of this opportunity. When the approval came for EZID to implement the fee-for-service model, about half of the groups and organisations that had done free trials moved into paying accounts within the first four months. CDL's relationships with some of the others evolved. For example, in connection with the individual UC researchers, the emphasis has gone from individual accounts into working with the campus libraries as EZID service providers. A number of UC campus libraries have now purchased university-wide subscriptions so they can provide identifier services to their entire research community.

To date, EZID has acquired attention and new clients beyond the UC campuses without actual marketing, although effort has gone into outreach in several other forms, including webinars, conference speaking engagements, social networking and word of mouth. The team also gets referrals from the DataCite main office in Hanover, Germany, because the DataCite website attracts responses. These may be directed to CDL based on the factors mentioned above. A marketing campaign of some kind is a highly desirable next step, pending resource availability.

Lessons learned

EZID's path toward cost recovery was motivated by the exigencies of budgetary constraints and it may be that these constraints were not only tangible but also attitudinal. With repeated messages related to budgetary reductions being given at the organisation level, it was relatively difficult for individuals to think completely freely about how to implement the business plan. Thus, when selecting a methodology for handling the financial exchanges between CDL and its clients, options that might have represented real expenditures were not explored. This led to a reliance on the existing library licensing apparatus and the in-house billing system. These have functioned adequately without doubt, and they work well for CDL's services that involve asset or content storage. They may be more complex than necessary, however, for a more 'lightweight' product like EZID. Adopting the readily available method was easy and fast, and from that perspective quite beneficial to the start-up needs of the project. Still, there are times when the idea of potential clients clicking on an online licensing agreement and then paying with PayPal sounds very appealing.

Six months into the implementation of the pricing model, it is clear that the carefully crafted subscription categories are a better fit for some client segments than others. Medium and large educational institutions and governmental agencies seem to find the sizing to be appropriate. Small schools and small non-profit organisations are more difficult to serve with the EZID cost model as it currently stands. These entities may be in a difficult position, because they often do not have adequate resources to run their own identifier service. Perhaps at some point in the future, if the cost recovery strategy has been highly successful, it will be possible to revisit the rate structure in such a way as to better accommodate these smaller institutions. A further observation is that there really is no single 'academic community', but rather an array of academic communities with different constraints and opportunities. Some of these communities are geographic and some are academic domain specific. This suggests that some flexibility and an attitude embracing continuous learning are important assets for libraries and librarians implementing a cost recovery solution.

Looking ahead

The EZID team looks ahead to future developments that fall into three categories: feature extensions, infrastructure improvements and service delivery. As a user-facing service, EZID has a development roadmap for enhancements aimed at improving the services offered to clients. The general themes underway at the time of this writing include a redesigned user interface with support for activity reporting and browsing, identifier services that increase support for the research lifecycle such as tombstone pages,[23] and the addition of other identifier schemes. Provision of support for domain-specific schemes will allow researchers to work with the identifier scheme(s) they prefer for the majority of the research cycle, only shifting to a DOI upon submission for publication, for example.

Behind the scenes, the EZID infrastructure is being strengthened. As the service matures, clients expect to see a professional-level business continuity plan in place. Therefore a primary goal at present is to establish a robust network for replication of the services underpinning the ARK service as well as the EZID management layer. The DOI service is already built upon an internationally distributed infrastructure.

Lastly, an important direction for the financial sustainability of EZID is to extend the service delivery model. Software systems providers can generate revenue in more than one way. The hosted solution model may be the primary revenue channel for EZID, but it was always the intention of the team to offer a second channel loosely based on the Red Hat[24] idea. In other words, for an additional annual charge, this 'super' client would get a branded version of EZID and the ability to sign up clients of their own (along with related administrative abilities). Certain arrangements and requirements have to be met by such a client, to be sure, but this mechanism represents an opportunity for strengthening existing partnerships and creating new bonds where none existed before.

Running a library service while recovering its costs can be a daunting enterprise. But being budget driven can provide some real advantages. EZID's economic imperative has been as a strong teacher about marketing, teaching the team to talk about library services in new ways. Equally, it has given priority to the formal improvements in procedures, documentation and infrastructure that are necessary for business continuity under any circumstances. And, it has opened doors to new kinds of partnerships with new kinds of partners. EZID is in the process of tracking costs and income so that, over the next couple of years, it can determine whether or not the service can indeed pay for itself, but, meanwhile, the process of trying has already generated returns.

Notes

1. The CDL was founded by the University of California in 1997. It is part of the Office of the President and serves all ten campuses of the university. For more information, see: *http://www.cdlib.org/*.
2. *http://n2t.net/ezid*
3. Application programming is needed for two software programs to communicate with one another. For EZID's API documentation, see: *http://n2t.net/ezid/doc/apidoc.html*.
4. For more information about LSRNs, see: *http://lsrn.org/*.
5. For more information about DataCite, see: *http://datacite.org/*.
6. ARKs can be deleted, unlike DOIs. In addition, the ARK server has a feature called 'suffix pass-through'. Assume that a large object, A, has 10,000 small components arranged in a hierarchy, as in A/B/C. It is possible to get an ARK for the large object, registering its location with EZID, and have the rest of the hierarchy pass through. For example, if A is mapped to the location L, then component A/B/C will automatically be mapped to L/B/C. The DOI resolver does not do this.
7. H.A. Piwowar, R.S. Day and D.B. Fridsma (2007) Sharing detailed research data is associated with increased citation rate', *PLOS ONE*, 2 (3): e308. Online at: *http://www.plosone.org/article/info:doi/10.1371/journal.pone.0000308*.

8. G. Kolata (2010) 'Sharing of data leads to progress on Alzheimer's', *New York Times*, 13 August.

9. A.M. Pienta, G.C. Alter and J.A. Lyle (2010) *The Enduring Value of Social Science Research: The Use and Reuse of Primary Research Data*. Paper presented at 'The Organisation, Economics and Policy of Scientific Research' workshop, Torino, Italy, April. Online at: *http://hdl.handle.net/2027.42/78307*.

10. For example, see NSF (2010) 'Scientists seeking NSF funding will soon be required to submit data management plans'. Online at: *http://www.nsf.gov/news/news_summ.jsp?cntn_id=116928*.

11. Development costs have been partially defrayed by generous support from the Gordon and Betty Moore Foundation (see: *http://www.moore.org/*).

12. The Council of University Librarians is composed of the University Librarians from each of the ten campuses and the Executive Director of CDL. For more information, see: *http://libraries.universityofcalifornia.edu/about-uc-libraries*.

13. DataONE's aim is 'to ensure the preservation and access to multi-scale, multi-discipline, and multi-national science data' (see: *https://www.dataone.org/*).

14. Dryad is an international repository of data underlying peer-reviewed articles in the basic and applied biosciences (see: *http://www.datadryad.org*).

15. For information about CrossRef, see: *http://www.crossref.org/*.

16. This process is called getting a Name Assignment Authority Number, or NAAN. For more information about NAANs, see the CDL Curation wiki entry at: *https://wiki.ucop.edu/display/Curation/NAANs*.

17. The ARK server is known as NOID, which stands for Nice Opaque IDentifier minter and resolver. For more information, see *https://wiki.ucop.edu/display/Curation/NOID*.

18. 'Pro forma describes a presentation of data, typically financial statements, where the data reflect the world on an "as if" basis.' See: *http://economics.about.com/od/economicsglossary/g/proforma.htm*.

19. For information about the IDF, see: *http://www.doi.org/*.

20. For more information about the Purdue University Libraries, see: *http://www.lib.purdue.edu/*.

21. For a description of the Carnegie Classifications, see: *http://classifications.carnegiefoundation.org/descriptions/basic.php*. The CDL size breakdown for commercial clients is based on the Bloomsbury Business Library – Business & Management Dictionary categories for commercial firms.

22. For more information about OSTI, see: *http://www.osti.gov/*. At the time of writing, it is understood that OSTI will be providing services to certain US government agencies.

23. A tombstone page is a web page returned for a resource no longer found at its target location of record. The tombstone may provide 'last known' metadata, including the original owner.

24. For a discussion of the merits of this approach, see: N. Munga, T. Fogwill and Q. Williams (2009) 'The adoption of open source software in business models: a Red Hat and IBM case study', SAICSIT Conference 2009, pp. 112–21. Online at: *http://www.informatik.uni-trier.de/~ley/db/conf/saicsit/saicsit2009.html#MungaFW09*.

Case Study 11

Adding e-books and audiobooks to the search experience

How one vendor addressed customer needs and created a better e-book system for libraries

Michael Gorrell

Abstract. The case study describes and explores various costing and pricing models for content and service delivery from the point of view of a major library supplier.

Keywords: access, content, costing models, e-books, EBSCO, EBSCO*host*, patron driven, pricing models

Introduction

EBSCO Publishing (EBSCO) has been a long-time research database provider but with the acquisition of NetLibrary from OCLC in March 2010, EBSCO embarked on a new mission, to incorporate e-books and audiobooks into the EBSCO*host*® research experience. Librarians had been encouraging EBSCO to add e-books to its list of offerings for years, and with the addition of NetLibrary, the time had come. EBSCO saw the opportunity to help libraries maximise their investments in e-books and databases by allowing both resources to be discovered and used within the same unified user experience. Having established the EBSCO*host* platform as the most used research platform as a database aggregator, the goal was to enhance the interface to make way for the unique needs of e-book and audiobook searchers. Drawing on its extensive experience in developing successful, user-tested, highly usable interfaces, the EBSCO team was up for the challenge of seamlessly integrating e-books and audiobooks in ways that allowed their value to shine. In addition to making interface enhancements, EBSCO realised that it could leverage its relationships with publishers to add more e-book and audiobook content as well as to expand the licensing models that were currently in place.

The process

One of the first things done after the acquisition was to establish a NetLibrary Advisory Council. This advisory group was used to solicit new ideas as well as to vet EBSCO's product teams' ideas. Several surveys, e-mails and webinars were conducted, allowing the EBSCO team to understand the needs and expectations of librarians of all types, worldwide. Using this effective feedback cycle along with its traditional methods of usability testing and focus groups, a design for the user experience emerged that met the goals of the team:

1. Allow searching and usage of e-books and audiobooks to be done from within EBSCOhost and EBSCO Discovery Service (EDS).
2. Make the user experience as natural for e-book/audiobook users as it is for database users.
3. Allow special features and attributes of e-books and audiobooks to be highlighted where appropriate.

In March of 2011, a year after the acquisition, the research culminated in the launching of a preview site, giving EBSCOhost and NetLibrary customers a view of what was to come. The final migration of e-books and audiobooks from NetLibrary to EBSCOhost was completed in July 2011.

Searching on EBSCOhost

In moving e-books onto the EBSCOhost platform, one of the key value propositions for librarians was to be able to leverage resources with which their users are already familiar. This meant that searching e-books (and audiobooks) should be natural within EBSCO*host*. From choosing databases to setting limiters to using result list controls, users should be able to find e-book content easily. This was achieved by having all e-books aggregated into an 'e-book Collection' EBSCO*host* database. Likewise, audiobooks are available to users via an 'Audiobook Collection' database. Standard EBSCO*host* limiters, facets and so on apply. These new collections fit seamlessly into the EBSCO*host* experience.

Standard EBSCO*host* features were now available to e-book and audiobook users, including saving, e-mailing, viewing citations and bookmarking results. The implementation team worked hard to make sure that pain-points in the previous platform were addressed. One highly anticipated improvement to the search experience was the rapid decrease in the number of steps required to download e-books and audiobooks – designed to provide a more intuitive and easy to accomplish, step-by-step process for end users. Functionality added includes allowing users to explore the table of contents (TOC) easily from the result list or the detailed record – in the NetLibrary interface a user had to access the full text (meaning the title was unavailable for other users to view) in order to view the TOC. EBSCO also invested in the addition of BISAC categories (user-friendly subject headings) to all e-book and audiobook records to increase findability.

Landing pages for both e-books and audiobooks were key features for the librarians that weighed in on features. They wanted an attractive, functional way to browse the content in their collections – something that would stand up well to Amazon and other commercial services. In addition to these features there were many that *came for free* as e-books and audiobooks were added to the platform. These include a fully 508c[1] accessible experience that offers COUNTER compliant reporting and permalinks to page numbers, and extensive branding options. And EBSCO is not finished. In 2013 EBSCO will include the addition of EPUB content. Adding EPUB content expands the number of front list titles available on EBSCO*host* and enhances the downloadable e-book program.

Improving content and access

As much as creating an excellent user experience was an important goal, the growing importance of e-books in library collection development required a second set of improvements designed for librarians, including increased access to content, improved and expanded access models and a more intuitive way for libraries to manage their collections and serve their end users.

Content

Currently EBSCO provides 300,000 e-books and audiobooks. EBSCO's content licensing team has been working with publishers since the acquisition of NetLibrary to increase the content available on the EBSCO*host* platform and to negotiate new access models. At this point, thousands of e-book titles are being loaded each month from hundreds of leading publishers including e-books in more than 30 languages.

E-books and audiobooks available on EBSCO*host* aim to serve the needs of all libraries and their users whether they are serious academic researchers looking for the latest information on a subject (from which he or she will now see e-book and audiobook results integrated with periodical content) to public library patrons looking for an e-book or audiobook to download to the latest mobile device. Mobile access is becoming a requirement for libraries and currently Adobe's solution facilitates download for e-books on EBSCO*host* allowing access from most dedicated e-book readers and other devices, including Sony, Nook, Samsung, iPad, iPhone and Android phones. The continuing growth of e-books and audiobooks available on EBSCO*host* will see the expansion of titles serving the needs of academic, medical and corporate users while adding more popular fiction and non-fiction titles for public libraries.

Access

Publishers, concerned with how e-books would impact their business, initially set up access models that were cautious and restrictive: one book, one user (1B1U) was the most common access model and users accustomed to downloading what they wanted online were left to wonder how an electronic resource could be 'checked out' of the library.

With the move to the EBSCO*host* platform, EBSCO has also been able to introduce a three user model (1B3U) and an unlimited user model (1BUU). Upgrade options are also a part of the new models being introduced. For instance, a library with a three user model could upgrade to an unlimited model when librarians determine that there is sufficient demand for a given title. The upgrade option, combined with Patron Driven Acquisition (PDA), allows libraries to expand the access to a title and offer it to each user without delay with a *pay as you go* mindset for the acquisition specialist.

Patron Driven Acquisition (PDA) is another library-focused initiative being expanded and improved by EBSCO. With PDA, money is set aside and librarians determine which books should be exposed to patrons – all at no initial cost. After the titles have been added to the online collection, patron usage determines which books are actually purchased. Publishers have worked with e-book aggregators to determine what defines usage and therefore how PDA purchases are triggered. When EBSCO acquired NetLibrary, PDA and its triggers were not commonly known or understood. However, in the subsequent years PDA has become more accepted and EBSCO has worked with publishers to implement industry standard rules determining usage. Titles are only triggered for purchase when a patron has actively pursued a means to view an e-book with the intent to read or use the content, including when the user:

- views an e-book for more than ten minutes;
- views more than ten pages of an e-book;
- prints, e-mails or copies and pastes a portion of an e-book page;
- downloads an e-book.

Since saving money and limited budgets have become a way of life for libraries, PDA promises to be a way to add to a collection without the initial investment and risk of buying the wrong books. With PDA for e-books and audiobooks on EBSCO*host*, librarians select e-book titles appropriate to the interests of their patron base – whether it is content from a specific publisher, frontlist content in a specific subject area or titles that are not in the library's print collection. With PDA, the librarians decide which titles are made available to their patrons, again making PDA part of collection development. The next step is to expose that content to patrons. The bibliographic records are loaded into the library catalogue, allowing users to discover e-book titles by browsing or searching the library collection. At the same time those titles automatically become part of the e-book Collection and Audiobook Collection on EBSCO*host*. As patrons find the titles and use them, libraries take ownership of these titles and funds are either deducted from a deposit or libraries are billed.

An enhancement that EBSCO is pursuing is a Smart PDA feature, which provides additional ownership options. Smart PDA allows a site to allow patron usage to not only determine the initial purchase of a title through PDA, but also allows that site to ensure that no user will ever be denied access while preserving the lowest cost possible. At the time of PDA set-up, titles are initially set up as 1B1U and an upgrade path is established as the list is created. For example, collection development staff might determine that they want to initially purchase at 1B1U, then if a second user needs to use that same title, the library would automatically purchase a 1B3U upgrade. Then, if a fourth simultaneous user ever came along the library would then purchase an unlimited license (1BUU) – all done in an automatic unmediated way.

Libraries could also choose an upgrade path that went immediately to unlimited use (1BUU). These upgrade paths and the initial purchase level can be set at a title-by-title basis if desired. These upgrade options prevent patrons from encountering a situation where e-resources are 'checked out' and lets libraries eliminate turnaways, i.e. users seeking an e-book or audiobook that is checked out or in use by another patron or researcher, and provide better access and service for the end user.

Using Smart PDA users never need to 'wait' for an e-book and libraries never pay for more access than is needed. Smart PDA lets librarians provide the ultimate in patron-driven acquisition with minimal overhead encountered by the library.

Patron-driven lease – the answer to inter-library loan for e-books?

Similar in concept to PDA, the Patron Driven Lease (PDL) programme allows libraries to select titles that are exposed to their patrons, but when a title gets triggered the library 'leases' the title rather than buying it. The cost of a lease is a percentage of the ownership price, saving libraries money. The same usage triggers apply, but titles are 'owned' by the library for shorter periods of time, as for example:

- 1 day
- 7 days
- 14 days
- 28 days.

PDLs provide an e-equivalent to inter-library loan and offer a great opportunity to expose even more content to patrons at a controlled price. When PDA or PDL title lists are set up, the library can establish a not-to-exceed ceiling, controlling their overall financial liability.

Subscription collections

EBSCO will be offering collections that can be subscribed to by the library. These are not titles that are owned by the library, but rather are collections of e-books that are analogous to full-text databases. The mix of content in these collections is likely to be less current than the titles that might be purchased but can provide excellent value and allow libraries to greatly widen the e-books that their patrons can use. EBSCO is also developing e-book anthologies that contain high-interest titles in several different subject areas, available to libraries on a subscription basis.

Collection development on EBSCO*host*

EBSCO is committed to providing easy tools to acquire and manage e-books and audiobooks and plans to continually enhance the EBSCO*host* Collection Management Tool (ECM) and expand the acquisition models by which libraries can acquire e-books. Librarians can now use ECM or YBP's GOBI3 to make purchasing decisions for the more than 350,000 titles available from EBSCO and they can acquire them by title-by-title purchase, by purchasing or subscribing to a number of new collections, by creating PDA lists and by making e-books available via short-term loan.

Current features that remain include popular features designed to ease collection development such as Subject Sets, Standard Collections and Custom Collections. Subject Sets are prepackaged sets of titles chosen specifically for their subject appeal. EBSCO's collection development team members – librarians and collection specialists – use their expertise and knowledge to create collections and Subject Sets for libraries. To date, EBSCO has created more than 200 e-book Subject Sets. All of EBSCO's Subject Sets include titles published within the past three years and have no duplication among current or past offerings.

EBSCO also creates Standard Collections as a starting point for libraries looking to begin selecting a wider range of titles within a given discipline. More than 200 standard collections have been created, each of which has between 500 and 2,000 titles. EBSCO also helps libraries develop their collections by offering Custom Collections. These collections are built by EBSCO's collection development librarians and each one is based on the distinct needs of a given institution. Custom Collections work well for larger purchases. Librarians work with the EBSCO collection development experts. Content objectives are shared along with information about current collections and budgetary requirements to create custom collections for libraries to consider. These suggested titles become the basis of the decision-making process. Collections can be purchased in whole or refined to meet the unique needs of an institution. Ultimately, these remain 'title-by-title' acquisitions since librarians can elect to remove titles or add additional content as needed.

Once again, while the collection options remain, ECM is poised to take the place of TitleSelect and provide a simpler management experience for librarians. ECM will make it even easier for librarians to create or add to their collections on their own, build or augment collections with Subject Sets, create a profile (and be alerted when new titles or collections meeting the profile become available), participate in collaborative collection development with colleagues or work with EBSCO to create a custom collection.

Conclusion

EBSCO has answered the call of libraries to add e-books and audiobooks to its array of products. In doing so it has allowed libraries to enjoy greater value out of the platform that is already one of the most used. EBSCO*host* was enhanced to optimise the usability of e-books and audiobooks, and feedback was incorporated from thousands of librarians worldwide. EBSCO has also taken steps to a greater range of content and leveraged its excellent relationships with publishers to provide new ownership and leasing options to libraries. Based on this, libraries can maximise their investments in e-books and audiobooks.

Note

1. Web accessibility and navigation. The EBSCO*host* platform has been upgraded, working with accessibility experts, to move beyond 508 compliance making it a site that can be used by people with visual and other disabilities using screen readers and keyboard controls.

Case Study 12

Woodhead Publishing Online – Chandos Publishing Online

Martin Woodhead

Abstract. This case study also takes a publisher perspective on digital economics. The ability to offer digital products at marginal cost provided an important incentive to publishers in the early years of development. But, here again, thorough market research enabled the formulation of business models that facilitated a move from add-on to mainstream.

Keywords: business models, Chandos Publishing Online, e-books, market research, publishing, Woodhead Publishing Online

Introduction

Woodhead Publishing Ltd is a book publisher specialising in current science and technology in the fields of engineering, material science, textile technology, food science, bioscience, biomedicine, environmental technology, energy and mathematics. The company was established in 1989 and is based in Cambridge, UK. In 2009 the company acquired Chandos Publishing in Oxford, specialising in books on librarianship and information science. A total of 150 books are published per year across both companies.

Since the Internet became established in the mid-1990s, Woodhead has had to monitor the rapid changes which have taken place in the world of publishing and bookselling and to make many decisions about what paths to follow. This process is forever ongoing and there are no signs of the pace of change slowing up; if anything, the reverse. How does a mid-sized publishing company such as Woodhead monitor these constant changes? Luckily, the publishing industry and the customers it serves are very open with their experiences about technological developments in particular. Attending meetings and conferences provides a wealth of information, but in addition to this, Woodhead undertakes considerable market research, both quantitative and qualitative, to determine what kind of books its customers wish to buy and how.

The major development since the mid-1990s has, of course, been the digitisation of text and how best to deliver it to customers. The first step down the digital road was taken by Woodhead in 1996 when the general view among science, technology and medical (STM) publishers was that it would be sensible to capture all text as portable document format (PDF) files while typesetting took place. This was led by the rapid developments taking place at that time in journal publishing, but, for the humble book, a compact disc (CD) of PDF files seemed on the face of it to serve no purpose as e-books had not been invented. The CDs therefore gathered dust for several years, but as there was no additional cost from the typesetters to create them, there seemed nothing to lose. But then, around the turn of the millennium, Woodhead became aware of the early US-based e-book aggregators such as NetLibrary,[1] Ebrary[2] and Knovel[3] and all of a sudden those dusty CDs started to realise their magnificent digital potential. The decision to create PDF files of every book published from 1996 onwards enabled Woodhead to obtain a head start on many of its smaller competitors. Larger publishers who also published journals had in most cases taken a similar decision around the same time with their book publishing operations.

The e-book aggregators were hungry for content and deals were soon done with all the major companies, usually for short terms so that experience could be gained rapidly and changes made if necessary. This strategy resulted in Woodhead's sales of e-books via aggregators reaching 10 per cent of total sales in 2003, a level higher than many of its competitors both large and small had achieved at that time and which is only just being reached by some publishers today. Given that the PDF files were a no-cost by-product of the typesetting process (the original print book run absorbing all the costs), the profitability of this new e-business was very favourable. Additional e-book aggregators such as MyiLibrary[4] and Books 24×7[5] then arrived on the scene as well as aggregators specialising in, say, reference books, such as X-Refer, now Credo Reference.[6] Google Books[7] also arrived, offering yet another option as well as publisher owned e-book sites such as CRCnetBASE.[8] Despite these additions, Woodhead's e-book business remained stubbornly around the 10 per cent mark and so it was decided to determine why this was happening and what could be done about it.

Two patterns emerged. The first was the plethora of e-book aggregators, all with different business models. Second was the steady growth of e-books hosted by publishers themselves, particularly, Springer, John Wiley, Blackwell (later to merge to form Wiley-Blackwell), Elsevier, CRC Press and university presses such as Oxford University Press and Cambridge University Press. The e-book aggregators became increasingly difficult to handle, particularly when assessing large consortia deals with libraries, and so a feeling of losing control of valuable content gradually took hold. To make matters worse, piracy began to raise its ugly head, much of it coming, in Woodhead's experience and also that of other publishers, from one particular aggregator partner who became known in the trade as 'the leaky aggregator'. The time had therefore come by late 2007 to consider developing a new strategy to regain control and to start growing e-sales again. This was to lead to the development of Woodhead Publishing Online and its launch at the Frankfurt Book Fair in October 2010.

Woodhead Publishing Online, Phase 1: Market research

While Woodhead had gained valuable experience of the e-book market through its partnerships with aggregators, it had little knowledge of the technicalities of hosting and distributing e-content or whether its customers would be interested in purchasing Woodhead e-content. Other publishers' offerings and their often stated experiences were a source of valuable information and encouragement. However, only a detailed market research survey and assessment of potential hosting partners could determine whether Woodhead's content would be purchased and whether the prospect of the company's own 'electronic warehouse' would be a viable economic proposition.

Woodhead runs a 'tight ship' and so no one could be spared to undertake what was clearly a huge task. Instead, after much discussion, in the third quarter of 2007, it was decided to appoint an experienced STM publisher with previous digital experience to act as a consultant on the project. This proved to be one of the best decisions made. The combination of Woodhead's long experience of carrying out market research surveys among customers to determine what should be published, plus the consultant's knowledge of the STM digital market, produced a winning formula. Two market research questionnaires were created quickly, one aimed at librarians and the other at researchers and end users in universities, research institutes and corporations. Both sectors were emailed and encouraged to participate in the surveys, which were hosted by Survey Monkey. Key questions in the survey were:

- How was Woodhead content, whether print or electronic, perceived and used?
- How much awareness was there of e-content from Woodhead and other publishers?
- Was there a preference for aggregator platforms or publisher platforms?
- Was there a preference for an own selection of titles as opposed to subject collections? If subject collections were preferred, how many years of content should be included in a collection?
- What were the preferred functionality features?
- What were the preferred content features, for example the importance or otherwise of abstracts and keywords?
- How was content best discovered?
- What were the preferred business models, for example subscription versus perpetual access?
- How was digital rights management (DRM) viewed?
- What was the pattern of current e-book purchases?

The response to these questions was not only greater than expected but also very encouraging. One thousand librarians were contacted and 148 responded (15 per cent), while 4,000 end-users/researchers were contacted and 575 responded (14 per cent), resulting in a total response of 723 from 5,000 people contacted. In addition, qualitative research was carried out among 20 librarians through personal visits and telephone interviews.

Woodhead Publishing Online, Phase 2: The mission

The mission soon became clear – to produce a state-of-the art e-platform that could deliver Woodhead content to customers in the manner they demanded. If such a platform could be developed, the research indicated it stood a reasonable chance of success. The next task for the consultant was to analyse the results and to draw up a 'Request for Proposal' document to send to a selected list of prospective host platforms. The key findings from the market research were:

- There was clear evidence of sustained market growth for the electronic delivery of technical and scientific book content. Market analysts were reporting annual growth rates averaging 20 per cent and more.

- There was proven demand for Woodhead e-content among end-users and librarians.

- There was relatively low penetration of Woodhead e-content indicating a major opportunity.

- The most important functionality features were those that add value by facilitating research, for example discovery, search, inward and outward linking.

- The preferred content granularity for search and retrieval was at the chapter level.

- The ability for users to print and copy was a basic expectation among both end users and librarians.

- There was a preference for perpetual access and flexible purchase models (select titles) from librarians, although 30 per cent did indicate that they would prefer a subscription to a one-time purchase model.

- Librarians did not favour Digital Rights Management (DRM) solutions that required a software plug-in.

An assessment of competing platforms and aggregators indicated that the platforms with the highest market penetration in the target markets were the integrated book and journal platforms that were designed to support the research process.

A review of Woodhead's existing e-partners indicated a need to reconsider its partnering strategy so as not to conflict with the proposed 'value added' Woodhead offering. In particular, the revenue shares in the relationships with some aggregators needed renegotiation and the policy for making core content available via competing products required revisiting. The initial assessment of hosting partners indicated that potential partners lay on a spectrum, from those that rendered and distributed e-books with low value-added, to those that provided integrated services which supported the research process, most of those bringing experience of handling research journal content. Woodhead's most likely technology partner would come from this latter group. It was considered that Woodhead would require a technology partner that was able to provide the key back-office functions including managing access and entitlement, and e-commerce.

Based on the above findings, a requirements list was then compiled and shared with potential technology partners during February 2008 with a Request for Proposal (RFP) for review in March 2008. The plan was for a soft launch in the third quarter of 2008 and a full commercial launch in the fourth quarter – an objective which turned out to be very optimistic. The RFP process proceeded very smoothly, with considerable interest from most of the companies approached, which included Ingenta,[9] Semantico,[10] MetaPress,[11] MPS,[12] Atypon,[13] Ebray[14] and I-Group.[15] All complemented the project team on the thoroughness and professionalism of the RFP document but some had to decline on account of their being unable to meet the specification required. After several weeks of discussions, it was decided to offer a contract to MetaPress, a division of EBSCO Industries, based in Alabama, USA, and well known among librarians.

Platform development and lessons learned

Having chosen MetaPress, and after much discussion, it was thought that the Woodhead project team comprising heads of departments (HoDs) should be responsible for progressing the development of the platform which was given the working title of Saturn. The consultant was thanked for the excellent work carried out up to that stage and the HoDs got to work, or tried to. Dispensing with the consultant's services proved to be the main mistake made in the whole process. The consensus was that the executive members of the company needed to understand thoroughly and 'own' the new platform but, in the event, this set back development by at least 12 months. While the initial forecast might have been optimistic, a launch by the end of 2009 would certainly have been possible had the consultant been retained on the project. The remaining project team was unable to progress the development at anything like the pace required due to the demands of their normal responsibilities. This situation continued until the second quarter of 2009 when it was realised that help was needed badly. Luckily for Woodhead, an introduction was made to another consultant, and from that point onwards, the pace picked up considerably, leading to a soft launch at Online Information 2009 Conference and Exhibition[16] and a full commercial launch in October 2010.

Besides the demands of their existing jobs, where else did the Woodhead project team underestimate the time needed to develop the platform? The preparation of XML data to accompany every title to be loaded by MetaPress was a major factor. Although PDF files were available for all titles published since 1996, the addition of chapter abstracts, key words, digital object identifiers (DOIs) and other data proved very time-consuming.

Fortunately the e-rights were owned by Woodhead for all titles published since 1996, otherwise establishing these rights could also have proven very time-consuming. Developing specific functionality such as the Woodhead 'pick 'n' mix' option also took longer than expected, together with the decisions on finalising the business model.

Throughout this at times frustrating period, Woodhead was supported by an excellent partner in MetaPress who proved not only patient but also very willing to produce a high-quality platform with the features requested by Woodhead's customers. While the Woodhead platform is based on the tried and tested MetaPress platform used by many publishers, it contains significant differences to make it appeal to customers, such as the 'pick 'n' mix' option, linked references via CrossRef[17] and a transparency of business model and pricing which enables library and other customers to easily assess its value to their institution. At the same time the familiarity of the MetaPress navigation system and log in details have proved to be a considerable benefit.

Market response

Launched commercially in October 2010 at the Frankfurt Book Fair as Woodhead Publishing Online,[18] the response to the platform from prospective customers has exceeded expectations. Many leading universities and research organisations as well as corporations throughout the world have purchased Woodhead content either as subject collections, pick 'n' mix selections or individual chapter purchases or rentals. It has been a steep learning curve for all concerned, but an enjoyable one, and it has been a particular pleasure to work directly with many librarians and other customers instead of being one step removed as in the conventional print book business. Perhaps best of all as far as Woodhead is concerned, the 10 per cent e-sales plateau experienced during the first few years of the new millennium had doubled to 20 per cent by the end of 2011 and shows every sign of doubling again over the next 2–3 years, assisted by the launch of a sister site, Chandos Publishing Online[19] in early 2012.

Future developments

Where is all this going? Clearly e-book revenues are growing rapidly, not only for Woodhead but also for many other publishers. Will the book be the unit of STM content in the future or will it be the book chapter? If chapters become the main unit will they be published online as a database as soon as they are written, edited and typeset? Will content be updated online more regularly than with print? Will users want direct access to authors to discuss points arising from their material? Will there be video clips, audio clips and data that can be interrogated or manipulated? Will everything be open access and free of charge to users while editing, production and hosting costs still need to be covered? These and many other questions are constantly debated to ensure that Woodhead maintains and enhances the quality of its publishing for the science and technology community through working in partnership with its customers all over the world.

Notes

1. NetLibrary has recently been acquired by EBSCO Publishing: *http://www.ebscohost.com/ebooks/about*.
2. *http://www.ebrary.com/corp/*
3. *http://why.knovel.com/*
4. *http://www.myilibrary.com/*
5. *http://www.books24x7.com/books24x7.asp*
6. *http://www.credoreference.com/home.do*

7. *http://books.google.com/*
8. *http://www.crcnetbase.com/*
9. Now known as Publishing Technology: *http://www.publishingtechnology.com/*.
10. *http://www.semantico.com/*
11. *http://www.metapress.com/home/main.mpx*
12. *http://adi-mps.com/Solutions/digitalpublishingsolutions/digitalpublishings olutions.aspx*
13. *http://www.atypon.com/*
14. *http://www.ebrary.com/corp/*
15. *http://www.igroupnet.com/*
16. *http://www.online-information.co.uk/*
17. *http://www.crossref.org/*
18. *http://www.woodheadpublishingonline.com*
19. *http://www.chandospublishingonline.com*

A cost study of BMCC electronic reserves with a streaming video service

Sidney Eng

Abstract. This case study stresses the need to take risks in order to achieve the organisation's vision and core mission – in this instance to meet the needs of the students and other users of library services. Early funding models relied on donations; more recently, a share of student fees has produced a viable income stream, though there is still the challenge of non-core or earmarked funding. The author then looks in detail at his experience of developing a digital reserve collection and analyses the ways of identifying both the direct and the indirect costs of operations as an aid both to determining the most efficient and effective way of proceeding and to achieving sustainability.

Keywords: Borough of Manhattan Community College, cost analysis, electronic reserve systems, funding, streaming media, sustainability

Introduction

At the Borough of Manhattan Community College (BMCC), which is part of the City University of New York (CUNY) system, the faculty and staff take the challenge of meeting the educational needs of over 20,000 commuter students seriously by experimenting with service innovations. It is also one of the library's stated mission goals to leverage technology to deliver information services to support learning. In reality, there are few options available to us because of a combination of high demand for service, changing user culture and limited resources. Technology is used to overcome infrastructure constraints and a large student population.

In going over the history of library services, it is fairly evident that the library has not changed; what has changed are the means and technical refinements of delivering the collections to the users. From the nineteenth century until recently, library services continued to be characterised by the idea of collection building; the function of librarian curation adds value to the resources and the process of discovery. An emphasis on increasing self-service defines the library including the digital one (Buckland, 1992). Early adoption of technology sometimes posed risks. Service innovations occasionally suffered from inadequate planning or overshooting targets. But the vision and the motivation for helping students achieve learning outcomes are always the driving forces, making the appetite to take risk more acceptable. Over a period of ten years which coincides with the proliferation of web-based services, our library saw various applications such as database-driven web resources, remote proxy service, roving reference, streaming video, electronic reserves, 24/7 chat reference and online tutorials satisfy information seekers and reinvigorate the workplace and the staff. During this same period, library resources have remained constant in the face of a growing enrolment. Technology that is perceived to be the catalyst for change can be used to overcome inaction and provide a competitive edge.

We chose the service-oriented approach in regarding the digital library (DL) as something that is analogous to a physical library with extensive electronic resources over the Internet. While digital libraries (DLs) deliver new applications in a twenty-first-century user environment, electronic reserves are one of the many basic services that a library offers to its patrons. Researchers tend to focus on solving problems. These efforts are mostly technical, legal or social in nature. There have been fewer discussions concerning the costs and sustainability of digital library projects in general and the electronic reserve service in particular (Halliday and Oppenheim, 1999). The return on investment question is even more difficult to answer. What we do know is that electronic reserves are placed by some faculty at the top of the list among library services (Poe and Skaggs, 2007).

The DL is sometimes defined as content collected on behalf of a user community. This case study considers the cost aspects of DLs as illustrated by an electronic reserves service (Docutek ERes). The *raison d'être* of reserve services is to facilitate students' access to course-related materials assigned by the faculty. These digital files encompass various formats. In the current scenario, streaming videos were developed as a part of electronic reserves, providing additional functionality to patrons who often are away from the library, but their needs vary according to their programmes of study and the faculty who teach them.

Electronic reserve systems come in different flavours. It is not limited to the mere electronic substitution of the traditional print reserves offered by academic libraries. By incorporating new technology, including course management systems like Blackboard, the use of institutional repositories, new linking methods and streaming media, electronic reserves maintains its unique status in an array of library services in today's networked environment. More recently, sharing course materials through citation management software and iTunes evokes the spirit of social media (Cheung et al., 2010). But in essence, where a single application is concerned, the core concept remains that of bringing information and users together at points of need and on demand.

BMCC's initial motivation was that the College and the library are both space challenged. Digital library (we called it a virtual library back in the 1990s) services are considered a solution to overcome severe space shortages with an eye to expanding academic support to accommodate new study habits. A well received application has been instructional videos streamed to the classrooms, most of which are equipped with Internet access and basic projection apparatus.

BMCC was an early adopter of digital library organisation. We began building a hybrid library that included traditional and non-traditional services (Eng, 2001). We put e-reserves in the former category and the streaming video server in the latter in the project programme at the time when the president of the college declared a paperless library. In hindsight, this was quite arbitrary. With very limited staffing, we ultimately combined the e-reserve service and streaming video server project into one. The team comprised the chief librarian, a part-time programmer and a web developer.

Funding

The funding supporting the BMCC digital library project has gone through two different incarnations. In 1998, after a building was donated to the College, the College was touting a new paperless library in an urban community college (Young, 1998). To fulfil the then forward-looking vision, part of the job of the administration was raising funds through foundations, local officials and corporate giving. BMCC made the case by offering high-end information services to students and the community to bridge the digital divide perceived to exist at that time. But the role of the blue-sky planning was unavoidable because other than a campus commitment to a virtual library service, there were few models we could draw from. Without the constraint of preconceived notions, the sky was clearly the limit. Initially we had some success in getting attention and donations, and the chief librarian took an active part in meeting potential donors. This source of money was interrupted due to the events of September 11, 2001 when the nearly completed building housing the virtual library centre was damaged beyond repair. The College and the library needed to rely on a funding stream of a different kind.

The City University of New York Board of Trustees voted a policy of charging a technology fee in 2002. The current fee level is $100 per full-time student and $50 for part-time students per semester. Each year, every campus is required to establish a Student Technology Fee Committee and develop a technology plan. It certainly helps that the library has always had a seat on this committee. The revenue from this fee improves computer services for each campus in the CUNY system. Its main goal is to secure for the student body a level of technology essential to a high-quality education. This includes the acquisition, installation and maintenance of computer systems/networks, Internet support, printers, scanners and library services.

The library receives 10 per cent of the income from the student technology fee to augment its regular budget. Since its inception, and over the last few years, we have had a number of technology-related initiatives that proved to be popular as measured by surveys. It should be noted that both donation money and technology fee revenue are not core funding. The issue of non-core funding is that the use of the budget is restricted to what is being proposed. For example, a majority of the student fee revenue support for the library is restricted to database subscriptions. Since it is non-core funding, no salary for staffing was considered. Looking beyond the horizon, the management of new initiatives should consider annual support that is renewable. Shoestring budgets or underfunded initiatives are not a long-term budget strategy.

Docutek ERes is the BMCC Library's electronic reserve system. The reserve collection is made up of required readings or class assignments placed on reserve by filling out an electronic reserve request form. There are strict guidelines the faculty must follow in order to place and use the course materials. These materials can be of a variety of formats, including HTML, Word, PDF, websites and PowerPoint files. Streaming videos were developed as a part of electronic reserves. Streaming videos are quite popular with professors who have a required video students must watch but not enough time to show in class. We can upload those videos to the ERes course page; students can watch them anytime, anywhere. To extend the service, it makes little difference if the reserve material is an instructional film, a Word document or a PDF file; an efficient work procedure with effective communication has already been established (Eng and Hernandez, 2006). Book chapters, journal articles, syllabi, course outlines, reading lists, lecture notes, sample tests, copyright compliant websites and instructional videos are now among the materials which have expanded the traditional reserves offerings.

Our project began, as most library projects do, with an assessment of current library practice and a review of best-in-class service. The idea of streaming media to the desktop was influenced by the Scholar's Workstation of Indiana University-Purdue University Indianapolis (IUPUI) (Plater, 1995) except that the IUPUI's streaming to the desktop approach was still analogue by using a cleverly designed mechanical arm to fetch VHS tapes and put down to a player. The streaming was limited to the 60 workstations in the physical library. Once we found the available video server technology we were set.

The mechanics of streaming media at BMCC is the same as a now popular web-based digital recorder in the consumer market like TiVo[1] or Verizon FiOS.[2] Users are also familiar with streaming video on news and entertainment sites, thus rendering even college undergraduates informed users who know what to expect. BMCC originally turned to streaming video to create digital copies of heavily used items for preservation. Eventually, we changed our approach from scheduled classroom streams to on-demand student viewing, providing such use observed copyright guidelines. By making library videos available online we could save faculty and students valuable class time. Students could view required videos from any computer at their convenience, from home or on campus (Eng and Hernandez, 2006). This project enabled the library to reach students whose work and class schedules prevented them from visiting the library when it is open – thereby extending library services without extending staff hours.

The appeal and advantages of streaming video are many. Users can multitask and control the stream as they would on a DVD player: they can pause, stop, fast forward and rewind, giving students the ability to learn and watch at their own pace. Additionally, streaming video eliminates the need to wait for the entire clip to download, since one watches the clip while it is being downloaded. One can further suggest that the technology of streaming promotes copyright protection, since streamed videos are not saved to remote computers. No digital copy is being made.

Technology

The library took on the technical aspects of the streaming, then added the links on password protected pages. Students are required to agree to a copyright statement before they can access the materials. The ERes system, hosted locally, was installed with the help of the systems programmer in California. We knew the advantages of video streaming but were not experts in our understanding of the technology. The ideal solution was a server with a built-in graphic interface that combined storage, encoding and re-compression features. After research and correspondence with existing users, we chose a web-based appliance that was a combination of hardware (basically a powerful computer with a dual video interface card and a TV tuner) and a software solution (SuperView video server). The pre-configured application accompanying the server is easy to use. The interface made digitising videos as simple as connecting a DVD player and clicking 'Record'. The SuperView digitises videos in the Windows Media Player format and allows for restricted access to recordings and the re-compression of existing recordings to optimise file sizes. This server appliance is menu driven and is set up to be managed remotely. Later, our web developer found a way to integrate the video server into the ERes system. Doing so allows patrons to use the same password protection of one single log-on. Statistical reports will be derived from the ERes alone. The developmental and maintenance costs of technical staffing were reduced.

Cost analysis, as illustrated in Table CS13.1, involves both direct and indirect costs of running an operation. The difference between the two is that direct costs are attributable to a specific activity or department. Indirect costs (sometimes also known as overheads) are shared by more than one operational unit. Both direct and indirect costs include categories such as salaries, equipment, supplies, furniture, computer networks and so on. Since the indirect expenses are shared, in order to

Table CS13.1 Costs model: direct investment as represented by the first-year application (2001–2)

Hardware start-up for E-Reserves	
Compaq Proliant server, dual NICs, media backup and built-in fax machine	$6,700
SuperView (Axonix) video server, VHS-DVD deck and tuner, Gigabit Ethernet	$5,790
UPS (uninterrupted power supply)	$300
Monitor and AB switch	$250
Docutek ERes software (installation, first-year license and fax module)	$9,145
Scanning equipment	$350
Total	$22,535
Indirect hardware cost for the project	
HTTP server	$5,500
Workstation	$2,300
Server mounting racks	$500
Cabling and networking	College supplied
Staffing	Shared while setting up the infrastructure, existing staff were then redeployed to manage the project

create an accurate picture of the true costs to the library, the first task should be to determine the proportion of shared expenses assigned to the respective work units. Often this step is omitted by budget planners because the library is part of a much larger enterprise where the overhead is shared. The library anticipates what we in CUNY call the OTPS ('other than personnel spending') budget a year ahead. Considering the cost of maintaining infrastructure alone, it is often arbitrary to segment out who uses what amount. It is easier to determine the charge of photocopying than the consumption of bandwidth. Charge-backs or charge-outs are often a pre-determined accounting exercise.

I would like to highlight two related issues that have an impact on budget formulation. Library managers often overlook the principle of capital expenses and depreciation. Because libraries are not-for-profit organisations, these items are often hidden from plain sight. Capital outlays that extend over a period of time are mistaken as a one-time expense. From the budget standpoint, equipment is usually counted in the year when it is purchased; depreciation and replacement costs are not factored in. In our project we encountered two situations where hardware end of life and the maintenance of the legacy system created the unusual challenge of finding suitable replacements. As it turned out, a few years after the initial installation, our video server stopped being supported because the manufacturer went into the more lucrative consumer electronics business. We had to learn quickly to rebuild the system and fortunately discovered that a newer version of the software was available for download from the Internet – crisis averted. In the long haul, we had to figure out a way to recreate an equally affordable solution that is also easy to use.

Sustainability

The end of life of the servers always looms around the corner. There is always the reality that the investment in technology will be superseded a few years down the road. Both the hardware and software have gone through several iterations. The library's budget is approved a year in advance by the provost and is itemised. When the server hardware is no longer supported or actually ceases to work, there is no available budget to replace the unit. The current plan is virtualisation, a process which puts multiple servers on the same hardware backed up by an identical virtualised unit, thereby adding redundancy and minimising multiple hardware costs.

What is obscured from our consciousness are staffing costs in experimental projects. In my library, personnel costs account for over half of the annual budget. With the exception of the allocation for part-time workers, the size of the staff is approved by the administration to the exact number, with little change from one year to another. Conceptually, staff could be considered a fixed cost, a partial cost item or no cost at all if it is absorbed by another cost centre. The team that initiated the project consisted of the chief librarian, a redeployed cataloguer and a support person from the cataloguing department. Once the service was off the ground, both the chief librarian and the cataloguer were replaced by a website coordinator who spent two-fifths of her time running the service and student workers who would do the scanning and recording. The reason this miniscule level of staff can manage such a project adequately is that we have automated some of the processes and are being proactive. Before the semester starts, the coordinator contacts the faculty about service and policy to encourage their cooperation. She also lets them know that their course materials will expire or be purged at the end of the semester. It was difficult in the beginning to enforce compliance. Eventually everyone understood our motivation and the benefit of planning ahead. In our example, much of the scanning function is done by part-time technical service employees when they are not otherwise busy. We have replaced the sole professional staff member with a website person who was originally hired as a copy cataloguer. Our staffing budget has not been increased. There are also important public service functions associated with any reserve service which resulted in changes in the workflow.

Schmidt (2002) outlines the typical workflow for a reserve service in a library. Twelve steps were listed for print reserves compared to a four-step process for electronic reserves (see Table CS13.2). In this model,

Table CS13.2 Steps for processing reserve material

Paper-based system	Electronic reserve system
1. Instructor submits materials for reserve	1. Instructor submits materials for reserve.
2. Library processes materials for circulation.	2. Library processes materials for scanning.
3. Library processes copyright clearance.	3. Library processes copyright clearance.
4. Library files materials for access.	4. Library scans and mounts materials on server.
5. Library makes materials available for checkout.	
6. Student requests materials at desk.	
7. Library retrieves materials.	
8. Library checks materials out to student.	
9. Student uses materials	
10. Student returns materials to desk.	
11. Library files materials.	
12. Repeat steps 6–11.	

libraries control the process of copyright clearance, which includes tracking, contacting, persistent URLs and proxy issues. The front-end of an electronic reserves service calls for providing accurate and timely information to the patrons. Educating the faculty and students becomes as important as coming up with technical solutions in the back office. The decision of who is responsible for copyright clearance will affect the economics of e-reserves.

Electronic reserves permissions costs

Reserve collections raise important copyright concerns. Electronic copies of course materials call for greater scrutiny because perfect copies can be reproduced and distributed easily. Streaming media is a special case because copyright laws were originally very specific about preventing the reproduction of digital files. The little discussed US Digital Millennium Copyright Act of 1998 shifted the balance between the interest of free access and fair use regarding electronic documents and would have affected the day-to-day practices of electronic collections (Lee and Wu, 2007).

Traditionally copyright laws imposed restrictions on public performance/ public showing of copyrighted works, with the exemption of use by faculty and students in a face-to-face situation. This exemption was based on specific fair use requirements. Internet transmission of such display was explicitly prohibited. Under these circumstances, some of our streaming practices would have been questionable.

This was reversed with the enactment of the TEACH (Technology, Education and Copyright Harmonization) Act of 2002 which extended the rights of educational institutions to use copyright protected materials in distance education. The TEACH Act indicates that it is not copyright infringement for teachers and students at an educational institution to transmit displays of copyrighted works if certain conditions are met (Eng and Hernandez, 2006).

The storage of the collection poses another fair use problem. Clearly, repeated use of an article or a book chapter from semester to semester violates the 'spontaneity' guideline as well as producing negative market effects. To the extent that the reproductions are protected by copyright, libraries typically handle copyright issues in two ways (Gasaway, 2002).

1. To establish an institutional policy to ensure that users comply with copyright, many libraries in the US follow the reserve guidelines established by the American Library Association (ALA.) Applying the principle of fair use and/or classroom exemption, libraries are allowed to make copies for educational purposes. 'Too often, libraries have been the passive recipients of faculty requests for reserve materials' (Gasaway, 2002).

2. The foolproof solution is to pay royalties to copyright holders. The Docutek ERes system has a management interface to allow the library to track and transact copyright clearance more seamlessly. But obtaining copyright permission is a very expensive undertaking. According to reports from the University of Colorado, Washington State University and Penn State University, the cost ranges from a low of $35 to a high of $86 per reading (Holobar and Marshall, 2011). Penn State University also reported an extreme situation where it had paid $5,000 in copyright licences for a single high enrolment course in 2008 (McCaslin, 2008). Adding to this the staff time spent on managing and tracking the process makes it prohibitive for many smaller institutions.

CUNY's centralisation of cataloguing created an opportunity for the redeployment of staff time. While keeping the same head count, the only in-house cataloguing involves our textbook, gifts and paperback book programme. All digitising is carried out by technical services staff who have already digitised required readings. Adding the electronic reserves programme brought new responsibilities to the staff and allowed them a higher level of interaction with college faculty and staff. The updated roles of technical services made the case that new technologies may enhance job viability. One study reports 'increased levels of value in the job/viability in the job market for all levels of staff' and theorises that expanding responsibility has given technical services workers increased value (Smith and Etcheverria, 2004). It is unnecessary to put a price figure on staff morale and well-being. The spectrum of DL experiments ranges from libraries with small budgets combined with staff enthusiasm and sweat labour to the multi-million dollar projects supported by national funding agencies, such as the National Science Foundation or the Institute of Museum and Library Services. However, from a cost accounting standpoint, they are not dissimilar, despite whatever scope they may fall into.

There have been many case studies and histories about the earlier adopters, particularly those early large-scale projects supported by government agencies. The early research determined the themes, the nomenclature and its new terminologies, and policies for further funding (Greenstein and Thorin, 2002; Griffin, 2005; Pomerantz et al., 2008). But local initiatives are also effective in demonstrating patron enthusiasm and success. DIY projects usually follow a practical scale. For example, Jane Gibbs's 'Doing It Yourself: Coventry University Library's Streaming Project' (2009) recounted the collaboration among information technology, library department and e-learning office staff. After testing the user demand, the media librarian found the needs of staff to match capacity. She also found that ongoing institutional support was less than forthcoming. Relying on other teams was also found in a study reported by a team at the University of South Carolina, Columbia. The launch of their scanning project cost $28,198.60, not counting the cost of staff or capital service, but there were many resources in kind offered by other departments. By hiring student interns instead of part-time help, she saved almost 50 per cent on salaries. Using the expertise and knowledge of the staff within the library also saved money (Boyd and Creighton, 2006).

Not many of these reports consider the costs to sustain an ongoing service or to institutionalise expansion. The impression is that many typical library initiatives are undertaken without securing the explicit financial backing of the institution. Because of the deliberately small experimental scale and limited duration, money is usually diverted from other areas to support these activities. This is understandable because library administrators are unsure about potential outcome. The path to success, reflected by improving or expanding the service, is full of bumps and detours. First, we have to test the idea, explore the alternatives, validate the assumptions and confirm the performance; then we need to find ways to do it efficiently. In the application of a non-standard service in terms of technology or expertise, there often is not any reliable evidence you could draw from to justify expenses.

Halliday and Oppenheim (1999) offered a systematic analysis of several economic models of DLs in the UK context. In order to keep the scope of the study manageable, they excluded many cost factors: infrastructure, metadata, multimedia costs, price of resources, cost to users and costs associated with system performance. While the study covered other aspects of an economic model, the discussion of electronic reserves was centred on a national reserves programme that would not be easily duplicated. Still, it was a pioneering study, particularly on the production and delivery of electronic journals. They offer this helpful observation: 'Economic issues tend to be tested after solutions have been found to the more pressing technical, cultural and legal issues because no library manager or user would consider paying for a service that had not been shown to be technically sound, legal and useful' (Halliday and Oppenheim, 1999). This was exactly the scenario we realised.

Using our own example, there are several important issues for a manager. It makes sense to construct a cost analysis that includes all relevant costs in the beginning. The second step is to compare yourself to the best similar projects you may find in other libraries or cost centres in other parts of the library. A literature search will reveal many accounts of DIY projects offering psychological and material support. The third is to accumulate useful data to institutionalise the service by obtaining support (Dougherty, 2008).

It is advantageous to position the library initiative within the bigger strategic plan of the institution. The basic idea of strategic planning is to allocate campus resources to achieve institutional goals and objectives. Where does the campus want to go and what roads will it use to get there? Every campus component competes for resources. The institution can only support a select list of projects and opportunities. It is important to align the library's mission to the strategic plan of the college in order to gain consensus and strategic priorities.

Several reports cited by Halliday and Oppenheim (1999) studied the cost factors of digital resources to the users themselves, apart from the libraries. These factors include the costs of owning better computing equipment, time to learn the new platform or interface, and the time to travel to the library when the online resources are unavailable (Halliday and Oppenheim, 1999). More directly, a cost–benefit analysis of the Virginia Historical Inventory Project with funding from the Library Services and Technology Act looked in detail at the quality of accessing original documents and images and dramatic savings were realised. The analysis provided for three scenarios of on-site use, delivery via US surface mail and remote online use with associated costs. The collection maintained over a million images and documents for researchers. The unit cost in terms of each model dropped significantly from on-site to online use. The costs to library of staffing are found to be higher per transaction with on-site users and least with online users (Byrd et al., 2001). The investment justified the costs.

Lessons learned

We have combined a turnkey system ERes with a pre-configured video server that required minimal technical expertise. The library can now affordably provide all students instant access to course-related resources or the entire video library over the local area network or across the Internet. Measured against software cost alone, it cost $0.051 for each document page used and $0.118 for each course page visit in our e-reserves system in 2010. A video file is counted as a document page. This appears to be a bargain.

There are several reasons cost studies are a useful evaluation method for library managers, as observed by Dougherty (2008). Researching alternative courses of actions can provide a better understanding of current activity, determine the actual cost of the new activity, justify a budget request or provide a tool to contain costs. Evidence from the University of Illinois, Urbana-Champaign shows the increased usage of electronic reserves from print reserves by students from 0.08 to 38 times per document. Faculty use of the electronic reserve service also increased. Not only are more faculty members using library course reserves, they are also placing more documents with increased frequency (Laskowski and Ward, 2003). By popular demand, Brown University Library announced in 2007 that they would add streaming media to their electronic reserves (Kurtzman, 2007).

In order to sustain the project, we must obtain adequate funding. Baker and Evans aptly provided this warning: 'It may be the case that start-up costs are minimal, but long-term costs may be substantial and likely to be ongoing, for example with regard to staff training/ development and operations ...' (2009). Once the service becomes popular, the faculty demands will be higher and the usage more diffused. Some consideration of the publicity benefit or bragging rights factor may be valid. However, the ultimate goal is to provide a service in ways that engage students and enhance teaching and learning.

Electronic course reserves captured materials that many libraries had not considered either primary or permanent. But they were considered the 'first line' of course information that students were told to read. This early development prompted Butler (1996) to refer to the electronic collection as a progenitor of digital libraries. According to Butler, the course reserves application fulfils several criteria for a digital library. These criteria include high demand and item transaction activity (so the system could justify its investment). Both providers and users could understand the content of the digital collection as one way to convert a particular part of the library collection to be more accessible. Technically it is feasible to manage with a smaller staff because of the limited collection size and definable scope (Butler, 1996). Changing technologies introduced new approaches to e-reserves within the context of a new user culture. The success of the service has challenged the ability of the providers to seek different means to deliver service. Many looked to integrate e-reserves into Blackboard or other platforms to cut cost and staffing (Escobar, 2010; Goodson and Frederiksen, 2011; O'Hara, 2006; Poe and Skaggs, 2007). Significant savings in staff time and other resources can be achieved by eliminating duplicate systems and shifting the requirements for copyright clearance. This is a debate whose outcome may well be decided by economic considerations.

Notes

1. *http://www.tivo.com/*
2. *http://www.verizon.com/fios*

References

Baker, D. and Evans, W. (2009) 'Digital library economics: the key themes', in D. Baker and W. Evans (eds), *Digital Library Economics: An Academic Perspective*. Oxford: Chandos Publishing.

Boyd, K.F. and Creighton, A. (2006) 'Building a digital library on a shoestring', *Computers in Libraries*, 26 (6): 14–20.

Buckland, M.K. (1992) *Redesigning Library Services: A Manifesto*. Chicago: American Library Association.

Butler, B. (1996) 'Electronic course reserves and digital libraries: progenitor and prognosis', *Journal of Academic Librarianship*, 22 (2): 124–7.

Byrd, S., Courson, G., Roderick, E. and Taylor, J.M. (2001) 'Cost/benefit analysis for digital library projects: the Virginal Historical Inventory Project', *Bottom Line*, 14 (2), 65–75.

Cheung, O., Thomas, D. and Patrick, S. (2010) *New Approaches to E-reserve: Linking, Sharing and Streaming*. Oxford: Chandos Publishing.

Dougherty, R.M. (2008) *Streamlining Library Services*. Lanham, MD: Scarecrow Press.

Eng, S. (2001) 'Visualizing the virtual library: from techno-stress to cutting edge', *Inquirer*, 8: 15–21. Online at: *http://lib1.bmcc.cuny.edu/facres/inquirer/inqSp01Vol8pdf.pdf*.

Eng, S. and Hernandez, F.A. (2006) 'Managing streaming video: a new role for technical services', *Library Collections, Acquisitions, and Technical Services*, 30: 214–23.

Escobar, H. (2010) 'Reserves through Sakai: University of Dayton's primary tool for electronic reserves', *Journal of Interlibrary Loan, Document Delivery and Electronic Reserves*, 20 (4): 253–61.

Gasaway, L.N. (2002) 'Copyright consideration for electronic reserves', in J. Rosedale (ed.), *Managing Electronic Reserves*. Chicago: ALA.

Gibbs, J. (2009) 'Doing it yourself: Coventry University Library's streaming project', *Art Libraries Journal*, 34 (3): 21–5.

Goodson, K.A. and Frederiksen, L. (2011) 'E-reserves in transition: exploring new possibilities in e-reserves service delivery', *Journal of Interlibrary Loan, Document Delivery and Electronic Reserves*, 21 (1/2): 33–56.

Greenstein, D. and Thorin, S.E. (2002) *The Digital Library: A Biography*. Washington, DC: Digital Library Federation, Council on Library and Information Resources.

Griffin, S. (2005) 'Funding for digital libraries research, past and present', *D-Lib Magazine*, 11 (7/8). Online at: *http://www.dlib.org/dlib/july05/griffin/07griffin.html*.

Halliday, L. and Oppenheim, C. (1999) *Economic Models of the Digital Library: Report to UKOLN*. Loughborough University.

Holobar, J.C. and Marshall, A. (2011) 'E-Reserves permissions and the Copyright Clearance Center: process, efficiency, and cost', *Portal: Libraries and the Academy*, 11 (1): 517–31.

Kurtzman, A. (2007) 'Course reserve system goes streaming', *Brown Daily Herald*, February, 28. Online at: *http://www.browndailyherald.com/campus-news/course-reserve-system-goes-streaming-1.1674650#*.

Laskowski, M.S. and Ward, D. (2003) 'The impact of implementing electronic reserves on staffing and service', *Journal of Interlibrary Loan, Document Delivery and Information Supply*, 13 (3): 15–28.

Lee, L.A. and Wu, M.M. (2007) 'DMCA, CTEA, UCITA . . . oh my! An overview of copyright law and its impact on library acquisitions and collection development of electronic resources', *Acquisitions Librarian*, 19 (1/2): 83–97.

McCaslin, D.J. (2008) 'Processing electronic reserves in a large academic library system', *Journal of Interlibrary Loan, Document Delivery and Electronic Reserves*, 18 (3): 335–46.

O'Hara, E. (2006) 'Eliminating e-reserves: one library's experience', *Technical Services Quarterly*, 24 (2): 35–43.

Plater, W.M. (1995) 'The library: a labyrinth of the wide world', *Educ Comm Review*, 30 (2). Online at: *http://net.educause.edu/apps/er/review/reviewArticles/30238.html*.

Poe, J. and Skaggs, B. (2007) 'Course reserves: using Blackboard for e-reserves delivery', *Journal of Interlibrary Loan, Document Delivery and Electronic Reserves*, 18 (1): 79–91.

Pomerantz, J., Choemprayong, S. and Eakin, L. (2008) 'The development and impact of digital library funding in the United States', in D. Nitecki and E.G. Abels (eds), *Advances in Librarianship: Influence of Funding on Advances in Librarianship*. Bingley, UK: Emerald Group Publishing.

Schmidt, S.J. (2002) 'Staffing issues for electronic reserves', in J. Rosedale (ed.), *Managing Electronic Reserves*. Chicago: ALA.

Smith, V.T. and Etcheverria, K. (2004) 'Staffing trends in academic library technical services', in B.L. Eden (ed.), *Innovative Redesign and Reorganization of Library Technical Services*. Westport, CT: Libraries Unlimited.

Young, J.K. (1998) 'A community college uses windfall to create a library without books', *Chronicle of Higher Education*, A23–4.

National Academic Research and Collaborations Information System in the Netherlands

Arjan Hogenaar

Abstract. This case study brings together many of the key themes discussed in Chapter 3, in particular: sustainability, resource allocation, the main costs associated with digital library service provision and cost-effective decision-making in order to ensure the best possible deployment and use of resources to meet stated aims and objectives.

Keywords: cost-effective decision-making, funding, NARCIS, resource allocation, sustainability

Introduction

The National Academic Research and Collaboration Information System (NARCIS) is a portal giving access to all kinds of research-related information from the Netherlands. The development and maintenance of the portal is an activity of the Data Archiving and Networked Services Institute (DANS),[1] but was initiated by the Royal Netherlands Academy of Arts and Sciences (KNAW).[2] There is a shared responsibility for the content between DANS, the Dutch universities, the Netherlands Organisation of Scientific Research (NWO)[3] and the major scientific institutions in the Netherlands. NARCIS is a free service and the budget for its maintenance and development is a regulatory task of DANS. The NARCIS portal fits well in the programme of the SURF Foundation[4] to promote access to scientific information. Therefore frequently NARCIS has been able to profit from SURF Foundation grants. In relation to cost-effectiveness, NARCIS is being developed using open source software and standards. By doing so, vendor lock-in will be prevented and international cooperation is made easier. In the near future, the use of persistent identifiers will become more and more important. A rough indication is given of the costs involved, split into direct and indirect personnel costs, costs for hard- and software, miscellaneous costs and indirect costs.

NARCIS: a description

NARCIS[5] is a portal giving access to a range of information sources. Started in 2006, NARCIS has now been developed into a central access point for research-related information in the Netherlands. Since February 2011, NARCIS has been a service of DANS. The most important information sources in the portal are the contents of the publication repositories of the Dutch universities and major scientific institutions and the contents of the DANS dataset repository, EASY.[6] In addition, overviews of current and completed research, Dutch researchers and their expertise and Dutch scientific institutions (together, the former Dutch Research Database, NOD) may be consulted via NARCIS. As NARCIS has become a service of DANS, a complex system of responsibilities has been evolved. DANS is responsible for the content of the components EASY and the Dutch Research Database, while the individual universities and scientific institutions are responsible for the content that has been harvested by the NARCIS portal.

Detailed information on the NARCIS portal is described in a 2006 paper,[7] available in the repository of the Royal Netherlands Academy of Arts and Sciences (KNAW).

NARCIS is an initiative of four major players in the Dutch scientific information field: KNAW, the NWO, the Association of Universities in the Netherlands and the SURF Foundation. The rationale behind this initiative was the fact that information related to Dutch research was scattered and difficult to find. The service has been maintained by KNAW between 2006 and 2010.

DANS

DANS is an institute under the auspices of KNAW which is also supported by the NWO. Since its establishment in 2005, DANS has been storing and making research data in the arts and humanities and social sciences permanently accessible and has a specialist department for research and development that can also carry out activities for research groups.

An important activity carried out by DANS is the setting up, managing and continued improvement of the user-friendly archiving system, EASY. EASY is open to all researchers in the arts and humanities and social sciences and it allows them to permanently store their data and to search data themselves. In other words, the objective of EASY is to be the electronic repository for data from the social sciences and the arts and humanities.

Free service

NARCIS is a free service, so it has no direct revenues from its users. The model for NARCIS fits well in the mission statement of KNAW:

> The Academy promotes quality in science and scholarship and strives to ensure that Dutch scholars and scientists contribute to cultural, social and economic progress.

NARCIS plays an important role in the elaboration of the goals of this mission. Therefore it was decided to develop NARCIS as a free service. Society as a whole – and the scientific community in particular – will profit from the investments in NARCIS. This makes it difficult, however, to give exact figures of costs and benefits.

There have been plans in the past to develop tailor-made paid services. The complex composition of the portal makes it difficult to decide who the owner is of specific data. To avoid possible legal problems, this idea has been abandoned.

Funding

The development and maintenance of NARCIS is funded by DANS. DANS itself is funded by the governmental organisations NWO and KNAW, though there is some extra funding. NARCIS has a collaborative partnership with the publisher SDU[8] in the production of an annual paper version of the Dutch Research Database: *Universiteiten en Onderzoeksinstellingen in Nederland*. For major new developments, DANS seeks to fit with national or international programs (SURF Foundation, European Union). By doing so, in many cases 50 per cent of the development costs will be covered by grants. Several KNAW scholars have understood the importance of the funding proposal in this area and have written proposals with NARCIS as one of the main topics. So far, three proposals have been awarded. In that sense, indirectly money is being paid for NARCIS.

Sustainability

In discussing the sustainability of the NARCIS portal, one has to make a distinction between the sustainability of the service and the sustainability of the data accessible via NARCIS. The *service* is being maintained by DANS. DANS already plays a major role in the field of data persistency so one may assume DANS is willing to continue this service. For the *data* the situation is complicated. The National Library of the Netherlands is responsible for sustainable access to the open access publications described in NARCIS, whereas DANS itself is responsible for the sustainability of the datasets described in EASY (and in NARCIS). Recently PersID published an interesting report on this subject.[9]

There is one problem to overcome: there is no arrangement yet for the sustainability of the research information (the information on researchers, research institutes, projects and programmes). Within the DANS organisation, attention will be paid to this problem in future years. It is foreseen that it will be a hard task for DANS to arrange a budget for the realisation of sustainable research information. The solution will be through the development of close collaboration with the other major players in this field (KNAW, NWO, Dutch universities).

Cost-effective decision-making

During the start-up phase, no services like NARCIS existed in most Western countries. At that time, KNAW had to make many decisions on its own. Cost-effectiveness was an important aspect from the start. It was decided to build the system on open source software to prevent vendor lock-in. Meanwhile, it was possible to compare different systems in Europe, the US and Australia. NARCIS relies on standards in use in the information field such as the protocol for metadata harvesting OAI-PMH and the metadata format DIDL/MODS. By doing so, it was possible to take advantage of international developments. For instance, the new hot topic 'enhanced publication' is built on the *de facto* standard OAI-ORE[10] and the representation of records is via RDF/XML. The costs for the development and maintenance of new standards for the Netherlands alone was too high, although it is sometimes a hard job to translate typical Dutch situations into the broader standards. Decisions on further developments were based on user studies in order to adapt the service to a real existing demand. As explained before, it was, and is, the intention of DANS to fit its developments with (inter-)national granting opportunities.

Responding to future developments

Sustainable access is becoming more and more important. Portals like NARCIS can only remain valuable if there is a guarantee that resources retrieved via this service are available in the long run. The costs for long-term preservation do not directly influence the NARCIS cost model, as NARCIS is just the access point to objects that are available elsewhere. In an indirect way, NARCIS has to react to this wish regarding sustainable access. The most important development in this respect is the introduction of persistent identifiers for authors, objects and organisations.[11]

These persistent identifiers are also crucial in the development of enhanced publications.[12] Enhanced publications are composed of traditional publications and/or datasets and/or audio/video fragments and the like.

NARCIS has already adapted its infrastructure to make it possible to harvest and refer to these complex objects. Besides, the persistent identifiers may be used to provide usage characteristics of (complex) objects. Cost models for the maintenance of persistent identifiers are becoming complicated. All partners in the Dutch scientific infrastructure will have to contribute. Furthermore – with regard to cost-effectiveness – there will need to be an investigation into the profitability of joining international standards in this field.

Resource allocation

Because NARCIS was a service of KNAW in 2010 it is difficult to give an exact resource allocation. This section will offer a rough overview. Naturally, in a service like NARCIS most costs are personnel related. Of the total budget 75 per cent of the costs are salary costs. A distinction is made between direct and indirect activities.

The *direct activities* are as follows:

- *Checks for completeness* – to ensure the completeness of descriptions in the NARCIS portal on a daily basis.

- *Metadata control* – checks of the correctness of the descriptions of publications in the NARCIS portal. Special attention is being paid to the metadata fields 'open access' and 'dissertation', as NARCIS has special entrances for these descriptions.

- *Formatting and modifying the homepage* – adaptation of the homepage to the contents of the components of NARCIS and feedback from its users.

- *Delivery control of text and images* – checks on how texts and images delivered to NARCIS will be presented.

- *Agreements with suppliers* – renewal of agreements with the suppliers of the research-related information on a regular basis.

- *Regular consultations, meetings with the community* – regular consultations and meetings to discuss defects, use cases and the direction of the development.

- *Monitoring and maintenance of the system (IT)* – IT personnel are needed to check the availability and performance of the system.

- *Production management* – the information scientists and IT personnel cooperate in planning new developments, performing user studies.

Apart from these direct activities, indirect activities may be identified separately. We define here indirect activities as the activities of employees who are not directly involved in the production of NARCIS but are necessary for facilitating the service and for making it more efficient. Such employees are, for instance, supervisors, accountants or communication consultants.

The *indirect activities* are as follows:

- *Administrative management* – activities related to payroll, recruiting, maintaining vendor relations and so on.

- *Communication* – producing communication plans and communication-related activities (such as the distribution of newsletters, the organisation of information and publicity meetings, the production of flyers and contact with the media).

- *Financial management* – controlling the expenditures and setting the annual budget for NARCIS.

- *Security management* – trust is a main aspect of the service. Therefore the security staff (as part of the central IT services) check and report security issues.

- *Legal management* – legal issues may arise, for example in conflicts of interest with publishers, researchers or institutions.

- *Support and facilities management* – the provision of a good working environment.

Other costs related to the maintenance of NARCIS

- *Purchases*. A complex system like NARCIS is built on up-to-date hard- and software. Servers have to be replaced every two years and software for harvesting, indexing and searching has to be renewed several times a year.

- *Miscellaneous supplies costs*. In particular costs for materials used in projects.

- *Other indirect costs.* Water and energy supply, telephone costs, maintenance, rent, etc.

In the near future it will be possible to have a good indication of these costs as well. From this preliminary overview it can be calculated that the total annual costs for NARCIS are about €500,000, of which approximately €400,000 are personnel costs and the remaining €100,000 cover the cost of hard- and software plus maintenance. The total income is dependent on the number of projects NARCIS is involved in but averages €50,000 per year.

Discussion

The starting of a national service like NARCIS is not a big problem. The costs are limited to the purchase of hard- and software and the making of arrangements with the information suppliers. For these information suppliers the costs are even more restricted, because all they have to do is to make sure their data are harvestable. The real problems start after a few years, when people have become familiar with the service and have begun to ask for additional features. Asking is simple, but realising is dependent on cooperation with the suppliers. Therefore extra time and money is needed both at the NARCIS level and at the level of universities and scientific institutions. At this time, NARCIS is on the threshold of a new era with persistent identifiers, linked data and enhanced publications: all developments that researchers have requested. These are new challenges, not only technically, but also for the cost model of the service. Implementing all these new features is too expensive for a single organisation. Therefore a portal like NARCIS needs a national approach, in which all scientific partners contribute to its maintenance and development.

Notes

1. *http://www.dans.knaw.nl*
2. *http://www.knaw.nl*
3. *http://www.nwo.nl/*
4. *http://www.surffoundation.nl/en/Pages/default.aspx*
5. *http://www.narcis.nl*
6. *https://easy.dans.knaw.nl/ui/home*

7. E. Dijk, C. Baars, A. Hogenaar and M. van Meel (2006) *NARCIS: The Gateway to Dutch Scientific Information*. Online at: *http://depot.knaw.nl/5631/1/Paper_ELPUB_2006.pdf*.

8. *http://www.sdu.nl/Pages/default.aspx*

9. PersID (2011) *PersID – V: Sustainability*. Online at: *http://www.persid.org/downloads/finalreports/PersID_Report_Part_5_final.pdf*.

10. Open Archives (2008) *ORE User Guide – Primer*. Online at: *http://www.openarchives.org/ore/1.0/primer*.

11. P. Doorenbosch and B. Sierman (2010) Paper presented at the Open Repositories Conference, Madrid, Spain, 6–9 July. Online at: *http://or2010.fecyt.es/Resources/documentos/GSabstracts/InstitutionalRepositories_LongTermPreservation_etc.pdf*.

12. M. Hoogerwerf (2009) *Durable Enhanced Publications*. Paper presented at the Proceedings of African Digital Scholarship and Curation, Pretoria, South Africa, 12–14 May. Online at: *http://www.ais.up.ac.za/digi/docs/hoogerwerf_paper.pdf*.

4

The universal library: realising Panizzi's dream

Derek Law

Abstract. Derek Law provides an overview and analysis of the case studies that form an integral part of this book. He also sets digital libraries – and their key tasks of aggregation, infrastructure and collection building, preservation, service and tools provision, standards development and maintenance – into their historical, environmental, political and economic context. The growing emphasis on collaboration and partnership – as evinced by the project narratives in this book – is noted. Reference is also made to new (digital) publishing models and the economic aspects in particular. The drive towards sustainability is seen as being of paramount importance throughout the case studies and Law's summary concludes with a listing of the key elements of likely success, as described by the practitioners who have contributed to this handbook.

Keywords: aggregation, collaboration, digital publishing models, economic models, funding, longevity, partnerships, sustainability

Introduction

Sir Anthony Panizzi famously organised the British Museum Library based on his 'Ninety-One Cataloguing Rules' in 1841. Behind his passionate attention to detail lay an equally passionate philosophical belief in the importance and value of libraries to all: 'I want a poor student to have the same means of indulging his learned curiosity, of following his rational pursuits, of consulting the same authorities, of fathoming the most intricate inquiry as the richest man in the kingdom.'[1]

This principled view of the function of libraries and their collections still resonates today – at least with librarians – and remains at the heart of the drive to move libraries into a digital world. However, recent public discourse has come to be seen as being dominated by the big beasts of the new information landscape and by their aggressive and often crude lunges to occupy the information space. Four recent examples demonstrate this very visible appetite for confrontation.

In the United States in early 2012, the proposed Research Works Act pitted publishers against scientists and led, among other things, to a proposed boycott of Elsevier by 7,500 scientific authors as a response to the company's support for the Act. The language soon became heated: 'The US Research Works Act would allow publishers to line their pockets by locking publicly funded research behind paywalls'[2] and the weight of public disapprobation, much of it organised through social networking, soon forced a withdrawal of the Act and a hasty climbdown by Elsevier.[3] Almost at the same time, another publisher, Penguin,[4] withdrew from its partnership deal with OverDrive,[5] the largest provider of e-book and audiobook lending to libraries, citing security concerns. OverDrive works with about 7,500 public libraries in the United States and over 1,000 publishers, and has access to over 100,000 works which it lends to library users. Most commentators felt it had more to do with feared loss of sales than with security.[6]

Nor is this dystopian landscape confined to libraries and publishers. Behemoths such as Google can also behave in what are seen as arbitrary and authoritarian ways. In the latest row over personal privacy the change in Google's privacy settings has sparked government-led requests to force the company to change, using legal coercion if necessary. France has asked European data authorities to investigate this pooling of user data, which began on 1 March 2012.[7] And finally one might consider the anguished debate over 'Wikileaks' and whether the US legal system should pursue Julian Assange. Liberal and respected columnists such as Clay Shirky fret over the balance between transparency and privacy and over how to make governments accountable.[8]

And yet behind this very visible, very public and apparently violent clash of information cultures, a quiet transformation has been going on which the case studies in this book collectively describe. We can see the different sectors of the information world working together. We can see the aggregation of resources, the building of portals and services, the creation of new resources. And behind this sits a sharp-eyed concern with return on investment (ROI) and business models, applying just as much to the public sector as to private business. This partnership approach may be less visible and less vocal, but it is infinitely more effective.

Each of the case studies in this handbook describes in detail a single initiative, but collectively they present a picture of an emerging ecosystem where existing and new players in the information world not only coexist but actively support each other in a sophisticated and complicated environment. In order to summarise the themes which emerge it is sensible to explore particular aspects. But almost all of the projects have multiple facets which involve at the very least the need to have some kind of sustainable economic model and the need to aggregate resources, and so their division may seem somewhat arbitrary. Additional examples will also be introduced to demonstrate that these are not isolated examples but rather exemplars of a steady and ineluctable movement to a new world where Panizzi's dream can be realised.

Aggregation

Historically, libraries and librarians have been zealous advocates of aggregation. Beginning with union catalogues, this has led to one of the great if unsung triumphs of international diplomacy, which is enshrined in the International Federation of Library Associations' (IFLA) twin programmes of Universal Bibliographic Control and the Universal Availability of Publications. These have been based not just on the necessary adoption of common standards but on the acceptance of a common philosophy which is the direct descendent of Panizzi's ambition. Thanks to the success of these programmes, it is broadly possible to identify any book or article ever published in any language and in any country, to request it through one's home library and to have the work, or a copy of it, delivered to that library within a short space of time. We take this astonishing feat for granted and yet there is no inherent reason to have, say, a public library in Lithuania receive an article from a medical library in Hawaii. But the system manages this extraordinary achievement routinely.

The habit of cooperation seemed to have been sidetracked for well over a decade. But after a period when library groups and consortia became perhaps over-focused on cooperative purchase, we can again see the emergence of the aggregation of resources and adding value to them as a hugely important phenomenon. This time aggregation focuses as much on the sharing of collections as the listing of them.

Two studies refer to two quite different models. accessCeramics (Case Study 5) displays a number of interesting characteristics. Firstly, it is image-based and images have proved a powerful educational tool for twenty-first-century users. Secondly, it is, at least in a loose sense, user created, although there is a vetting process for contributions. And thirdly, it sees adding value to institutional brand and reputation as a powerful benefit. Like most of the activities described it has been created with much charitable and grant support. But the paper also gives a very honest sense of the financial challenges such a project faces when run by a small institution.

But there are other forms of aggregation. One is the re-creation of a document which has been scattered. One such example is the Codex Sinaiticus. The Codex is an ancient, handwritten copy of the Greek Bible which came to the attention of scholars in the nineteenth century at the Greek Orthodox Monastery of Mount Sinai. It became scattered with further material discovered in the twentieth and even twenty-first centuries. Parts of the Codex are held in four libraries around the world. The principal surviving portion is now held by the British Library. A further 43 leaves are kept at the University Library in Leipzig. Parts of six leaves are held at the National Library of Russia in Saint Petersburg. Further portions remain at Saint Catherine's Monastery on Mount Sinai. A major project[9] has preserved, digitised, transcribed and 'reunited' this important manuscript and made it available on the Web.

A second is the creation by institutions of a collection which had not previously existed. A small example of this is the Red Clydeside collection in the Glasgow Digital Library.[10] During the period between 1910 and 1932 the city of Glasgow was witness to an unparalleled wave of working-class protest and political agitation which challenged the forces of capitalism and also, on occasion, directly challenged the state itself. This was strongly suppressed by governments fearfully watching what was happening in St Petersburg and Moscow. The events and people who shaped this period forged an enduring legacy which still remains part of the political and social fabric of the city to the present day, and which is known quite simply as Red Clydeside, but the clandestine nature of this movement left its records scattered and fragmented. The Glasgow Digital Library then collected and digitised some 220 items drawn from local archives and special collections to build a coherent record of what had happened almost a century previously.

The third and most ambitious model is the assembly and enrichment of known collections from multiple international sources. Emory University has done this for the Atlantic Slave Trade.[11] The Voyages database assembles searchable records collected by scholars from all round the Atlantic basin and has value added through the addition of maps, images, data and name indices for individual Africans who were transported. Seen as a dynamic rather than a completed project, scholars who discover new information can add it to the database and thus share it with their colleagues.

Building infrastructure: the long haul

The sort of aggregation just described focuses on what historically has been seen as special collections and archives – rare and unusual material. But just as much consideration is needed when considering the ordinary: the material which has formed the vast physical bulk of what was stored in paper-based libraries and for most libraries that is journal literature. Again quite new and complex models can be seen to be emerging. We have moved very rapidly from a time when shared library storage was the hot agenda item to considering models where resources are stored in what might be considered a version of the Cloud and made accessible to multiple user categories, each with differing rights. The growth of JSTOR[12] (see Case Study 1) is perhaps the best example of this. It now has a widely known brand name, a positive reputation and a huge client base, and with 7,000 participating institutions, holdings of 1,500 academic journals and 600 million accesses a year its growth has been phenomenal. It is also a broad community resource which is creating sustainable business models which are shaped by the needs of several groups – libraries, publishers and scholars – and not just one. And again it embraces change and adaptability rather than stasis as the new digital landscape develops, changes and matures.

The growth of multinational science publishers has tended to disguise the fact that these are in the strict sense aberrant forms. The backbone of scholarship and scholarly publishing remains the small learned society. Project MUSE[13] (Case Study 2) recognised this almost twenty years ago and has explored how smaller journals in the humanities and social sciences could afford to have a digital presence. And the resource pressures on these societies can be as much technical as financial. How are they to gain access to competences and standards and to make decisions well outside their professional domain? MUSE has, of course, now moved beyond journals to e-books, but it again displays all the benefits of collaboration, aggregation and partnership and the recognition of a linked ecology from researcher to reader with different partners using different skill sets to manage the process of dissemination.

Longevity

One of the beauties of copyright libraries is that their mission is evident and simple. Give them a copy of a book or even a manuscript and they will endeavour to keep it forever. And they have done this effectively for literally hundreds of years so far. And even when war, tempest or age prevents this, there will usually be copies somewhere else. How different the fate of computer files and digital objects. Technological obsolescence, media ephemerality and the content deletion policies of computer centres all conspire to offer very little in the way of guaranteed preservation. Some of the responses are described elsewhere in this book, but we can already see that this is both a complex issue and one where cooperation and collaboration have been in play for some time. Again the following examples show the power of working together.

The wonderfully titled LOCKSS (Lots of Copies Keep Stuff Safe), based at Stanford University Libraries, was initiated in 1999 and is an international community initiative that provides libraries with digital preservation tools and support so that they can easily and inexpensively collect and preserve their own copies of authorised e-content. LOCKSS uses open source software and support to preserve today's web published materials for tomorrow's readers while building their own collections and acquiring a copy of the assets they pay for instead of simply leasing them. It is a decentralised digital preservation infrastructure. LOCKSS preserves all formats and genres of web published content.

PORTICO (Case Study 8) was set up in 2005 and is another example of the partnership model bringing together libraries, publishers and funders. As of 2012[14] it preserved 12,555 e-journal titles, 123,586 e-book titles and some 46 digitised historical collections, working with 140 publishers (representing over 2,000 societies and associations) and 728 libraries. This simple list of numbers shows an impressive requirement for collaboration but conceals the huge activity which goes on underneath to create a sustainable economic model.

The KEEP Project,[15] funded by the European Commission, looks at the preservation of emulation environments which will allow access to all sorts of digital outputs which form the cultural heritage of the late twentieth century and beyond. Using computer games as its test bed it has shown many of the systemic difficulties which are emerging in the preservation of digitally born resources. At least some of these stem not from technical difficulties but from such things as copyright legislation framed in what now seems a different world.

Reducing the data burden relies on promoting data interchange standards, so that data is held once. This facilitates systems integration both across the institution and within wider stakeholder groups. It fosters the community cloud. This will never eliminate keeping data on site and on campus but will reduce data volumes. This can both save money and add value. The Chronopolis network described by Minor and Kozbial (Case Study 6) is a perfect example of this. The project leverages high-speed networks, mass-scale storage capabilities and the expertise of its partners to provide a geographically distributed, heterogeneous, highly redundant archive system.

Tools and services

Digital environments add a new dimension to what libraries can do. Technology allows us to explore and develop new services to meet changing user needs and to match the way they work, live and use technology. Expectations of immediacy are driven by everything from instant book purchases on Kindles to confirmed restaurant reservations for the same evening. Mobile technologies have led to a step shift in user experience and expectations. The study from the Borough of Manhattan Community College (Case Study 13) is a perfect expression of this, where its electronic reserves and streaming video service are tailored to meet the needs of 20,000 commuter students. Almost as important is that their stated mission is to leverage technology to innovate in support of learning. A more recent development has been to look at providing the infrastructure which allows others to contribute. Perhaps the most obvious form of this is portals, two of which are described in the studies by Smith (Case Study 4) and Hogenaar (Case Study 14).

As is often the case, the Netherlands has developed an interesting and clear national structure in the NARCIS system, which Hogenaar describes. It has a clear focus – research – and is based on a number of collaborating institutions representing different but closely related communities. They have combined to create a portal which sits comfortably within the SURF Foundation, which, like JISC in the UK, links all researchers. It is an excellent model of what can be achieved by building on existing relationships. Smith describes a portal framework for humanities scholars based on a grant-funded study carried out at Emory University. Again, the key element of the study is that the framework is designed to encourage community engagement and to respond to expressed user needs. It also begins to address one of the major challenges facing cultural heritage bodies in a digital age – the identification and exposure of 'hidden' collections.

Perhaps the largest portal of them all is Europeana,[16] another EU-funded project. It provides a single access point to millions of books, paintings, films, museum objects and archival records that have been digitised throughout Europe. It is an authoritative source of information coming from European cultural and scientific institutions and links to over 20 million objects coming from more than 1,500 institutions in 32 countries. But its very size has uncovered other issues. Although it is an astonishing example of collaboration, aggregation and standards development it has had more difficulty in defining its audience and their needs. This in turn has led to some complicated and arguably needlessly arcane issues between Europeana, the Europeana Libraries Project and the European Library over who should hold and provide access to which content.

Standards issues have been at the core of library cooperation for generations. From cataloguing rules to MAchine Readable Cataloguing (MARC), from Dublin Core to the Open Archives Initiative – Protocol for Metadata Harvesting (OAI-PMH), the creation and more importantly the application of standards has driven forward library cooperation. And this will remain the case. One such tools and standards issue is addressed by Starr in her description of EZID (Case Study 10). Persistent identifiers are a long-standing issue in the digital world. While standards such as the Digital Object Identifier (DOI) have come from the commercial world, it is less common to see standards emerging from the library world, in this case the California Digital Library. Most importantly it recognises the sheer variety of the things libraries collect, which range well beyond the books and journals which dominate the traditional publishing world. EZID can assign identifiers to anything: scientific datasets, technical reports, audio files and digital photographs, for example.

Born-digital collection building

Johnson and Palmer (Case Study 3) describe the experience of the University Library at Indiana University-Purdue University Indianapolis.

A key element here has been working with local community groups to aggregate their skills with collections wished for locally by the community. Although not all of them are in the strict sense born-digital, it is again the development of partnership models which has led to success. Indeed it allows them to describe such collaboration with one of the most striking phrases in this book: 'organic relationship development has been wildly beneficial'.

Perhaps the largest growth of born-digital material lies in institutional and subject repositories. OAIster[17] claims to contain over 25 million records from over 1,100 institutions. These include records for digitised (scanned) books, journal articles, newspapers, manuscripts, digital text, audio files (wav, mp3), video files (mp4, QuickTime), photographic images (jpeg, tiff, gif), datasets (downloadable statistical information), theses and research papers. OpenDOAR[18] (the Directory of Open Access Repositories) lists over 2,000 repositories, just over 80 per cent of which are institutional with the number steadily growing, and almost half in Europe. These provide access to 10 million items. With most of the material crawled by Google and available through Google Scholar[19] searches, this has become a powerful mainstay of the new ecology. The repository movement is closely aligned to the Open Access movement, which has proved hugely contentious. But irrespective of views on Open Access, repositories are here to stay.

Monographs

Most discussion on the digital environment tends to focus either on journals or special collections. Much less thought seems to have been given to the monograph, which historically has been the backbone particularly of humanities and social science scholarship. The emergence of e-books and the flailing search by major publishers for a sustainable economic model has disguised some interesting developments. One fascinating aspect is covered in Gorrell's study on e-books and audio books (Case Study 11). It has been suggested[20] that only 29 per cent of library patrons have e-readers and that while so many publishers refuse to make e-books available to libraries, librarians would do better to wait until the hugely volatile market has settled down and focus resources on the needs of the majority. But the EBSCO model which Gorrell describes offers libraries a very attractive combination of aggregation, professional support and technical skill. As importantly, this new medium is not seen as separate, different and awkward, but is integrated into an existing platform with which users will be familiar. Again the key is aggregation, but this time of delivery platforms and tools. And most importantly of all, libraries are seen as partners for the delivery of a commercial product and not as museums of the book.

There are well known projects which are delivering collections of digitised free e-books, but they do tend to focus on the aggregation of content rather than the integration of delivery mechanisms. The oldest of these is the Gutenberg Project,[21] which has been running since 1971, is run by volunteers, has over 38,000 books and is adding 100 titles a week, but there are now major sites such as Many Books,[22] Munseys,[23] Feedbooks[24] and Open Library.[25]

OAPEN (Open Access Publishing in European Networks)[26] began as a publisher-led but EU-funded project to explore the feasibility of publishing scholarly monographs in a sustainable open access model. It now has around 1,000 monographs listed on its website, mainly from university presses. Perhaps unsurprisingly given its humanities background, the principal aim is the sharing of knowledge rather than the maximising of profit, but sustainability is a key driver. In this open access model the monograph is made freely available – readers (or their libraries) do not have to pay to read it online, rather the costs of the publishing process (for example, peer review, typesetting, marketing) are recovered through alternative routes such as research grants, institutional funding or perhaps through readers purchasing print editions or particular formats for their iPad or Kindle. The project is now being extended more widely to the UK. OAPEN-UK[27] is an Arts and Humanities Research Council and Joint Information Systems Committee (JISC) funded project exploring the issues impacting upon the publishing of scholarly monographs in the humanities and social sciences. OAPEN-UK has two strands: an open access pilot gathering data on the usage, sales and citations of 60 monographs, and a wider research project which explores the environment for open access publishing. The project is working with Taylor & Francis, Palgrave Macmillan, Berg Publishers, Liverpool University Press, University Wales Press, research funders and universities, to understand the challenges and steps required to move towards an open access publishing model for scholarly monographs.

A different model again is described by Woodhead (Case Study 13), whose mid-sized firm specialises in science and technology monographs and has been buffeted by the pace of technological change. But again key messages about partnership and flexibility come through. The company has made huge efforts to find out what the market wants and then deliver that, rather than attempting to dictate what it shall have. It has then chosen to work in partnership with an aggregator, again ensuring that customers will interact with an existing delivery platform aimed at supporting the research process.

Funding

Higher education libraries have not hitherto had to undertake a great deal in the way of financial planning. In the United Kingdom, for example, the library budget is typically last year's figure plus (or sometimes minus!) a few per cent. Until very recently the Library was seen simply as a necessary if expensive part of the fabric of any university. Of course the budgets were and are very well and very professionally managed, but little was needed in the way of business planning and such revenue generation as was undertaken tended to be either for endowments or was a way of paying for new services whose costs were readily identifiable, whether photocopying, inter-lending or online searching. Libraries inhabited a dependency culture where sustainability was not a consideration. In essence the library was simply a top-sliced cost from the university budget, or delegated to faculties as is often the case in continental European universities (Law, 2010).

We do, of course, know quite a lot about existing library costs – at least about direct costs – for example through the long-time series of Society of College, National and University Libraries (SCONUL) statistics in the UK. But it is important to note that these simply do not cover indirect costs such as estate, heating and lighting, security and maintenance and building amortisation costs, which are both increasing costs to the institution and costs which may look quite different for digital libraries. Nor has there been any significant analysis of these figures. Indeed, the whole issue of total cost of ownership is a hugely neglected topic (Law, 2009). Charles Bailey's comprehensive bibliography of scholarly economic publishing gives evidence of this.[28] Only 14 pages out of over 450 – barely 3 per cent – cover the economic issues associated with the whole digital environment.

This neglect may be changing and indeed many of the studies in this handbook offer comment on the business models they have explored or adopted. And two notable trailblazers do offer insightful views on aspects of the economic model. The study by Griffiths and King (Case Study 9) summarises work undertaken over two decades and explores the important topic of return on investment. This analysis of tools and metrics allows a fascinating exploration of such important metrics as contingent valuation and return on investment which are increasingly valuable tools in exploring and explaining the indirect benefits libraries can bring to their parent organisations.

A newer name to enter the battleground of the costing of scholarly publishing is the economist John Houghton. His seminal report (Houghton et al., 2009) opened up the debate on the costs of scholarly publishing, the profits of publishers and where the costs should lie. His study (Case Study 7) considers the work he has done since then in other countries, which confirm the thesis that there are alternative models to the historic ones and that these alternative models must be explored.

While most of the authors of studies focus on financial matters, there are two striking discussions, on the accessCeramics financial model (Case Study 5) and on the Chronopolis network (Case Study 6). Dahl describes how many projects begin, with local enthusiasm and grant funding. But as the resource grows new financial models must be explored. It should be noted that accessCeramics has shied away from subscription models, in part on principle, and the paper clearly articulates the options and difficult choices it faces in making content available. Chronopolis also began as a grant-funded programme but has made decisions to seek a mixed-funding economy for the future. This quite different approach reflects different stakeholder groups and different types of data. But what is perhaps most striking with these as with the other studies is the degree of sophisticated economic understanding that underpins their thinking. The digital economy is not just about raising funds but about concepts as varied as monetisation, cost–benefit analysis and intangible institutional benefits.

Conclusion

The diverse range of contributors to this handbook demonstrates that the information world is populated by a naturally collaborative set of innovators. For over a decade they have slowly grappled with transient technology and developing and changing standards, while absorbing huge shifts in the forms and nature of communication. But throughout it all they have begun to create linkages which allow us to begin to perceive the emerging shape of a viable information new world, where no one group dominates, where collaboration is to the advantage of all and where we still have valuable products and services to offer users in the prosecution of their lives. The mantras listed in the study of Project MUSE pithily sum up the lessons learned and therefore bear repeating. If the digital world were old enough to have grandmothers, these would be the pieces of good advice that they would recite and pass on:

- Develop the rationale for ongoing investment into the platform.
- Build a robust stable of key stakeholders from all communities.
- Listen to your customers and build relationships based on trust.
- Communicate extensively in person and one-on-one with partners.
- Know your readers, editors, authors, researchers, students and librarians.
- Embrace the digital chaos of tomorrow – do not fear it.
- Invest in your people.
- Commit to project management.

But most of all, if we work together, the universal library is an achievable goal and not an unrealisable dream.

Notes

1. Quoted in Louis Fagan (1880) *The Life of Sir Anthony Panizzi, K.C.B.* Remington & Co.
2. *http://www.guardian.co.uk/science/2012/jan/16/academic-publishers-enemies-science*
3. *http://www.elsevier.com/*
4. *http://www.penguin.co.uk/*
5. *http://www.overdrive.com/*
6. Laura June (2012) 'Penguin kills library ebook lending deal with OverDrive', *The Verge*, 13 February,. Online at: *http://www.theverge.com/2012/2/13/2795791/penguin-kills-library-ebook-lending-deal-with-overdrive.*
7. *http://www.guardian.co.uk/technology/2012/mar/01/google-privacy-policy-changes-eu*
8. Clay Shirky (2010) 'Wikileaks and the long haul', 6 December. Available at: *http://www.shirky.com/weblog/.*
9. *http://codexsinaiticus.org/en/project/*
10. *http://gdl.cdlr.strath.ac.uk/redclyde/*
11. *http://www.slavevoyages.org/tast/index.faces*
12. *http://www.jstor.org/*

13. *http://muse.jhu.edu/*
14. *http://www.portico.org/digital-preservation/the-archive-content-access/archive-facts-figures*
15. *http://www.keep-project.eu/ezpub2/index.php?/eng*
16. *http://www.europeana.eu/portal/*
17. *http://www.oclc.org/oaister/about/default.htm*
18. *http://www.opendoar.org/*
19. *http://scholar.google.com/*
20. Bobbi Newman (2012) 'Should libraries get out of the ebook business?', *Librarian by Day* blog. Available at: *http://librarianbyday.net/2012/03/07/should-libraries-get-out-of-the-ebook-business/*.
21. *http://www.gutenberg.org/*
22. *http://manybooks.net/*
23. *http://www.munseys.com/*
24. *http://www.feedbooks.com/*
25. *http://openlibrary.org/*
26. *http://www.oapen.org/home*
27. *http://www.oapen-uk.jiscebooks.org*
28. Charles Bailey (2011) *Scholarly Electronic Publishing Bibliography 2010*. Houston, TX: Digital Scholarship.

References

Law, D. (2009) 'Digital library economics: aspects and prospects', in D. Baker and W. Evans (eds), *Digital Library Economics: An Academic Perspective*. Oxford: Chandos Publishing.

Law, D. (2010) 'Digital libraries in higher education', in M. Collier (ed.), *Business Models for Digital Libraries*. Leuven: University of Leuven Press.

Houghton, J., Rasmussen, B. and Sheehan, P. (2009) *Economic Implications of Alternative Scholarly Publishing Models: Exploring the Costs and Benefits*, Report to the Joint Information Systems Committee (JISC). Online at: *http://ie-repository.jisc.ac.uk/278/*.

Index